N

QUICK

REFERENCE

THE LIFE
OF CHRIST

Publishers since 1798

Thomas Nelson Publishers
Nashville

Published in Nashville, Tennessee, by Thomas Nelson, Inc.

Portions of this work were published previously as *The Life of Our Divine Lord,* Zondervan Publishing House, 1958; *Beginnings in the Life of Christ,* rev. ed., Moody Bible Institute, 1975.

Unless otherwise indicated, Scripture quotations are from the *New King James Version of the Bible* (NKJV), © 1979, 1980, 1982, Thomas Nelson, Inc., Publishers. Other translations quoted are the *King James Version* (KJV); the *New International Version* (NIV), © 1978, the New York International Bible Society (used by permission of Zondervan Bible Publishers); the *New English Bible* (NEB), © 1961, 1970, and the *Revised English Bible* (REB), © 1989, both by The Delegates of the Oxford University Press and the Syndics of the Cambridge University Press (used by permission).

Library of Congress Cataloging-in-Publication Information

Vos, Howard Frederic, 1925–
    The life of Christ / Howard F. Vos.
      p. cm. — (Nelson's Quick reference)
    Includes bibliographical references and index.
    ISBN 0-8407-3363-1 (pbk.)
    1. Jesus Christ—Biography. I. Title. II. Series.
BT301.2.V64 1994
232.9'01—dc20
[B]   93–41924
                                                    CIP

Printed in the United States of America
1 2 3 4 5 6 7 8 — 00 99 98 97 96 95 94

To

Emmagene B. Vos

Contents

MAJOR LOCATIONS AND DISTANCES IN THE LIFE OF CHRIST

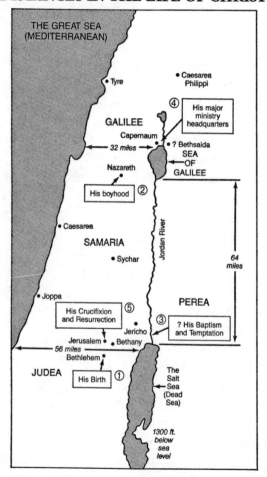

An Opening Word

In some circles of Western civilization there is a tendency to despise and reject the cultural impact of Jesus Christ's earthly life and ministry. After all, He lived almost 2,000 years ago and preached an ethic that would seem to have little relevance for a hurly-burly world in which might appears to make right and in which power politics commonly govern the affairs of nations. Millions find Him irrelevant and know Him only as a curse word. So widespread is this negative view of Jesus Christ and the Bible which portrays Him that it is common to speak of a "post-Christian era."

But just at the time that modern enemies of Christ, like Voltaire in the eighteenth century, are congratulating themselves on the imminent demise of Christianity, there is amazing new vitality of the Christian faith in the world. For example, some compute the conversion rate in Latin America at three times the natural birth rate, and it is asserted that in Africa, evangelical Christians may compose half of the adult population of the continent by the year 2000. Reports also paint a remarkable picture of church growth in Korea, as well as a steady increase in China's underground church since Communism came to power in 1949.

Then there are the endless reports of spiritual hunger in the former Soviet Union. Possibly this great land which did not participate in the Protestant Reformation and other revivals will now have its turn. The

Jesus film has made a phenomenal impact and has contributed to large numbers of conversions wherever it has gone, especially in Africa. In 1993 the Lausanne Statistics Task Force reported that in a world of 5.5 billion people, there are now 540 million Bible-believing Christians, for a total of 10 percent. Even in supposedly "post-Christian America," a Gallup poll released in 1989 indicated that 31 percent of all adult Americans claimed to have had a "born again" experience. And some statisticians have concluded that there are probably as many Christians in the world today as have lived during the entire history of the church put together.

Parallel to this growth of Christianity in the world is a decline in the once-prevalent belief that the reason and science of the West promised a kind of salvation for all who followed their direction. Despite this promise, it is clear that a sense of guilt and fear of death and the future are as prevalent today as ever. The "peace dividend" of the end of the Cold War eludes us as numerous small but horrific regional conflicts testify to the unchanged fallen nature of humanity. Millions need forgiveness of sin and the love of God in human relations. And in their search for release from the bondage of sin and power for daily living, millions are turning to Jesus Christ. Thus, from a spiritual perspective, a study of the person and work of Christ is as relevant today as it ever has been.

Moreover, those with cultural or historical interests will certainly recognize the impact of Jesus Christ on Western civilization. No doubt they will agree with Jaroslav Pelikan that "Jesus of Nazareth has been the dominant figure in the history of Western culture" since His birth in Bethlehem.[1] Or they may agree with Malcolm Muggeridge that "whatever is truly admirable" in the achievements of art, literature, music, and architecture, the quest for knowledge and the pursuit of justice derives from the coming of Jesus into the world almost 2000 years ago.[2]

For the most part, writers on the life of Christ have concerned themselves almost exclusively with the story of His earthly ministry and have focused the spotlight all too frequently on His humanity. In this present work there is a departure from the usual approach to the life of Christ. The narrative of His life is clearly summarized in a way that is unencumbered with the usual digressions and interruptions required when all aspects of his life and ministry are discussed in chronological order.

Following a topical approach, other chapters deal with such subjects as the historical and geographical context of Christ's earthly ministry, the nature of His person, His message, parables, miracles, and persons in His life. Throughout, the book bears full recognition of His deity and the fact that the thirty three years our Lord spent on earth were but a fleeting moment in comparison with His eternal existence as the Second Person of the Trinity. Moreover, Christ's interest in humanity did not terminate with His ascension. His present ministry on behalf of His own is a subject of numerous New Testament portions, as is His predicted return. Separate chapters deal with His present and future activity.

Furthermore, the message of Christ has practical

ethical values for the contemporary believer. The apostle John declared: "He who says he abides in Him ought himself also to walk just as He walked" (1 John 2:6). This study, then, quite logically concludes with a chapter on the implications of the life of Christ for the daily walk of the believer. A consideration of His life constitutes more than a mere academic exercise; it should change one's daily walk. To this end the present work has been written.

NOTES

1. Jaroslav Pelikan, *Jesus Through the Centuries* (New Haven: Yale University Press, 1985), p. 1.

2. Malcolm Muggeridge, *Jesus The Man Who Lives* (New York: Harper & Row, 1975), p. 7. See also Bruce Bernard, *The Bible and Its Painters* (London: Macdonald & Co., 1988).

ONE

The Fact of Christ's Life on Earth

DID Christ really live on earth? Or does the idea that He did have its origin in myth? "Such a foolish question!" exclaims the Bible believer. "Isn't time divided into B.C. and A.D.? And doesn't the Bible supply proof enough?" For some, yes. But many skeptics have doubted the truth of the New Testament claim. Some still doubt, even after the publication of such widely accepted works as Shirley Jackson Case's *Historicity of Jesus*.[1] So, in beginning a study of the life of Christ, it is useful to restate some of the evidence for believing that Christ really lived on earth.

Probably the earliest testimony to the historicity of Christ is that of the apostle Paul. In his early years a violent opponent of Christ, Paul had to be convinced of the truth of Christ's activities and His claims; hence his witness is especially valuable. Very likely most of his letters were "mailed" before the first of the four gospels was written. As a result of modern discovery, the Pauline epistles enjoy an increasing reputation for validity among critical scholars. It is of no little significance that such a great liberal as Shirley Jackson Case could declare, "The genuineness of the principal Pauline epistles is among the most generally accepted conclusions of what may be called modern critical opinion."[2] Paul had much to say in his epistles about the earthly ministry of Christ. By way of illustration,

he referred to His incarnation (Romans 1:3); His institution of the Lord's Supper (1 Corinthians 11:23–
26); His provision of eternal life (Romans 5:15–21);
His crucifixion (1 Corinthians 2:2; Galatians 2:20);
and His death, burial, and resurrection (1 Corinthians
15:3–8). Paul's statements about the life of Christ are
minimal, however, compared to those in the gospels.

Although the value of the testimony of the gospels
to the life and ministry of Jesus Christ has been dis-
puted, critical opinion concerning them has been
forced to change in recent decades too. Critics used to
say that the gospels came into their present form long
after Christ lived on earth, perhaps during the third
century. By implication, or direct statement, they
taught that much of the information in the gospels
concerning Jesus was legendary, having developed during the century or two after His death. Now, however,
on the basis of evidence from the papyri, we know
that the New Testament was written in first-century
Greek. An indication of the change in scholarly opinion appears in the declaration of such an outstanding
liberal theologian and archaeologist as Millar Burrows
of Yale that "the books of the New Testament were
written in the first century."[3]

Sir Frederic Kenyon, former director of the British
Museum, placed the date of John near the end of the
first century and the rest of the gospels about the time
of the fall of Jerusalem.[4] An eminent New Testament
scholar, John A. T. Robinson, of Trinity College, Cambridge, reversed himself on many of his earlier radical
views in 1977 and concluded that the New Testament
books were written between A.D. 47 and 70.[5] Having

been written so soon after the events they record, the gospels should be reliable in content. At least, many who knew Jesus well would still have been alive and could have contested any errors of fact in the gospel narratives.

While biblical testimony concerning the historical Jesus is taking on increased validity, there is supporting evidence in several early Roman and Jewish sources. One of the earliest Romans to comment on the person of Christ was Tacitus (A.D. c. 60–c. 120). An orator and a politician, he is best known as a historian. The *Annals,* one of his historical works, is of particular importance for the present study. Written near the end of his life, the *Annals* contains a history of the Julian emperors from Tiberius to Nero (A.D. 14–68). In the section on Nero, Tacitus briefly describes the persecution of Christians, and in the process names their leader: "Christus, from whom their name is derived, was executed at the hands of the procurator Pontius Pilate in the reign of Tiberius.[6]

Pliny the Younger (c. 62–c. 113), while governor of Bithynia and Pontus in Asia Minor (modern Turkey), was faced with the issue of how to treat Christians, who were by then an illegal sect. About A.D. 111 or 112 he wrote to the Emperor Trajan for advice on the subject. In describing Christians he said: "But they declared that the sum of their guilt or error had amounted only to this, that on an appointed day they had been accustomed to meet before daybreak, and to recite a hymn antiphonally to Christ, as to God, and to bind themselves by an oath, not for the commission of any crime but to abstain from theft, robbery, adul-

tery, and breach of faith, and not to deny a deposit
when it was claimed.[7] While this does not provide any
detail concerning the person of Christ, it does attest
to His existence—at least as far as these early Christians
were concerned.

When Pliny went to Asia Minor to serve as governor of Bithynia and Pontus, he took along as his
correspondent the biographer and historian Suetonius
(c. 75–160). Suetonius' chief work was the *Lives of the
Caesars* (Julius to Domitian), of which only fragments
remain. In his *Life of Claudius* appears this statement,
"Since the Jews were continually making disturbances
at the instigation of Chrestus, he [Claudius] expelled
them from Rome."[8] The interpretation of the passage
in its context must be either that a disturbance had
been caused by a Jew named Chrestus, who was living
in Rome at the time, or that a controversy had arisen
between Jews and Christians over Christ and certain
doctrinal issues. Many accept the latter and feel that
this is a testimony to the existence of Christ as early as
the middle of the first century. Both the Greek and
Latin words for Christian sometimes are spelled with
an *e* rather than an *i* in New Testament manuscripts,
and it is possible that Christus was also sometimes
spelled Chrestus. That Claudius did expel the Jews
from Rome is confirmed in Acts 18:2.

Another Roman witness to the person of Jesus
Christ is Lucian of Samosata in Syria (c. 125–c. 190),
whom many regard as the most brilliant writer of
revived Greek literature under the Roman Empire. In
his later years he held a government post in Egypt. Of
particular interest to us is his satire on Christians and

their faith, published under the title *The Passing of Peregrinus,* about 170. He describes Christ as the originator of "this new cult" of Christianity and mentions that he was "crucified in Palestine" for having originated the cult.[9]

Greatest of the early Jewish historians was Josephus (A.D. 37?–100). Among his writings were the *History of the Jewish War, Antiquities of the Jews,* an *Autobiography* and *Against Apion.* In the *Antiquities,* finished in A.D. 93, a much-disputed passage describes Jesus Christ:

> Now there was about this time Jesus, a wise man, if it be lawful to call him a man; for he was a doer of wonderful works, a teacher of such men as receive the truth with pleasure. He drew over to him both many of the Jews and many of the Gentiles. He was [the] Christ. And when Pilate, at the suggestion of the principal men amongst us, had condemned him to the cross, those that loved him at the first did not forsake him, for he appeared to them alive again the third day; as the divine prophets had foretold these and ten thousand other wonderful things concerning him. And the tribe of Christians, so named from him, are not extinct at this day.[10]

Obviously, this is a rather evangelical-sounding statement for a Jew of Josephus' standing to have made. Some have held, therefore, that the entire passage is an insertion made by a Christian; and the fourth-century church historian Bishop Eusebius of Caesarea has been suggested as the one responsible. It is commonly believed now that Josephus probably

made some reference to the existence of Jesus in this
passage and that we have here a doctored-up account
rather than a complete interpolation. Some have even
tried to restore the Josephus passage to its original
wording.

In this connection, Professors Shlomo Pines and
David Flusser of the Hebrew University in Jerusalem
reported on a tenth-century Arabic manuscript which
contains a rendering of the debated passage very different from the traditional one. The Arabic rendering,
which they believe to be the original, reads as follows:

> At this time there was a wise man who was called
> Jesus. And his conduct was good, and [he] was
> known to be virtuous. And many people from
> among the Jews and other nations became his
> disciples. Pilate condemned him to be crucified
> and to die. And those who had become his disci-
> ples did not abandon his discipleship. They re-
> ported that he had appeared to them three days
> after his crucifixion and that he was alive; accord-
> ingly, he was perhaps the messiah concerning
> whom the prophets have recounted wonders.[11]

Whether or not this wording is Josephus' original is
beside the point. It hardly seems possible that a person
of Josephus' breadth of knowledge could have avoided
completely a reference to Jesus of Nazareth in a reasonably complete history of the Jews. Moreover, later on
in his account he spoke of James as "the brother of
Jesus, who was called Christ.[12] This unembellished
statement has a ring of authenticity and may be accepted as a bona fide witness to Jesus' life on earth.

Early Jewish tradition also confirms the existence of Jesus of Nazareth. The code of religious law, called "the traditions of the elders" or the Mishnah, was compiled about A.D. 200. Thereafter a commentary grew up around it which is called the Gamarah. The Mishnah and Gamarah together are usually known as the Talmud, and the Babylonian form of the Talmud is longer than the Jerusalem form. The Talmud makes a number of hostile references to Jesus, and most of them speak of Him as "One" who did such and such. One of the more specific allusions to Jesus appears in the tractate Sanhedrin (43a) of the Babylonian Talmud:

On the eve of the Passover, Jesus of Nazareth was hung. During forty days a herald went before him crying aloud: "He ought to be stoned because he has practiced magic, has led Israel astray and caused them to rise in rebellion. Let him who has something to say in his defence come forward and declare it." But no one came forward, and he was hung on the eve of the Passover.

This passage clearly attests Jesus' existence, implies His miraculous work ("practiced magic"), and indirectly refers to His death by crucifixion ("hung") rather than the usual execution by stoning.

In the light of all this assured or apparent testimony to the historicity of Jesus, skepticism has had to beat a retreat. However scholars or popular interpreters may evaluate the person of Jesus today, rarely will one ever completely deny His existence. Admitting, then, that

He lived on earth at the beginning of our era, let us look at the preparation of the world for His coming.

NOTES

1. Shirley Jackson Case, *The Historicity of Jesus*, 2d ed. (Chicago: U. of Chicago, 1928). For other defense of the historicity of Jesus, see Gary R. Habermas, *The Verdict of History* (Nashville: Thomas Nelson, 1988); Josh McDowell and Bill Wilson, *He Walked Among Us* (San Bernardino: Here's Life Publishers, 1988); Josh McDowell, *Evidence That Demands a Verdict* (San Bernardino: Here's Life Publishers, 1972), Vol. I; and E. M. Blaiklock, *Who Was Jesus?* (Chicago: Moody, 1974).

2. *Ibid.*, p. 178.

3. Millar Burrows, *What Mean These Stones?* (New Haven: Amer. Sch. of Oriental Res., 1941), p. 54.

4. Frederic Kenyon, *The Bible and Archaeology* (New York: Harper & Bros., 1940), p. 288.

5. John A. T. Robinson, *Can We Trust the New Testament?* (Grand Rapids: Eerdmans, 1977), p. 63.

6. Tacitus *Annals* 15.44.

7. Pliny the Younger *Correspondence of Trajan, Epp.* 10.96.

8. *Life of Claudius*, XXV.4.

9. Lucian *Passing of Peregrinus* 1.11.13.

10. Josephus *Antiquities* 18.3.3.

11. Peter Grose, "New Evidence on Jesus' Life Reported," *New York Times,* February 13, 1972, pp. 1, 24.

12. Josephus 20.9.1. For discussion of the authenticity of this passage, see McDowell and Wilson, *He Walked Among Us,* pp. 38–40.

TWO

The Preparation of the World for Christ's Coming

HISTORY, it seems, was ripe for the coming of Christ and His birth in Bethlehem. The apostle Paul declared, "When the fullness of time had come," or, "When the right time finally came" *(Good News for Modern Man)*, "God sent forth His Son, born of a woman, (Galatians 4:4). Not only did Paul speak by inspiration, but, living in that time, he understood, as we cannot, how everything fit together to provide a proper context, or "right time," or "fullness of time," for Christ to be born. He was able to make the impact He did because to some degree the world was ready for Him and what He had to offer.

Greek Cultural Contribution

The Greeks had made a cultural contribution to Christ's coming. As early as the Formative Age of Greece (c. 800–500 B.C.), colonies of Greeks had established themselves in Spain, southern France, southern Italy, Egypt, Cyrenaica (modern Libya), Cyprus, Asia Minor, and all around the Black Sea. Of course they brought with them their political, social, and economic institutions, and the religion, language, and other elements of Greek culture. When Alexander the Great and his successors, the Seleucids of Syria and the Ptolemies of Egypt, arose in the fourth century B.C., they built on that foundation and extended the hold of Greek culture over the entire area from the Eastern Mediterranean to the Indus River. When Rome completed her conquest of the Italian peninsula in the third century B.C., she fell under the spell of the Greek culture of southern Italy and adopted it as her own. Thus the Romans never did develop a distinctive culture of their own but rather a Greco-Roman culture, which spread throughout the whole Mediterranean world.

As Christianity came on the scene and heralds of the gospel made their way across the Roman Empire, they did not suffer culture shock as modern missionaries do; there was only one basic culture for the entire empire. Moreover, this Greco-Roman culture had a single language: Greek. To be sure, official documents and decrees were issued in Latin, and regional languages, such as the Aramaic of Palestine and Syria, continued to be spoken at home, but the language of business and ordinary communication was Greek. As the books of the New Testament made their appearance in Greek, they were immediately understandable to the whole Mediterranean world.

Another contribution of the Greeks which helped prepare the world for the spread of Christianity was city building. Alexander the Great had built cities as bastions for securing the countryside. There troops and government officials were stationed and the business of a region was transacted. And from the cities the superior culture of Hellenism could be disseminated. Alexander's successors also built cities; and the Romans, seeing the advantages, built cities until the entire Mediterranean world was urbanized. What had been used for the spread of the "gospel" of Hellenism, Paul took up as a means to spread the gospel of the grace of God. Paul's strategy for reaching the Roman world with the gospel was an urban strategy. He spent varying amounts of time in many cities, the longest being Corinth (eighteen months) and Ephesus (over two years).

Roman Political Contribution

The Romans made a political contribution to preparing the world for the coming of Christ and the Church. They united the Mediterranean world, which meant that there could be an easy flow of people across the entire region. The large number of places from which Jews gathered in Jerusalem for the Feast of Pentecost is a case in point (Acts 2:5–11). And the movement of the apostles from province to province was not difficult. Today, however, a host of sovereign nations constitute the Mediterranean world; each requires passports and visas, and one cannot even travel from Jerusalem to Syria or Libya or to other countries of North Africa.

Not only did Rome permit a free flow of people around the Mediterranean area, but she encouraged or facilitated that movement with her magnificent road system. That famous highway system got its start back in the fourth century B.C. and enjoyed rapid expansion during the first Christian century. By around A.D. 100 it comprised some 250,000 miles of paved or improved roads, a distance ten times around the earth at the equator. The familiar saying that "all roads lead to Rome" rose from the fact that a milestone stood in the Forum at Rome with a record of distances, by road, from Rome to chief cities of the empire.

Another Roman political contribution was Roman citizenship and Roman law. The first large-scale extension of Roman citizenship in provincial areas came under Julius and Augustus Caesar. The expansion continued throughout the first Christian century until finally, under Caracalla in 212, Roman citizenship was available to all free persons in the empire. Citizenship conferred special rights and privileges, as well as duties.[1] What this status meant is well illustrated in the experience of the apostle Paul at Philippi (Acts 16:35–40) and later in Jerusalem (Acts 22:22–29). Subsequently it gave him the right to appeal to Caesar as to the supreme court of the empire (Acts 25:11–12).

Another Roman political contribution was the *Pax Romana,* or "Roman Peace." The *Pax Romana* did not mean elimination of war, for there were several armed conflicts during the period (27 B.C.–A.D. 180). Rather, the *Pax* involved the exercise of sufficient military power to keep that world in some semblance of order and tranquility, to keep the lid on the political and social cauldron of the Mediterranean world. And there was also the *Pax Augusta* (the peace of Augustus), the peace, prosperity, and stability that his imperial administration was able to confer on that world.

Jewish Religious Contribution

The Jews made an important religious contribution to preparing the world for Christ by establishing synagogues. Usually considered to have originated in Babylonia during the Exile, synagogues were organized wherever Jews lived in substantial numbers. Jewish districts existed in all the major cities of the Roman Empire at the time of Christ. An educated guess is that there were about one hundred fifty synagogues scattered across the empire early in the first century. Whatever the number, these institutions were lighthouses of monotheism in a polytheistic world. Moreover, they stood for a high ethical standard in a world without moral absolutes. The Scriptures these synagogues possessed were usually written in Greek, rather than Hebrew, in a translation known as the Septuagint, produced in Alexandria, Egypt, between 250–150 B.C.

As a result, many Gentile seekers after truth became "God-fearers" or "proselytes" to the Hebrew faith and later to Christianity. Hints of their number and their receptivity to the Gospel appear in the New Testament. Some came to Jerusalem for the great Feast of Pentecost (Acts 2:10). One rose to a position of leadership in the church at Antioch of Syria (Acts 6:5). An Ethiopian eunuch, highly placed in the court of his land, had also heard about the Hebrews' God and eagerly responded to the Gospel (Acts 8:26–39). Numerous proselytes seem to have embraced the Gospel at Antioch of Pisidia (Acts 13:43), and a "great multitude" of proselytes, or "God–fearing Greeks," at Thessalonica believed in Christ and became members of the church there (Acts 17:4).

Another way in which Judaism prepared for the

coming of Christ was through its expectation of a
Messiah. Anticipations of a Messiah who would deliver God's people Israel appear throughout the Old
Testament. He is presented as Moses' Prophet "like
unto me," Isaiah's "suffering Servant," Jeremiah's
"Branch," Daniel's "Son of Man," and as the coming
of God Himself to deliver His people. During the
later intertestamental period, after Israel fell under the
domination of Rome, the setting up of Messiah's
kingdom was interpreted in largely political overtones.
Christ's disciples had a hard time conceiving of Jesus'
kingdom as a spiritual one. James and John and their
mother thought of it as a literal or political entity soon
to occur and one in which they might sit on His right
hand and His left (Matthew 20:20–22; Mark 10:35–
39).

Yet one more way in which Judaism prepared for
the coming of Christ involved a concern for salvation.
The Law of Moses was doing its work. All the Law
could really do was condemn. More and more it became evident that men and women could not live up
to the standards of God. They became increasingly
impressed with their own sinfulness. The Law was
indeed a tutor or pedagogue to lead them to Christ
(Galatians 3:24–25). As is clear from the New Testament, there was nothing in official Judaism—that of
the Sadducees, Pharisees, or scribes—which brought
heart satisfaction. So people were open to a new,
the way of God's grace through faith in Christ.

Although the Jews were primarily responsible for
the religious preparation for the coming of Christ, and

though the Son of God became incarnate as a Jew, the Romans and Greeks also made religious preparations for His coming. The Romans did this by their conquests; in defeating various peoples they contributed to a loss of faith in their gods, who were perceived as unable to protect them. Thus the Romans, unwittingly, helped to create a spiritual vacuum.

The Greeks made a religious preparation through the speculations of their philosophers, who generally undermined the older polytheistic religions by their skepticism but then failed to provide a satisfactory alternative. Positively, Plato and his followers taught that reality existed not in this present temporal world of the senses but in the world of the spirit, where the highest ideals of the good, the beautiful and the true exist. Some philosophers concluded that behind all the multiplicity of gods there must be a monotheistic being. Zeno and the Stoics developed a high ethic that in many ways approached the New Testament ethic. So philosophers generally were repudiating the old polytheistic cults, some were discovering a monotheistic being behind the welter of gods that people worshiped, some were teaching the immortality of the soul, some were developing elevated ethical systems, and some, such as Epicurus and Zeno (the Stoics), sought a more personal relation to God, or Being, in the universe. They all in their ways both reflected and helped to create a hunger for a personal relationship with a God who could provide eternal life and enablement to live out an ethic that would embrace all human relationships.

NOTE

1. For an especially good discussion of Roman citizenship, see A. N. Sherwin-White, *The Roman Citizenship,* 2nd ed. (Oxford: The Clarendon Press, 1973).

THREE

The World into
Which Christ Came

The Political Situation

IT WAS September 2, 31 B.C. After some weeks of maneuvering, Octavian, with a force of 90,000 men and about 400 warships, had bottled Mark Antony and Cleopatra in the Bay of Actium in western Greece. Antony had an army equal to Octavian's and a fleet of about 500 warships. But because many of Antony's men seemed to feel that they were fighting for an Egyptian queen and not for Rome, they defected in considerable numbers to Octavian. Moreover, Antony's forces were decimated by disease. The great battle which some ancient historians concocted apparently never took place. Only a few of Antony's ships fought at all. Cleopatra managed to escape with a small squadron and fled to Egypt; Antony also escaped and followed her there. Most of the navy and the entire army went over to Octavian within a day or two. Octavian had broken the back of his opposition and was soon to become undisputed master of the Roman world.

Herod the Great of Judea deserted Antony and went to Rhodes to meet Octavian and acknowledge his sovereignty. Since he had been such an active supporter of Octavian's arch foe, Herod could not easily explain himself out of an embarrassing situation. He decided to tell the truth. He frankly admitted his friendship for Antony, described the support he had given him, and promised Octavian the same loyalty if allowed to keep his kingdom. Herod's charm won Octavian over. He agreed to march in state down the coast of Palestine on his way to deal with Antony and Cleopatra in Alexandria. Herod saw that nothing was lacking. To help his cause, he sent a gift of a very large sum of money to his new master. On hearing the news of Antony's suicide and ultimately Cleopatra's, Herod breathed more easily, and he was soon rewarded with extended domains for his demonstrations of loyalty to Octavian.

Augustus as Emperor

Octavian had established his claim to the political inheritance of Julius Caesar. His victory brought to an end a century of civil war. With the cessation of hostilities, the great *Pax Romana* began. In 27 B.C. Octavian (by now given the title of Augustus) became the first emperor of Rome (actually he preferred to be called *princeps,* or *first citizen*), and The Eternal City now governed an empire rather than a republic. Everywhere, Augustus was hailed as founder of a new golden age, and he spared no effort to make the hope a reality. Piracy virtually disappeared from the high seas. Robbery greatly declined on land. He brought a general stability to the frontiers. Settled conditions permitted flourishing commerce throughout the empire.

As the first citizen of the empire, Augustus controlled all phases of government, and as commander-in-chief of the army he controlled the military. The army was the real power of the empire. Organized and trained by Octavian, it had been responsible for bringing him to power. The 5,000-man Praetorian Guard provided him with a personal task force; stationed as it was at the edge of Rome, it served to remind the Senate and the people who was boss. In the empire at large Augustus maintained an army of about a third of a million men. These were distributed principally along the Rhine and Danubian frontiers and in Syria and served mostly to protect the frontiers rather than to maintain the power of the emperor. The navy policed the Mediterranean, the Black Sea, and the Danube.

Augustus shared the rule of the provinces of the empire with the Senate, even as he did the responsibility of administration in Rome. In general, senatorial provinces (such as Sicily) were those most thoroughly Romanized and therefore needed only a few local police to keep order. Imperial provinces, on the other hand, required legionary forces to enforce the Roman will.

In all provinces, governors and other officials received a salary during Augustus's reign, thus removing one of the great causes of extortion during the days of the Republic. In addition to these two classes of provinces, a number of client kingdoms existed within the empire. While Rome controlled the foreign relations of these principalities, they enjoyed a great deal of local autonomy. Judea and Galatia, among others, fell into this category in Augustus' day; but before the end of his reign he transformed them into provinces. As part of his effort to tidy up the empire and to estimate resources for purposes of taxation and military recruitment, Augustus ordered a comprehensive census of the population and an evaluation of property in each of the provinces (Luke 2:1–2). Evidently, however, a census could be taken in the various provinces as conditions permitted or dictated, rather than occurring at the same time everywhere.(See Chapter 8.)

At home, Augustus turned his attention to problems that the Senate had never been successful in handling during the days of the Republic. For instance, he established police and fire departments. To solve the problems of grain supply and the needs of the large number on public dole, the Senate turned over to Augustus the responsibility of obtaining adequate grain stores from various parts of the empire. By the time Christ was born, perhaps as many as two hundred thousand (about one-fifth of the population) were on public welfare rolls in the capital!

Tiberius

Before his death, Augustus adopted Tiberius (a stepson by his third wife) as his son and associated Tiberius with himself in ruling the State. Upon the death of Augustus in A.D. 14, Tiberius refused to regard himself as emperor until the Senate ratified the choice. The new emperor (who ruled A.D. 14–37) had become embittered and suspicious during the years of mistreatment at the hands of Augustus (Tiberius had not been Augustus' first choice as his successor), and his personality caused him no end of trouble with the Senate and the people of Rome. Finally, he grew tired of this friction and retired to Capri in A.D. 26 (the year he appointed Pilate procurator of Judea) and left the rule of the city to the commander of the Praetorian

Guard. Whatever inability he demonstrated in ruling Rome, Tiberius compensated for it by able administration of the empire, where peace and prosperity continued.

Herod the Great

While Augustus was setting the Roman house in order and rehabilitating a somewhat impoverished empire, Herod the Great was hard at work in Palestine, justifying the confidence that the emperor had placed in him. Herod was important to Augustus in at least three spheres. First, his military expeditions east of the Jordan largely succeeded in subjecting the wild Bedouin there, and made possible the formation of the Roman province of Arabia.

Second, he furthered the cultural aims of Augustus, who wanted to develop a uniform Greco-Roman culture for the entire empire. Herod succeeded in Hellenizing Palestine as the Seleucids had never been able to do. He supported the cult of the emperor and built temples to Augustus. He rebuilt Samaria, renaming it Sebaste (Greek for Augustus). Characteristic Hellenistic structures he built there included temples, a theater, and a hippodrome. To furnish his domain with an adequate port, Herod built Caesarea on the site of Strato's Tower and named it for Augustus. There he constructed a breakwater and quay that constituted an engineering feat remarkable for his day. In the town itself, a temple to Caesar dominated the skyline; and a theater, amphitheater, and hippodrome provided for other aspects of a Hellenistic society. Even in Jerusalem he built a theater, and near the holy city an amphi-theater.

Third, Herod effectively controlled Palestine for Rome—an accomplishment of which his descendants and the Roman procurators were to prove incapable. To keep the country under control, he built fortresses at Alexandrium, Hyrcania, Herodium, Masada and Machaerus.

At the same time that he supported emperor worship in Palestine, Herod was engaged in rebuilding the Jewish temple—a project he was never destined to finish. Begun in 20–19 B.C., it had been under construction for 46 years by the time Jesus began His ministry (John 2:20), and it did not reach completion until A.D. 64, only to be destroyed in A.D. 70 by the armies of Titus. For this project Herod spared no expense. Outside of the building of Caesarea, it was his crowning achievement. Generally improved economic conditions during Herod's reign permitted other building activities, among which were a number of public works, a summer palace at Jericho, and architectural gifts to the cities of Syria, Asia, and Greece, where he erected theaters, stadiums, and temples to pagan gods. Such expenditures, made in a spectacular manner, served to combat the anti-Semitism so prevalent among the Gentiles and to prove to the world that he was as civilized as anyone. He also subsidized Greek scholars and philosophers to show his interest in intellectual pursuits.

In his personal affairs Herod was not so successful. Even before the Battle of Actium, they were seriously complicated. When Herod returned from his meeting with Octavian at Rhodes, he found the domestic kettle at the boiling point. His wife Mariamne, of the Maccabean or Hasmonean line, had grown to loathe him. Mariamne's mother, Alexandra, also hated him and plotted against him. On the other hand, Salome, Herod's sister, was determined to destroy the Hasmonean influence at court. Ultimately, Salome won out. At a mock trial, Mariamne was falsely convicted of unfaithfulness and treachery and sent to the gallows. Later, Alexandra was executed for real complicity in another plot.

After Mariamne's execution, Herod, who still loved her greatly, became temporarily insane. His physicians gave him up. Slowly, however, he recovered; but his old charm was gone. He became moody and suspicious. For a while there was peace in the household, but during the last decade of Herod's life contention again arose, this time among three of his sons. Finally Herod had all three of them executed. Shortly after the execution of the third, he died a painful death from what has been described as a combination of intestinal cancer and dropsy. Against such a background of murder and intrigue, it is no surprise that Herod would slay many infants at Bethlehem in an effort to destroy the newborn King of the Jews (Matthew 2:16).

Herod's Sons

Before he died, Herod made out a new will, naming Archelaus king of Judea, Samaria, and Idumea, Antipas tetrarch of Galilee and Perea, and Philip tetrarch of the region northeast of the Sea of Galilee. Since Rome really controlled the area, it was up to Augustus to decide whether or not the terms of the will should be followed. His decision was favorable, with the exception that Archelaus was made ethnarch instead of king and put on probation.

These three sons had varying success in their respective administrations. Philip proved to be an able ruler, but certainly the Gentile character of his subjects made the way smoother for him. His Hellenism would not have been well received by Jews. He built his capital at Caesarea Philippi in honor of the emperor and rebuilt Bethsaida and called it Julias in honor of Augustus's daughter. He ruled until his death in A.D. 34. Herod Antipas had mixed success with his domain. In A.D. 6 a rebellion occurred in Galilee; the Romans ruthlessly crushed it and permitted Antipas to remain at the helm. Later he built his capital at Tiberias, on the western shore of the Sea of Galilee. It was this Herod whom Jesus described as "that fox" (Luke 13:32), and before whom Jesus stood during Passion Week (Luke 23:7–15). He also executed John the Baptist (Luke 9:9; Mark 6:14–29). Later, in A.D. 37, the emperor Caligula removed Antipas from office and exiled him to Gaul.

Archelaus had the most trouble of all. He proved utterly incapable of handling the Jews of his realm and Augustus finally banished him to Gaul in A.D. 6. At that time the emperor changed the status of Judea and Samaria to that of an imperial province and appointed a procurator (resident at Caesarea) to govern the territory; this arrangement lasted until A.D. 41.

The Procurators

Five procurators ruled during the life of Christ: Coponius (A.D. 6–9); Marcus Ambibulus (A.D. 9–12); Annius Rufus (A.D. 12–15); Valerius Gratus (A.D. 15–26); and Pontius Pilate (A.D. 26–36). Little is known about the first four, and they have little significance for the life of Christ. As is well known from the New Testament message, Pilate permitted the crucifixion of Christ. One wonders, however, why he bothered to please the Jews on this occasion when he so violently outraged them at other times. Once, under cover of darkness, he smuggled into Jerusalem military insignia bearing the likeness of the emperor. A crowd of Jews went to Caesarea to remonstrate with him for their removal. Refusing them for six days, he finally ordered troops to surround them on the sixth day and threaten them with instant death if they did not disperse. They bared their necks and prepared to die, whereupon he finally relented.

On another occasion he robbed the Jewish temple treasury to obtain finances to build a new aqueduct to Jerusalem. This time he did not heed Jewish remonstrances and set the troops on the unarmed demonstrators, killing many. At the end of his regime he killed a large number of Samaritans who had assembled at Mount Gerizim to witness the unearthing of some sacred objects purportedly buried there by Moses. This proved to be his undoing, and he was sent to Rome for trial. The procurators never seemed to understand the Jewish mind, and Jewish outrage built up an increasing opposition to all things Roman until open rebellion flared in A.D. 66, with the resultant destruction of the temple and the holy city in A.D. 70.

A political party in Judaism that should not be overlooked were the Herodians. They were supporters of the dynasty of Herod, particularly of Herod Antipas, ruler of Galilee. Like the Pharisees, they stood to lose their position if the status quo were destroyed by the institution of Jesus' kingdom. Therefore they joined the Pharisees in an effort to trap Jesus and obtain his arrest and conviction (Matthew 22:16; Mark 12:13). They were pro-Hellenistic and supported Herod's promotion of Greco-Roman culture in Palestine.

The Geographical Background

The drama of history unfolds on the stage of geography. The stage where Christ performed His earthly ministry was the tiny land of Palestine. Aside from its great importance as a land bridge between Europe, Asia and Africa, this small territory is primarily significant for its religious impact. Here were cradled Judaism and Christianity; and here are found sites dear to the heart of Muslims as well.

Extending from Dan in the North to Beersheba in the South (1 Kings 4:25; about 150 miles) and from the Mediterranean to the Jordan (a strip of land some twenty five miles wide in the north and about seventy five in the south), Palestine is approximately the size of New Hampshire or Vermont. During much of the New Testament period, rulers of this area also extended their authority beyond the Jordan, to Perea and the area northeast of the Sea of Galilee.

Coastal Plains to Mountains

Even this small territory presents a varied terrain. Along the Mediterranean coast, nearly at sea level, lies the Maritime Plain, which divides from south to north into the plains of Philistia, Sharon, and Acre. Next come the foothills, or Shephelah or Piedmont, ranging from 500 to 1,000 feet high. Towering above them rise the mountains of the western ridge to an altitude of 2,000 to 4,000 feet. This area subdivides, north to south, into Galilee, Samaria, Judea and Idumea. Famous peaks of this range include Mount Tabor, near the southern end of the Sea of Galilee, about 1,925 feet high; Mount Gerizim in central Samaria, about 2,900 feet; and the five hills of Jerusalem, almost 2,600 feet.

Jordan Valley to Eastern Ridge

The next longitudinal division of Palestine is the Jordan rift, deepest "ditch" on the face of the earth. Beginning near 9,232 foot Mount Hermon, the Jordan rapidly descends almost to sea level at Lake Huleh (about four miles long by three miles wide, now farmland drained by the Israeli Government). Ten miles farther south it flows into the Sea of Galilee, almost 700 feet below sea level (its size is about thirteen miles long and eight miles wide). In the next 65 miles, the Jordan slithers over 200 miles of riverbed to dump its waters into the deepest declivity on earth. There lies the Dead Sea, about fifty miles long and eleven miles

wide. Its surface is almost 1,300 feet below sea level
with its deepest part reaching down another twelve or
thirteen hundred feet.

Like the western mountain ridge, the eastern ridge
rises two to four thousand feet. During the life of
Christ, this territory, anciently divided, north to
south, into Bashan, Gilead, and Moab, was known
as the Tetrarchy of Philip (with its areas of Ituraea,
Trachonitis, Batanaea, and Auranitis), Decapolis, and
Perea.

Jerusalem and Caesarea

As far as the Jews were concerned, Jerusalem remained the capital of Palestine in New Testament
times, and the Romans were forced to maintain some
administrative offices there. But the Roman seat of
government was Caesarea, located on the Mediterranean about twenty miles south of Mount Carmel.
This city, with its artificial harbor and long breakwater,
was built by Herod the Great and dedicated in
10–9 B.C.

Decapolis

One area requiring further comment is Decapolis
(see map, p. 30). As the name implies, it originally
was a region, or confederacy, of ten cities (Damascus,
Philadelphia, Raphana, Scythopolis, Gadara, Hippo,
Dion, Pella, Gerasa, and Canatha); but the number
varied from time to time, at one point including as
many as eighteen cities. The region of Decapolis mentioned in the gospels (Matthew 4:25; Mark 5:20;
7:31) was located south and east of the Sea of Galilee,

with the exception of Scythopolis, which lay west of the Jordan. Decapolis at the time of Christ covered roughly the area known anciently as Gilead, overlapping some of Bashan to the north and more of Ammon to the south. Several of the cities listed above (such as Damascus and Canatha) did not, then, lie within this district, but to the north of it.

The Decapolis cities were Hellenistic; some of them may have been founded soon after Alexander the Great conquered Palestine. The Romans freed these towns from Jewish control and gave them much local autonomy under the general supervision of the legate of Syria. To the Jews, the cities of Decapolis were important as centers for the spread of Greco-Roman culture, the entrance of which disunified the closely knit Jewish national culture. In contrast with the strictly Jewish cities of Palestine, they contained pagan temples, baths, amphitheaters, and other structures commonly seen in a Gentile city of the period. Their social and religious life also displayed the looseness of first century pagan concepts.

Religious Developments

In addition to his political reforms, Augustus turned his attention to religious and moral rehabilitation. He sought both to restore religious feeling to a prominent place in the lives of his subjects and to use religion as a prop for his political program. Besides the temples his generals or associates built or restored, Augustus himself restored or repaired over eighty of them. While the philosophers ridiculed the old Roman gods—a

Palestine in the Time of Christ

0   20   40
Scale of Miles

Most geographical locations discussed in pages 26–29 appear in this map.

general decline in the worship of the gods had set in by the time Christ was born—their followers were still numerous.

Roman Religion

Shortly after 200 B.C. another element entered the religious scene of the Mediterranean world: the worship of the goddess Roma, the personification of the Roman State. Ultimately, leaders of state shared deification along with the state. Beginning as it did in the Eastern provinces, this practice had as its background the god-king ideal of the ancient Near East, and inhabitants of the Eastern provinces had voluntarily deified such Roman rulers as Julius Caesar and Mark Antony. In fact, traces of Augustus worship can be detected as early as 29 B.C. Soon Herod the Great built temples to Augustus at Caesarea and Sebaste (Samaria). In 12 B.C. an altar to Roma and Augustus was established near the modern town of Lyons, France, and shortly thereafter near modern Cologne. Seeing the political value of emperor worship, Augustus accepted it and even fostered its development. Multitudes hailed him as a divine savior, responsible for the peace, prosperity, and security of the empire. Moreover, in 12 B.C. Augustus was elected Pontifex Maximus, or head of the state religion.

Mystery Religions

A third important element of Roman religion at the time of Christ was the mystery religions. These were called mysteries (*Mysterion* came from a Greek root meaning "to initiate") because the initiate entered them through an elaborate and secret ritual accompanied by an emotional stirring resembling a salvation experience. In this emotional upheaval, adherents fancied they became one with the mythical head of the mystery, who had died and risen again. By this token they could expect a blissful life in the hereafter. The mysteries provided the personal contact with the god and the emotional element missing in the worship of the old gods, the philosophies of the intellectuals, or the state cult. It is important to note that while there are superficial similarities between the mystery religions and Christianity, all the mystery religions had a mythical basis. None was related to a historical personage, as was Christianity. Nor did they require a new way of life or provide enablement for living that life, as did Christianity. Moreover, their deities usually were linked to the agricultural cycle, dying and rising again with the rhythm of the seasons, rather than dying and rising once purposefully to provide the basis for salvation from sin.

The Jewish Temple

As in the Old Testament, the temple stood at the heart of New Testament Judaism. Destroyed by Nebuchadnezzar in 586 B.C., it had been rebuilt by the returning exiles, dedicated in 515 B.C., and reconstructed by Herod the Great in 20–19 B.C. and following. In about a year and a half the sanctuary itself was completed, but the rest of the temple complex was not finished until A.D. 64. When Jesus made His trips to the temple, He saw a truly beautiful structure of white marble abundantly decorated with gold—a dazzling sight in the bright Palestinian sun. The temple area measured almost 600 feet east and west and a little over 600 feet north and south. It was divided into the outer court or court of the Gentiles and the inner court, subdivided into the women's court and the court of the Israelites.

Within the latter lay the court of the priests in which the sanctuary stood. This was divided into the Holy Place, and Holy of Holies. Only the priests entered the Holy Place, and only the high priest entered the Holy of Holies, and then only on the Day of Atonement. Central to the temple worship were the sacrificial offerings, including daily morning and evening sacrifices, special offerings on festal occasions, and myriads of private offerings to cover offenses mentioned in the Law.

Priestly Power

Consequently, there was always a substantial number of officiating priests moving about the temple. At the head of these descendants of Aaron was the high priest, who was the religious head of the Jewish people. As such, he negotiated with governments to which the Jews were subject. Also, he alone entered the Holy of Holies on the great Day of Atonement to offer sacrifices for all the sins unwittingly committed by his people. And he presided over the Sanhedrin, a court that handled all cases of infraction of the Law.

Since the Jews did not distinguish between civil and religious law, the power of this body was tremendous. The Romans did not violate their authority except in cases of treason or other major crimes. The priestly party in Judaism generally constituted the more wealthy classes, possessed the political power, and controlled the civil life during the Herodian period.

Forced to deal with Gentiles by virtue of their public position, the priestly party (constituting the group known in the New Testament as the Sadducees, so named after Zadok the priest—1 Kings 2:35) tended to make concessions to pagan ideas and practices. Being more open to Hellenizing influences, they became rationalistic and anti-supernaturalistic in their approach to theology. For instance, they denied the existence of angels and the resurrection (Matthew 22:23 ff; Acts 23:8). They believed the soul died with the body, so there was no room in their theological system for a future judgment. Probably they gave greater weight to the Law than to the prophets, but there is no evidence that they rejected the latter. However, they did reject the oral traditions which the Pharisees minutely developed. Since the Sadducees depended so heavily on the temple and the sacrificial system and on their social position around Jerusalem, it seemed almost a foregone conclusion that they would disappear when the temple and Jerusalem were destroyed in A.D. 70. Ministering alongside the priests were Levites (descendants of Levi; mentioned twice in the gospels—Luke 10:32; John 1:19). Since they were not descendants of Aaron, they could not be high priests, but they could assist them in various rituals.

The Synagogue

During the intertestamental period, when most Jews were dispersed throughout Mesopotamia and the

Eastern Mediterranean world, a new institution grew up to supply the cohesive element for Judaism that the Jerusalem temple had formerly provided. Known as the synagogue, it was the place of Sabbath gathering for study of the Scripture and prayer. Wherever as many as ten Jewish families resided, a synagogue was to be organized. Widely distributed by the time of Christ, synagogues assumed an important place in Jewish life, for in conjunction with them schools were frequently set up. The synagogue was the special sphere of ministry of the Pharisees, who, though numbering little more than 6,000 in Herod's day, had great influence and were the most vital Jewish party of their time.[1]

Pharisees and Sadducees

The Pharisees were separatists, the puritans of their time, and as such withdrew from evil associations or places of political leadership. They were laymen, while the Sadducees were priests. In further contrast to the Sadducees, they were supernaturalistic in doctrine—holding to the resurrection of the dead, and the existence of angels, and punctiliously observing the law, which they constantly elaborated by means of the oral law or "tradition of the ancients." Their undue concern over ceremonial washings, fastings, and the like brought them into conflict with Christ and His disciples. And their religious hypocrisy often earned them the condemnation of our Lord. Not all were hypocrites, however, as the interest of Nicodemus and Joseph of Arimathea demonstrate. The Sadducees tended to make concessions to the Greco-Roman culture of Palestinian officialdom. The Pharisees refused to do so, but centered their attention on strict observance of the Law.

Some pious Jews wearied of finding satisfaction in public life at all and turned to the monastic or ascetic life. Such were the Essenes, who were primarily located along the northwest side of the Dead Sea, although some lived in cities. They numbered perhaps 4,000 in all, if one accepts the testimony of Philo and Josepheus. Entrance into their communities was by certain rites of initiation; once a member, a man lived under very strict regulations, including community of all property. Generally speaking, the Essenes abstained from marriage, but some "marrying Essenes" are known. Their recruits, then, normally came from outside their ranks rather than by propagation.

Ascetics and Zealots

Not much was known about the ascetics of Palestine during this period until the discovery of the Dead Sea Scrolls, and more particularly until the excavation of the Qumran community near the scroll caves in 1951 ff. The inhabitants of Qumran, though possibly not Essenes, were certainly closely related to them. Qumran was occupied from about 150 B.C. until shortly before the fall of Jerusalem in A.D. 70. The nearby cemetery, containing graves of over one thousand persons, gives some idea of the size of the community.

Qumran

The Qumran *Manual of Discipline,* one of the best preserved Dead Sea Scrolls, is an interesting piece of ascetic literature. In addition to describing the rules of the sect, it reveals that they had a great interest in the coming of the Messiah and the establishment of the Kingdom of God. Theologically, Essenes were akin to the Pharisees, thoroughgoing supernaturalists and observers of the Law. They differed radically from the Pharisees in many interpretations of the Law, however. Like the Sadducees, the Essenes left no lasting impression on Judaism.

In the last few decades, a flood of interpretative literature on the Dead Sea Scrolls has appeared, much of it seeking to discover in the Qumran community antecedents of Christianity. Particularly frequent has been the suggestion that the "Teacher of Righteousness" of Qumran is to be linked in some way to the Messianic concept in the New Testament. In fact, some have viewed Jesus Christ as a sort of reincarnation of the teacher of righteousness, and they have sought to find anticipations of nearly every significant event in the life of Christ in Qumran descriptions of the teacher of righteousness, thus reducing the uniqueness of Christ. Some of the claims for the teacher seem to be greatly exaggerated, especially the one that he was expected to return. Moreover, it is hard to distinguish between the teacher of righteousness as an ideal and as an individual. Since topflight scholars are disagreed on identity and as to how to interpret Qumran references to him, we need not be unduly disturbed over his detracting from the uniqueness of Jesus Christ.[2]

Hopes for Messiah

Something was said above concerning the Messianic hope in Judaism. While the Old Testament predicted

a coming Messiah, the anticipation of a Messiah increased greatly during the intertestamental period.
Then, suffering under the heel of foreign oppressors,
the Jews began to look more and more for a coming
deliverer and the restoration of a national state. This
anticipation gave rise to a substantial amount of apocryphal literature, much of it apocalytic or prophetic in
nature (dating about 300 B.C. to A.D. 100).

The apocalypses did not picture a Messiah who
would suffer and die for the sins of His people, but
one who would serve as a political deliverer. An illustration of this concept is found in the attitudes of
Jesus' disciples, who had a hard time thinking beyond
a political kingdom to His coming death and resurrection. In brief, the apocalypses speak of a coming Messiah (some picture him as merely human and others as
supernatural), a final destruction of hostile heathen,
the establishment of a kingdom in Palestine, the new
heaven and new earth, and the resurrection and last
judgment. Though the apocalypses were an expression
of the more literate element in Jewish life, no doubt
many of the common people looked for a deliverer
too, especially as tension grew between Jew and Roman in the years preceding the Jewish wars and the
destruction of Jerusalem in A.D. 70.

Zealots

Another sect, religiopolitical in nature, were the
Zealots. In general, they agreed with the Pharisees in
religious matters, but recognized God alone as their
ruler. Therefore, they would not recognize foreign
rulers and advocated violence to liberate themselves

from Rome. Simon, one of Jesus' disciples, probably had once belonged to this party, as his name implies (Luke 6:15; Acts 1:13).

The Samaritans

While the foregoing summarizes the main elements in Judaism at the time of Christ, there was one more group in Palestine outside of Judaism that requires comment: the Samaritans. When Jeroboam split the kingdom after the death of Solomon, he introduced calf worship there. Later, Jezebel brought in Baal worship. As punishment for idolatry the Northern Kingdom went into captivity in 723/722 B.C. At that time the Assyrians deported many of the chief citizens and imported colonists loyal to them. Intermarriage brought about a people not strictly Jewish in blood or in religion. When the Jews returned from Babylonia and restored the commonwealth, they refused permission to the Samaritans to have a part in the temple worship, whereupon the Samaritans established their own worship center on Mount Gerizim.

In common with the Jews, they observed the Sabbath, circumcision, sacred feasts, and looked forward to a coming Messiah (who would in this case convert all nations to Samaritanism). But they accepted the Pentateuch alone, rejecting the rest of the Old Testament. They held that Mount Gerizim was the true abode of God on earth and transferred the occurrence of many sacred events from other sites to the Mount and its environs. John 4 makes it clear that there were few dealings between Samaritans and Jews in Jesus' day, at least as far as the most pious were concerned.

The Multi-cultural World of Jesus

As we close this discussion about the world into which Christ came, we are just as concerned about the world in which He and His followers functioned.

Jewish Faith

A reading of the Gospels impresses us that His was especially a Jewish world. He was circumcised the eighth day, dedicated in the temple on the fortieth day, brought up under the law, made a pilgrimage to Jerusalem at age twelve and paid due respect to the temple and synagogue.

Fluency in Greek

But there was more to His world than that. While His family may have commonly spoken Aramaic at home, Palestine was multi-lingual in Jesus' day. This is clearly evident from the fact that the inscription on the cross, "Jesus the Nazarene, the King of the Jews," (John 19:19) was written in Hebrew (Aramaic), Latin (the official language), and Greek (the universal cultural language). Joseph must have known Greek and must have spoken it frequently; his family must have grown up speaking it. If Jesus' half brothers, James and Jude, could write good Greek as they composed their New Testament epistles, Jesus must have known and used it too. Joseph would have found it easier to function in Egypt (when he fled there with Mary and Jesus after His birth) if he spoke Greek. Not only Jesus' family, but also His Jewish disciples Peter, John, and the tax collector Levi (Matthew) were also fluent in Greek, as their several New Testament books demonstrate.

Greco-Roman Cities and Commerce

Mention of Levi as a tax collector introduces another dimension of the wider experience of Jesus and His disciples. Matthew 9:9 in the King James Version correctly identifies Levi's activity; he was sitting at the "receipt of custom" when Jesus called him. That is, his place of business was a toll booth or customs office near the wharves of Capernaum. He collected tariffs or duties levied on goods shipped across the Sea of Galilee from the territory of Philip to that of Herod Antipas or on merchandise or goods in transit from Jerusalem to Tyre or Damascus. This detail helps to remind us that Galilee was not provincially Jewish. In fact, in the New Testament it is called "Galilee of the Gentiles" (Matthew 4:15). That is, it was heavily influenced by non-Jewish elements. As noted earlier, the region of Decapolis lay just to the east of the Sea of Galilee and Jesus ministered there; one city of this Greco-Roman league of cities, Scythopolis, lay to the west of the Jordan in the territory of Galilee proper. Also, Caesarea Philippi, the capital of Herod Philip (named for Augustus Caesar) northeast of the Sea of Galilee, and Tiberias on the western shore of the Sea in Galilee proper (named for the emperor Tiberius), a creation of Herod Antipas, were not very Jewish in their orientation.

The Example of Sepphoris

Especially pertinent to Jesus' own experience in Galilee, however, was the city of Sepphoris, Herod Antipas' capital of Galilee during Jesus' youth, which lay only four miles north of Nazareth. This city of perhaps 30,000 people, with its palace, forum, Greco-Roman theater, villas, temples and more provided a stark contrast to the sleepy village of Nazareth with its some four hundred inhabitants. Was Sepphoris possibly Jesus' "city set on a hill" (Matthew 5:14)? And was He able to people his discourses with merchants, government officials, wealthy landowners and more from his familiarity with this bustling non-Jewish center?[3]

To be sure, Jesus' world was largely rural and peopled with farmers, fishermen and shepherds, but there appears to be another dimension that is totally ignored. Not only do we need to take into account the impact on Galilee of the cities of Decapolis and Sepphoris and Tiberias and Caesarea Philippi, but also of the great city of Caesarea about twenty-five miles southwest of Nazareth and to a lesser degree rebuilt Samaria about twenty-five miles south of Nazareth. Both of the latter were also bastions of Greco-Roman paganism. Finally, New Testament Palestine was full of the influence of Greco-Roman (Hellenistic) paganism, as the non-supernaturalistic views of the Sadducees and others demonstrate.

NOTES

1. It should be remembered, however, that as good Jews, the Pharisees loyally supported the temple.

2. For discussion see William S. LaSor, *Amazing Dead Sea Scrolls* (Chicago: Moody, 1959), pp. 164–71, and the bibliography referred to on those pages. See also William S. LaSor, *The Dead Sea Scrolls and the New Testament* (Grand

Rapids: Eerdmans, 1972), Chapters 8, 9. LaSor has effectively dealt with assertions concerning the Teacher of Righteousness.

3. For a discussion of the excavation and significance of Sepphoris, see Richard A. Batey, *Jesus and the Forgotten City* (Grand Rapids: Baker, 1991).

FOUR

The Nature of the
Person of Christ

His Deity

IT IS not enough to demonstrate that Jesus actually lived in Palestine and to picture the world into which He came. He was more than man—more than a mere child of His age. He was the God-Man, the exalted Second Person of the Trinity incarnate. Scripture affirms our Lord's deity in at least eight ways.

His Names

The names given to the God-Man in the gospels are not empty titles. Each has a significance. Several indicate deity. As the *Logos* (or Word), John 1:1 ff., He is the expression or revealer of God. That the *Logos* is not some inferior being who merely conveys an impression of God to humanity is clear from the first verses of John's Gospel, where He is declared to be *eternal* and *God* Himself. Another term, *Son of God,* though employed in several senses in Scripture, sometimes denotes the essential deity of Christ. Examples of this appear in Matthew 11:27; 14:28–33; 16:16; and 26:63. In yet other passages Jesus is called *God*. Prophetically, Isaiah called Him "mighty God" (9:6), and said that John the Baptist would "make straight in the desert a highway for our God" (i.e., Christ, Isaiah 40:3). Isaiah also termed Him *Immanuel* (7:14), which Matthew interprets as "God with us" (1:23). Thomas, beholding Christ's wounds said, "My Lord and my God" (John 20:28); Jesus did not refuse this ascription of deity. Other New Testament passages referring the title of God to the Savior include Titus 2:13; and Hebrews 1:8; cf. Psalm 45:6. A fourth title, *Lord*, is sometimes applied to Christ in the New Testament in such a way as to be practically the equivalent of *God*. Significant verses on this point include Mark 12:36–37; Luke 2:11; 3:4; Acts 2:36; 1 Corinthians 12:3; Philippians 2:11.

His Claims

Although Jesus carried on His ministry largely in the power of the Holy Spirit and restricted the manifestation of His deity, He nevertheless made it quite clear who He was. To the Jews, who claimed Abraham as Father, He asserted, "Before Abraham came to be, I am" (John 8:58, literal translation). By this, Jesus taught there was a sense in which the idea of birth and beginning did not apply to Him; in Him was eternal existence (cf. Exodus 3:14). Not only did He always exist in the past, He also would continue to do so in the future. Jesus told the Pharisees, "The Son abides ever" (John 8:35, KJV). When our Lord gave the Great Commission to His disciples, He laid claim to another attribute of deity—omnipotence, when He declared, "All power is given unto me in heaven and in earth" (Matthew 28:18, KJV).

Two of Jesus' claims concerning His ministry also

indicate deity: the power to forgive sins, and the power of resurrection. His ability to forgive sins is intimated in John 8:36 (KJV): "If the Son therefore shall make you free, you shall be free indeed"; but it is more clearly stated in the narrative of the healing of the palsied man. On that occasion Jesus said, "The Son of man has power on earth to forgive sins" (Mark 2:10, KJV). And the scribes said, "Who can forgive sins but God?" (Mark 2:7 KJV). In regard to the resurrection, Jesus promised everyone who receives Him as Savior, "I will raise him up at the last day" (John 6:40, KJV). As Paul made clear in the argument of 1 Corinthians 15, the resurrection of believers is based on the resurrection of Christ. And Jesus avers that He has power to arise from the dead, as well as to raise others: "I lay down my life, that I might take it again. No man takes it from me, but I lay it down of myself. I have power to lay it down, and I have power to take it again" (John 10:17–18, KJV).

In a number of references, Jesus also asserts that God is His Father: Matthew 7:21; 10:32–33; 11:27; 12:50; 15:13; 16:17; 18:10, 19, 35; 20:23; 25:34; 26:29, 53; Luke 2:49; 10:22; 22:29; 24:49; John 6:37–40, 57; and 10:35–36. That this is tantamount to a claim to deity is obvious from John 5:17–18 (KJV): "But Jesus answered them, My Father works hitherto, and I work. Therefore the Jews sought the more to kill him, because he not only had broken the sabbath, but said also that God was His Father, making himself equal with God." Last, Jesus equates Himself with God: John 14:9–10, 23; John 5:19–27; and especially John 10:30, "I and my Father are one."

Evidence from His Works

Greatest of all our Lord's works that testify to His deity is His ability to forgive sins. In the last section on the claims of Christ, we noted His claim to possessing this power. His enemies recognized it as a work of God alone, for they said, "Who can forgive sins but God alone?" (Mark 2:7). And even in the minds of those of our generation who imperfectly understand the way of salvation, there is a general recognition that forgiveness of sins is a divine act.

Creation, too, is a work of God. While scientists have been amazingly successful in fabricating synthetic materials, they have not been able to produce life. Moreover, if human beings could produce life, they could hardly be given credit for the origin of the universe or even inorganic materials on the earth. Scripture attributes the creation of all things to Christ: "All things were made through him; and without him nothing was made that was made" (John 1:3).

It almost goes without saying that Jesus' work of resurrection is an evidence of deity; humanity is hardly able to prolong life, to say nothing of restoring it once it is gone. Likewise, His power over nature attests His deity. Even with modern instruments, scientists are scarcely able to predict the movements of storms; Jesus could quiet them (Mark 4:35–41). In fact, Jesus is not only master of nature, His power also causes all things to hold together (Colossians 1:17). This reference suggests that without Him atomic fission could occur; the laws of nature might become inoperative.

Perhaps healing diseased persons is not clear evidence of deity, but Jesus dealt with diseases doctors could not treat. For instance, the woman with the issue of blood had seen doctors for twelve years and still found no relief (Mark 5:25–26). The leper was incurable until Jesus healed him (Matthew 8:2–4; Luke 17:11–19). Moreover, Jesus restored defective parts of the body: blind eyes, a withered hand, lame legs, and deaf ears. Recognizably, too, His power over demons was supernatural. Satanic power is supernatural and can only be conquered by a superior supernatural force.

Acknowledgment of Satanic Forces

Even the demons recognized the deity of Christ and His authority over them. Evidence of this appeared on two occasions when Jesus healed demon possessed individuals. At Capernaum a demon cried out, "What have we to do with You, Jesus of Nazareth? Did You come to destroy us? I know who You are—the Holy One of God" (Mark 1:24). The demons at Gadara agonized, "What have we to do with You, Jesus, You Son of God? Have You come here to torment us before the time?" (Matthew 8:29).

Testimony of the Father

Jesus frequently spoke of His relationship to the Father and of the Father's interest in what the Son was doing on earth. On two occasions the Father rent the heavens and gave audible witness to this divine relationship. At the baptism He declared, "This is my beloved Son, in whom I am well pleased" (Matthew 3:17; cf. Mark 1:11; Luke 3:22). Similarly, at the transfiguration He asserted, "This is my beloved Son, in whom I am well pleased. Hear him" (Matthew 17:5; cf. Mark 9:7; Luke 9:35).

Evidence from His Attributes

In discussing Jesus' claims to deity, we saw evidence of His eternity and omnipotence (infinite power). In addition to these, the New Testament ascribes at least three other qualities or attributes to our Lord. Jesus Himself virtually claimed holiness when He said, "Which of you convicts Me of sin? And if I tell you the truth, why do you not believe me?" (John 8:46). Hebrews 7:26 and 2 Corinthians 5:21 are two other indisputable references. His omniscience (infinite knowledge) is indicated in several references, for instance: "For Jesus knew from the beginning who they were who did not believe, and who would betray him" (John 6:64). Moreover, He knew all about the woman of Samaria (John 4:17–19, 39), the ass's colt (Matthew 21:2), the upper room (Mark 14:15), Peter's denial (Matthew 26:34), Nathanael (John 1:47–50), and all men in general (John 2:24–25). The evidential value of Jesus' omniscience can be clearly discerned in John 16:30, "Now are we sure that You know all things, and have no need that anyone should question You. By this we believe that You came forth from God." Last, He is the immutable or unchangeable one: "Jesus Christ is the same yesterday, today, and forever" (Hebrews 13:8).

Realization of the Disciples

While the disciples were slow to grasp the full significance of Jesus' nature, on occasion they did recognize deity. After the incident of His walking on the water and Peter's attempt to do the same, the disciples in the boat worshiped, saying, "Truly You are the Son of God" (Matthew 14:33). They affirmed this at the time of Peter's great confession, "You are the Christ, the Son of the living God" (Matthew 16:16).

Testimony of Inspired Writers of Scripture

In addition to the foregoing evidence for the deity of Christ, several of the New Testament writers add items of value. To be sure, they assented to the claims of Christ, the witness of the Father, and the acknowledgment of satanic opposition; but they add comments which are pertinent here. Of all the gospels, John's gives the most exalted view of the person of Christ. Christ has always existed (1:1); He is God (1:1), and has enjoyed eternal and intimate fellowship with the Father (1:2, 18). He is the only begotten of the Father, has become incarnate, and made provision for the salvation of humanity (1:14; 3:16–18). Constantly in his gospel and first epistle, John affirms that He is the Son of God, the Light of the world, and the Savior. Paul calls Him the "Lord of glory" (1 Corinthians 2:8), and the "Son of God" who "gave himself for me" (Galatians 2:20). Paul also says that Jesus is "equal with God" (Philippians 2:6), and that "in Him dwells all the fulness of the Godhead bodily" (Colossians 2:9). The writer to the Hebrews describes Him both as God's Son (1:2) and as God (1:8). Certainly the New Testament leaves no doubt of His deity. Nor is there any question in the mind of the believer, into whose soul has shone the glorious light of salvation provided by the Lord of Glory.

His Humanity

With all of the emphasis on the *man* Jesus in recent religious writing, it hardly seems necessary to discuss the humanity of our Lord. Yet, historically, a full appreciation of Christ's deity has often brought with it a belief in a defective humanity. The early Church fought this error under such names as Apollinarianism and Docetism. Furthermore, a study of Christ's humanity should engender a new realization of the fact that He, as our Shepherd or High Priest, has gone through the experiences we face every day. Therefore He is fully able to sympathize with us in our need. That Christ was truly human may be seen from the fact that He possessed a real human body and a true human soul and spirit.

Evidence for a Real Human Body

To begin with, Jesus had a human mother and an ancestry. Mary was His mother in a real sense (Matthew 1:18; 2:14; 12:47; 13:55; John 2:1). In case motherhood alone be considered insufficient to prove the point, Paul asserts that He "was born of the seed of David according to the flesh" (Romans 1:3). Luke traces His lineage through the whole human family back to Adam (3:23 ff.). Certainly the nativity accounts in the Gospels leave no doubt that the birth of Jesus followed the normal conditions of human birth, and that He was therefore undeniably human. John, after describing so magnificently the deity of Christ, concludes: "And the Word became flesh and dwelt among us" (1:14).

After submitting to the normal conditions of human birth, Jesus experienced a normal human development. He was circumcised the eighth day (Luke 2:21), and He "grew, and became strong in spirit, filled with wisdom" (Luke 2:40; cf. 2:52). The Epistle to the Hebrews testifies that He "learned obedience by the things which he suffered" (5:8). Moreover, as our Lord came to maturity, He had the appearance of a man. In fact, His appearance must have been quite ordinary, or at least characteristic. Said the Samaritan woman at Jacob's well, "How is it that You, being a Jew, ask a drink from me?" (John 4:9). Apparently she knew His nationality from His appearance or speech.

To the two disciples on the road to Emmaus, He seemed to be merely another traveler (Luke 24:13 ff.). Mary mistook Him for the gardener (John 20:15). His synagogue hearers seemingly did not consider Him to be unusual, for they were astonished because He taught with authority (Mark 1:21). Even after the resurrection, He retained human appearance, saying to the disciples, "Behold My hands and My feet . . . handle Me and see, for a spirit does not have flesh and bones, as you see I have" (Luke 24:39).

As our Lord carried on His earthly ministry, He was subject to the limitations of the body. He grew hungry (Matthew 4:2), thirsty (John 19:28), weary (John 4:6), and slept (Matthew 8:24). Climaxing all of His work, He suffered and died. Last, human titles were given to Christ. His favorite was the "Son of Man," which He used of Himself over eighty times. He is also called the "man Christ Jesus," "Jesus, the Son of David," and "a man of sorrows."

Evidence for a True Human Soul and Spirit

But Jesus would not have been a complete man if the immaterial part of His being were somehow defective. Many in the early Church claimed this was true and said that the divine nature took the place of the human will and other human faculties. (For this they were condemned as heretics.) Four passages are particularly clear in demonstrating that He possessed a soul and spirit: "My soul is exceeding sorrowful" (Matthew 26:38, KJV); "Father, into thy hands I commend my spirit" (Luke 23:46, KJV); "He was troubled in spirit" (John 13:21, KJV), and "He groaned in spirit" (John 11:33, KJV). It seems clear in each case that the reference is to His human nature. In addition to specific teaching that Christ possessed a soul and spirit, Scripture attributes to Him human passions: love (Mark 10:21), compassion (Matthew 9:36), sorrow (John 11:35), and anger (Mark 3:5). But while Jesus was truly man, He was without sin, as several references attest (Hebrews 4:15; 2 Corinthians 5:21; John 8:46; Hebrews 9:14; 1 Peter 1:19; 2:22; 1 John 3:5, 7). This could be true because He was supernaturally conceived. Moreover, He never offered sacrifice for His sin and never prayed for personal forgiveness. Whenever displayed, His anger was righteous indignation.

Relation of the Two Natures in Christ

As soon as we establish the divine and human natures of Christ, we face the fundamental difficulty of the relation of the two natures in one person. That the two were brought together in a perfect union is obvious from Scripture. Our Lord never refers to Himself in the plural; nor is there an interchange of "I" and "thou" between the divine and human natures as is true of Trinitarian relationships. Several passages of Scripture refer to the two natures in Christ, but clearly refer them to one person (Romans 1:3–4; Galatians 4:4–5; Philippians 2:6–11). In these as well as others it is obvious that the divine Son of God was united to a human nature.

We have been talking about the union of the two natures in Christ, but as yet have not defined the term *nature*. In simple language, *nature* denotes the sum total of all the essential qualities or attributes of a thing. So, nature as applied to the humanity of Christ includes all that belongs to His humanity. As applied to His deity, it includes all that belongs to His deity. Personality is more than nature. We describe human nature as something common to all human beings, but a person is a nature with the addition of independent subsistence, individuality.

United, Not Fused

When the divine and human natures were united in the person of Christ, they did not lose their identity. They did not fuse into some third sort of entity, neither divine nor human. Christ the man was at the same time divine *and* human. The human nature always remains human and the divine nature always remains divine. Our Lord is therefore both God and man, no less God because of His humanity, no less human because of His deity. It is impossible to transfer the attributes of one nature to the other because a change of attributes would cause a change of essence. For instance, a human body cannot become omnipresent, because one of the main characteristics of a body is localization. In fact, infinity in general cannot be transferred to finite humanity. And if the finity of the human nature were transferred to the divine nature, it could no longer be divine.

This whole subject can become involved in deep theological and philosophical discussion, but it has practical results for every believer. In the first place, the union of the two natures insured a perfect, sinless person. To repeat a common illustration, the human nature, likened to a wire, by itself can be easily bent (caused to sin); welded to a steel beam (to which the divine nature may be likened), it cannot. This sinlessness is absolutely essential to all of His work as Savior. As a man, Christ could die for Himself or on behalf of another; only as God could His death have infinite value as He bore the sins of all mankind. His eternal priesthood, too, is based on the union of the two natures. As man, He could act on behalf of man and evidence human sympathy (Hebrews 4:5). As God, this priesthood is eternal and infinite (Hebrews 7:25). Third, His kingship is related to the union of the two natures. The Davidic covenant (2 Samuel 7) promised a king forever in the line of David. To be a descendant of David requires humanity; the eternal aspect of the covenant requires deity. David's Greater Son will one day return to rule on Mount Zion and in the New Jerusalem.

In summary: the true doctrine of the person of Christ requires belief in a real human nature, a true divine nature, and the union of the two natures in one sinless person, without confusion of attributes. The early church agreed on these aspects of the person of Christ in great ecumenical councils, especially affirming and spelling them out at the Council of Chalcedon (just east of Constantinople) in 451.[1]

NOTE

1. An especially good treatment of the person of Christ appears in John F. Walvoord, *Jesus Christ Our Lord* (Chicago: Moody, 1969).

FIVE

The Message of Christ

TO MANY, the essence of Christ's message appears in the Beatitudes (Matthew 5), the Lord's Prayer (Matthew 6), and the Golden Rule (Matthew 7:12). Those who stress personal commitment in Christian experience would add Christ's salvation message to Nicodemus (John 3), and the discussion of salvation and the Holy Spirit He carried on with the woman at Jacob's Well (John 4). Few realize, however, that the words of Christ recorded in the gospels present in outline a complete system of Christian doctrine. One may discover this by carefully working through the words of Christ as clearly identified in a red letter edition of the Gospels. He refers to the Scriptures, the Godhead, angels, salvation, man, the Church, and the future. In broad outline this is what He says about each.[1]

The Scriptures

Since none of the New Testament books was written until at least a decade after the death of Christ, to Him the Scriptures were the Old Testament books. For these He had a high regard. On several occasions He gave witness to the historicity of Old Testament characters or their acts. Some of these have been doubted by modern critics. He alluded to Jonah's having been swallowed by a great fish and to the repentance of Nineveh (Matthew 12:40–41), to the Queen of Sheba's Jerusalem visit (Matthew 12:42), to David's

eating the holy bread in the house of God (Matthew
12:3–4), to conditions in the days of Noah (Luke
17:26), and to the destruction of Sodom (Luke
17:29). In all, Jesus mentioned twenty Old Testament
characters and quoted from nineteen different books.

Second, Christ's attitude toward the Scripture is
seen in His frequent reference to fulfillment of prophecy. To Him, fulfillment naturally followed prophecy,
and His viewpoint therefore demonstrated His high
regard for Old Testament predictions (Matthew 5:18;
Luke 21:22). The scope of Old Testament prophecy
to which He referred included His ministry in general
(Luke 24:44), opposition to His ministry (Matthew
13:14–15; Matthew 15:7–8), His rejection and triumph (Matthew 21:42; Luke 20:17–18; 22:37;
24:25–27, 44–46), the ministry of John the Baptist
(Matthew 11:10), and the teaching ministry of God
(John 6:45).

Third, Christ *treated* the Scripture as authoritative.
To Satan, during the temptation, He said, "It is written" (Matthew 4:4, 7, 10). To the Jews, He said,
"Scripture cannot be broken" (i.e., annulled or ab-
rogated; John 10:35). On another occasion, Christ
alluded to a commandment in the Law as a commandment of God (Matthew 15:4). Again, Jesus testified to
the Mosaic authorship of the Pentateuch (Mark 1:44;
John 5:46–47; 7:19), a view which many deny. And
last, our Lord even referred to the canon as a whole.
In Luke 24:44, He spoke of the Law, Prophets, and
Psalms—the three divisions of the Hebrew Canon of
the first century A.D. Of course the third section included more than the Psalms; but since it was the

largest book in the section, it was used to stand for the section as a whole.

Jesus spent the whole of His public ministry expounding the Old Testament. Yet, as He used it to denounce the errors of His day, never once did He warn of supposed errors in the Scripture—which modern critics profess to find there. If there were such, He as the Omniscient One should have known about them. Whenever Jesus referred to the Old Testament—"the faithful and true witness" (Revelation 3:14)—did so in terms designed to inspire confidence in every word.

The Godhead

Among the many things our Lord had to say about God the Father are the truths that He is spirit (John 4:24), holy (John 17:11), righteous (John 17:25), loving (John 3:16; 17:23), omniscient (Matthew 10:29-30, Luke 16:15—even knowing the hearts of men), omnipotent (Mark 10:27; John 19:11; Matthew 19:26), self-existent (John 5:26), and dwells in heaven (Matthew 5:16). In relation to His creatures He is merciful (Luke 6:36), provident (Matthew 6:30 ff., Luke 12:24-29), rewarding (Matthew 6:4), and the giver of resurrection life (John 5:21). As to sovereignty, His will is done in heaven and He is Lord of heaven and earth (Matthew 11:25). Therefore, prayer is to be made to Him (Matthew 6:9).

The Godhead is not unitarian but trinitarian in nature. In His Great Commission, Christ gave the command to baptize in the name of the Father, Son, and

Holy Spirit (Matthew 28:19); other indications of triune relationship are numerous. Many passages speak of the Father's relationship to the Son. He commits all things into the hands of the Son (Matthew 11:27), loves the Son (John 5:20; 17:24), has given Him authority to execute judgment (John 5:27), sent the Son on His earthly mission (John 5:30, 36–37), and is one with the Son (John 17:11).

Not only does the Father sustain a paternal relationship to the Son, but also in dozens of references He is called Father in a general sense. These references should not be construed to teach a universal fatherhood of God, however. Christ Himself makes it clear: "No one comes to the Father except through me" (John 14:6). The new birth is essential. For Christ's relationship to the Holy Spirit, see below under "The Doctrine of the Holy Spirit."

The Doctrine of the Person of Christ

In the last chapter the nature of the person of Christ was discussed in some detail. Of necessity there is partial repetition here, but only such items are now included which may be inferred from the statements of Christ Himself. The Savior spoke concerning His person, present mission, and future activity. In respect to His person, He made it clear that He was both divine and human. The pages of the Gospels exude evidences of His deity.

Christ's Deity

Again and again Jesus of Nazareth claimed that God was His Father, obviously not in the same sense as He is to believers or of all persons by creation, but in *the unique* sense (Matthew 12:50; John 5:19 ff.; especially John 17; *et al.*).

On several occasions He referred to Himself as the Son of God (John 5:25; 9:35, 37; 11:4). He said that He came from the Father and was about to return to Him (John 3:13; 6:51, 62; 7:29, 33; 8:23, 42; 16:16, 28). He told the disciples things He had seen while with the Father (John 8:38). Moreover, He asserted that the temple was His house (Matthew 21:13), that all the Father had was His (John 16:15), and that He and the Father were one (John 10:30). As if all this were not sufficient claim to deity, our Lord promised to send the Comforter (John 15:26; 16:8). Certainly only a member of the Trinity could direct the affairs of another member of the Trinity. In performing His works, Christ often exercised divine power. He said, "Peace, be still" to the storm on the Sea of Galilee (Mark 4:39); "Lazarus, come forth," when the latter had been laid to rest in his tomb (John 11:43); and, "But that you may know that the Son of man has power on earth to forgive sins . . . I say to you, arise, take up your bed" to the man afflicted with palsy (Mark 2:10–11). Furthermore, Jesus claimed to be the Messiah (John 4:26). Certainly the Old Testament predicted a divine Messiah.

Last, it is evident from many things Jesus said and did that He possessed certain attributes or qualities which belong to God alone. He is self-existent, an uncaused being (John 5:26). He is eternal (John 8:58: "Before Abraham came to be, I am"—literal translation), all powerful (Matthew 28:18), omniscient

(Matthew 9:4; 26:18, 21, 34; Mark 2:8; Luke 19:30; 22:10–12), and life and the source of it (John 14:6).

Christ's Humanity

As to Jesus' humanity, there are also abundant indications. He referred to Himself constantly as the Son of Man. He spoke of His soul (Matthew 26:38; Mark 14:34), and of human dread as He faced death (Matthew 26:39; Luke 12:50). On the cross He agonized over God's forsaking Him (Matthew 27:46; Mark 15:34), and He cried, "I thirst" (John 19:28). He frequently referred to His sufferings, death, burial, and resurrection (Matthew 20:18–19, 22, 28; 26:2, 31–32; Mark 9:31; 10:33–34; 12:10; Luke 9:22; 17:25; 18:31–33; 24:46; John 2:19). And to demonstrate that He was true humanity after the resurrection, as well as before, Christ said to Thomas, "Reach your finger here, and look at My hands; and reach your hand here, and put it into My side. Do not be unbelieving, but believing" (John 20:27).

Jesus was not merely God and man; He was the God-Man on a mission. Consciousness of His mission permeated His every thought and move (Mark 1:38; 10:45; Luke 2:49; 5:32; 19:10; John 4:34; 9:4; 18:37). As He conceived it, His mission involved suffering, death, burial, and resurrection to pay the penalty of man's sin (for references see last paragraph), and a calling of sinners to repentance toward God and faith in Himself in order to receive salvation.

As He made clear, His message was a new one—built on grace. It was not some effort to patch up the old Mosaic order (Matthew 9:13, 16, 17; Mark 2:21–

22; John 3). Christ's mission also included setting up His kingdom. He offered Himself as King (Matthew 21:1–11; Luke 23:3) and was rejected. But He will come again, will judge humanity, and will reign (Matthew 16:27; 19:28; 21:44; 24–25; 26:64; Mark 14:62; Luke 9:26; 17:30; John 14:2–3). Meanwhile He is preparing a place for His own (John 14:2–3), and making intercession both for those who have received Him as Savior and those who will believe on His name (Luke 22:32; John 17).

The Doctrine of Salvation

While it may be asserted that Christ was and is greater than any of His works, certainly His greatest work was the redemption of mankind. Were it not for Christ's redemptive work, we could not know the essential greatness of the Second Person of the Trinity. According to the words of Christ Himself, the shedding of His blood constitutes the basis of salvation (Matthew 26:28). Granted that this is true, we are faced with the problem of how this act becomes efficacious for all, or is applied to them. His death becomes valuable because as man He could suffer man's penalty. But since one man could pay only his own penalty or that of another, a Savior of the human race must be more than a man. So, as the God-Man, He is infinite and can therefore pay the penalty for an infinite number of individuals.

Works or (and) Faith?

As to the application of Christ's work to the individual, there is something of a problem. In Matthew,

Mark, and Luke there appears on the surface to be a moral approach to salvation, while in John the approach is spiritual. That is to say, in the first three Gospels Jesus seems to teach salvation by works; while in John it is obviously by faith. For instance, in Matthew 19:21 Jesus enunciates to the rich young ruler the following conditions for salvation: "If you want to be perfect, go, sell what you have and give to the poor, and you will have treasure in heaven; and come, follow Me." Again, of the woman who washed His feet with her hair in Simon's house Jesus said, "Her sins, which are many, are forgiven" (Luke 7:47).

In dealing with a problem of this nature, we must remember that any admission by God of the value of human works for salvation would rob deity of the glory belonging to Him in providing salvation for humanity. Second, value assigned to human works in accomplishing salvation would violate the clear scriptural teaching concerning man's depravity in complete estrangement from God and his inability to do anything to get himself saved (e.g., Ephesians 2:8–9; Titus 3:5). Third, a detailed analysis of each passage which appears to teach salvation by works will demonstrate that Jesus merely utilized the work as an evidence or test of faith. Jesus tested the rich young ruler's devotion by the command to part with his earthly goods. Obviously the man's life was so wealth-centered that he could not put Christ in the place of primacy. For the fallen woman, her devotion was an indication of her faith and love. Did not Jesus Himself tell her, "Your faith has saved you. Go in peace" (Luke 7:50)? Certainly Jesus' clear emphasis on salvation by faith in the Son of God and His work outlined to Nicodemus (John 3) was not inconsistent with accounts from the other Gospels discussed above.

Repent and Receive

In His presentation of the salvation message, Jesus frequently urged His hearers to repent (Matthew 4:17; 10:7; Mark 1:15; Luke 13:3, 5). Because of incorrect popular usage, repentance is commonly misunderstood. The literal meaning of the Greek word translated *repent* means an *about face,* or revolutionary *change of mind* concerning God and His demands on us. The concept is well illustrated in 1 Thessalonians 1:9, KJV, where the same word is used in the original, "You *turned* to God from idols to serve the living and true God." Jesus also taught the indispensability of the new birth (John 3:3, 6–7). Again the literal translation is much more meaningful: "You must be born from above" (John 3:3). That is to say, by faith individuals receive Christ as Savior and a new divine life is imparted to them. Jesus is the only one through whom we can be saved (John 14:6), and no one who comes to Him need fear rejection (John 6:37).

As sinners place faith in Christ, they receive eternal life at that moment (John 5:24; 6:47, 54), and the Son intercedes with the Father on their behalf to keep them in grace (John 17:9–26). Jesus also declared that the Father performed a ministry in drawing unbelievers to the Savior (John 6:44, 65). As He preached salvation, Jesus ministered primarily to Jews; but He made it clear that regeneration was for all (Luke 24:47). Once sinners have put their faith in Christ, they are not left to their own devices. The Father may be depended on to make full provision for all their daily needs (Matthew 6:24–34). Moreover, believers have a responsibility to live in accord with their new life in Christ. Some of these principles are enunciated in the Sermon on the Mount (Matthew 5—7). Certainly discipleship is expected of them (Matthew 16:24–26; Mark 8:34–38; Luke 9:23–27). They are also charged with the responsibility to witness (Matthew 5:13–16).

Actually, Jesus had a great deal to say about how believers should live. He taught much of that in parables, which are discussed in the next chapter. Preeminently, his instruction for living the Christian life centered around three words: *faith, faithful,* and *love.* To "have faith in" is to put one's full confidence in. One is to put full confidence in God for salvation (John 14:1; cf. John 20:31; Mark 11:22), for power to accomplish tasks (Mark 9:23; 14:36), and for daily provision (Matthew 6:25–34). Then the believer is to be *faithful* in service to God. Jesus commends faithfulness on the part of all who serve Him (Matthew 24:35; 25:14–30; Luke 16:12), and He commands faithfulness to the end (Revelation 2:10). Jesus' supreme commandment for Christian living was, "Love the Lord your God with all your heart and with all your soul and with all your mind. . . . And . . . Love your neighbor as yourself" (Matthew 22:37–38, NIV). Rigorous application of this commandment makes most discussion of what one ought or ought not do as a Christian purely academic. It does, however, open the door to some serious thinking about what it means to love God and one's self. Many find it difficult or virtually impossible to love others because they do not really love themselves.

The Doctrine of Man

Concerning the doctrine of man, Christ asserted his origin by an act of divine creation (Matthew 19:4; Mark 10:6). Moreover, man and woman were made for each other, and once married were to remain that way until parted by death or for other specified reasons. So he denounced the easy breaking of the marriage tie (Matthew 19:8–9; 5:31–32). While He did not describe man's fall, Christ affirmed man's sinfulness. His nature is corrupt and from it proceeds all kinds of evil (Matthew 12:34–35; 15:11, 17–20; Mark 7:20–23; Luke 11:13). In addition to having a sinful nature, human beings are sinners by practice (John 8:7). Since they are sinners and have souls of great value (Matthew 16:26), they need to be born again (John 3:3, 5, 7) or they will perish (John 3:16).

The Doctrine of the Holy Spirit

When believers have experienced the new birth, they need the enablement of the Holy Spirit to live the Christian life. That the Holy Spirit is not merely an influence, but a person, is quite clear because He is spoken of as a person (John 16:13–15), and works as a teacher and guide, for which personality is a requisite

(John 14:26; 16:13). That the Holy Spirit is also divine is clear

- from His possession of the attribute of holiness;
- from His part in the divine work of salvation (John 3:5, 6, 8);
- from His association with the other members of the Trinity in the baptismal formula (Matthew 28:19);
- from the fact that sin against Him is regarded as even more serious than a sin against Christ (Matthew 12:31–32; Mark 3:28–30);
- and from His relationship to Christ.

He anointed Jesus Christ for His earthly ministry (Luke 4:18–21); Christ sent Him to minister in His stead after the Savior ascended (John 16:7); and after coming, the Holy Spirit testified of Christ (John 15:26).

Jesus also taught

- that the Holy Spirit had been instrumental in inspiration and revelation (Mark 12:36);
- that He would have a ministry of convicting the world of sin, righteousness, and judgment in the present age (John 16:8–11);
- that He would come to indwell believers permanently (John 14:16–18);
- that He would teach them the truths they should know and say (John 14:26; 16:13–15), especially in the face of trial and tribulation (Matthew 10:19–20; Mark 13:11; Luke 12:12);
- and that He would empower believers for ministry (Acts 1:8).

The Doctrine of Angels

While the New Testament alludes to the existence and ministry of good angels, and Christ spoke of them in connection with His return (Matthew 16:27) and in answering the Sadducees (Luke 20:36), Jesus did not discuss them very much. Since He constantly faced demon inspired opposition, what He said about angels related mainly to Satan and his fallen angels. From the temptation account (Matthew 4:1–11), it is clear that Christ believed in the personality of Satan, leader of the fallen angels; at least He treated Satan as a personal spirit. He recognized Satan as an enemy of the preached word, in His interpretation of the sower parable (Luke 8:12).

He declared that His unregenerate opponents were in the grip of Satan: "You are of your father the devil" (John 8:44, KJV). He predicted the judgment and fall of Satan (Luke 10:18; John 12:31). He saw the influence of Satan in Peter's opposition to His suffering and death (Matthew 16:23). He foretold the satanically inspired plot to betray and crucify Him (John 14:30). Jesus also taught that there were degrees of evil among the fallen angels—evil spirits (Matthew 12:45; 17:21; Luke 11:24–25). But Jesus did not merely teach concerning Satan and his henchmen. He cast out demons from many people and released the victims into a new and living way. His power over demons was absolute.

The Doctrine of the Church

Our Lord made one reference to the Church: "You are Peter, and upon this rock I will build my church;

and the gates of hell shall not prevail against it'' (Matthew 16:18, KJV). From this verse two things are clear: the founding of the Church was yet future, and the gates of hell would not be able to stand against the victorious onslaughts of the Church. As to the identity of the rock upon which the Church would be built, there is less certainty. Some have held that it is Christ, others Peter, and still others the confession of Peter—the Christian message.

An interpretation which seems to do justice to all the facts runs something like this. In saying, "You are *petros* and on this *petra* (see Greek of this passage) I will build my church," Christ meant, "You, Peter, are a little sliver *(petros)* of rock, and on this big rock *(petra)* composed of many slivers or layers I will build my church."[2] Ephesians 2:20 supports this interpretation. There we discover that the Church is built on a foundation of apostles and prophets. Peter, then, would be one of the apostles (one of the pieces of rock or cut stones) who historically constitute the first row of stones laid in building the Church.

The Doctrine of the Last Things

There are at least six elements in Jesus' teaching concerning last things: resurrection, judgment, reward, everlasting punishment, the second coming and the order of events at the end of the age.

1. He taught a resurrection of both believers and unbelievers, the one to life and the other to damnation (Luke 20:35–37; John 5:29; 6:54).

2. In regard to judgment, His main emphasis was on a day of reckoning sometime in the future (Matthew 7:22–23; 10:15; 11:22, 24; 12:36; Luke 10:14), but He became more specific in the Olivet discourse, where He placed a judgment after the tribulation (Matthew 25:31 ff.).

3. Jesus was also rather general in statements about rewards for the just (Matthew 20:1–16; John 5:29), but on one occasion He specifically told the disciples that they would sit on twelve thrones in His Kingdom (Matthew 19:28; Luke 22:29–30).

4. On numerous occasions our Lord unequivocally asserted His belief in everlasting punishment (Matthew 18:8–9; Mark 9:43–48; Luke 10:15; John 5:29); and nowhere did He intimate a second chance or annihilation.

5. He frequently mentioned His second coming too—usually in general terms (Matthew 16:27; Luke 12:40; John 14:3), but in the Olivet discourse He was more specific (Matthew 24:29–30).

6. This brings us to a brief consideration of the order of events at the end of the age as He outlined them. For the most part these appear in the Olivet Discourse (Matthew 24—25; cf. Mark 13 and Luke 21). These chapters must be related to Daniel 9:27, which describes the Tribulation period: at the beginning of it the world prince will make a covenant, or treaty, with the Jews; in the middle of the period he will break the covenant and cause the sacrifice in the temple (evidently to be rebuilt) to cease until the end of the Tribulation, when the prince will be judged.

In Matthew 24, severe trials are predicted which obviously are the beginning of the Tribulation (v. 8); in verse 15 there is reference to the breaking of the covenant mentioned in Daniel 9:27, with a desecration of the Jewish religious center and termination of the sacrifices and ritual; then comes the Great Tribulation (the last half of the period). This is followed by the second coming of Christ (vv. 27–31). After an interlude of illustrative parables on the subject of His coming, Christ returns to more specific teaching on the subject in Matthew 25:31 ff.

There He points out that judgment will follow His return, and those found righteous will enter the kingdom (v. 34), evidently the millennial Kingdom. The wicked will be turned into everlasting punishment. The fact that this coming is posttribulational does not eliminate the possibility of a pretribulation coming as well. Much more information on the order of events at the consummation of the age may be found in the writings of Paul and John, which must be brought into the account for a full-orbed understanding of this doctrine. Chapter 12 deals with this subject more fully.

NOTES

1. See chapter 6 for further details on some of these doctrines. An interesting supplement to this chapter is Herbert Lockyer's *Everything Jesus Taught* (New York: Harper & Row, 1976).
2. In classical Greek, *petra* on occasion describes a large flaked rock, from which flakes or slivers (*petros*) may be broken.

SIX

The Parables of Christ

SOME have the impression that parabolic or proverbial speech was an invention of Old or New Testament writers, and that this instructional gimmick was limited to them. This is not the case. While the origin of parabolic speech is unknown, its use has been widespread. Several peoples of the ancient Near East commonly used parables, and Hebrew rabbis were particularly fond of the method. In certain areas of the Near East proverbial or parabolic speech is prevalent today.

Definition of a Parable

To provide a completely satisfactory definition of a parable is no easy task; nor is it necessary to try to do so here. The time-honored definition of a parable as an earthly story with a heavenly meaning is useful, but not quite adequate. The Greek word *parabolē* means a *comparison* or *analogy*. A parable is then a comparison or analogy drawn from daily life or nature and used to disclose a spiritual truth. These short fictitious narratives about well known human experiences were plausible analogies to those to whom they were addressed.

For example, Jesus' hearers were quite familiar with a sower who went out to sow, a shepherd who went out to seek a lost sheep, or a rich man who served a great banquet. Thus it was easy for Jesus to compare

the sowing of seed to the spreading of truth, or the
shepherd seeking a lost sheep to the Savior's seeking a
lost sinner, or a rich man sending invitations to a
banquet to His invitation to a spiritual banquet. Parables may take the form of brief figurative sayings, simi-
les, metaphors, or stories.

The Purpose of Parables

Jesus, as the master teacher, knew how to present
easily understood lessons to His hearers. Not only
could He put profound truths in understandable language, but also He arrested their attention, held their
interest, and facilitated their learning by means of stories. Starting with an account of some experience in
life, He vividly portrayed the message He sought to
impart. Moreover, parables aided Him in driving
home a truth or an accusation of guilt or wrongdoing.
As Hunter observes, "The parable, by its very nature,
is hard to contradict. Demanding an opinion on its
own human level (the two debtors is a good example),
the parable finds an opening which makes the hearer
lower his guard and leaves him defenseless. Then, before he is aware of it, the sword thrust is home."[1]

While the parables were a teaching aid when the
Lord wished to instruct His disciples or a crowd of
seekers, their spiritual meaning was hidden from His
enemies. Mark 4:11–12, KJV, is particularly significant
in this regard:

And he said unto them, unto you it is given to
know the mystery of the kingdom of God: but

unto them that are without, all these things are done in parables: that seeing they may see, and not perceive; and hearing they may hear, and not understand; lest at any time they should be converted, and their sins should be forgiven them.

Jesus never denied the truth to the spiritually responsive, but often dealt with those who had hardened their hearts against Him in parables. Note how many times Christ spoke to the scribes and Pharisees in parables. Yet even in such cases they generally got the point of what He was trying to say and frequently winced under the stinging attacks (see Matthew 21:45).

Principles of Interpretation

While it is impossible here to explain in detail how to interpret parables, four principles will prove useful.

1. Normally, each parable has one particular truth to teach. Interpretative efforts should be directed toward discovering that one truth. Significance need not necessarily be attached to details, and when those details are interpreted, they should be interpreted in the light of the main truth.
2. The meaning of a parable may be discovered by the interpretation furnished by Christ Himself (as in the case of the parable of the sower, or the wheat and tares, Matthew 13); by a study of the context, the circumstances under which they were spoken or the persons to whom addressed; by a compari-

son of the various passages where the parables appear when they are repeated in a second or third gospel; or by a consideration of Bible customs in an effort to understand the local color or customs alluded to in the parables.

3. Parables should not be treated as sources of doctrine but merely as illustrations of doctrine clearly revealed elsewhere in Scripture. If this principle is not carefully followed, a fallacious interpretation of one parable could lead to serious doctrinal error. In this connection, we must be careful not to interpret any parable in such a way that it will contradict other clear teachings of Scripture.

4. Parables are pre-Cross and were uttered in a Jewish context. Their interpretation must not be allowed to obscure the principles of grace. Salvation is by faith and not by human works.

The Meaning of Our Lord's Parables

Scholars vary widely in the number of parables they see in the Gospels. Their lists range from about thirty to eighty, depending on whether they include seeming parables not described by the term *parable,* and whether they include shorter parables and parabolic illustrations. Fifty two are discussed here, divided into nine categories. Some of the shorter ones are included out of a desire to throw light on difficult passages. In a few cases, assignment of a parable to one of these categories is somewhat arbitrary. In each case the story of the parable is not told in detail but described in conjunction with the interpretation. Scripture references are noted in every instance so the reader can follow the interpretations with an open Bible.

1. Parables Concerning the Message of God in the World

Nature of the Message

After his conversion, Matthew gave a banquet in his home for Jesus. During the meal, the Pharisees and disciples of John the Baptist criticized Him for eating with publicans (tax collectors) and sinners, and especially for failing to fast. Jesus' answer took the form of a parable. He said that no one uses new cloth to patch an old garment, nor does he put new wine into old bottles (wineskins). New cloth is not shrunk. When an old garment is patched with it, shrinkage tends to make the tear worse. New wine placed in old wineskins will cause skins to burst because they already have been stretched about as far as possible during a previous fermenting process.

The point of the parable is that Jesus has come with a new message of grace, as opposed to the old legal order (represented both by the Pharisees and John the Baptist). The gospel, which is gracious in character, is not merely something tacked on to the Law system; nor can it be adapted to the old worship forms. It is a new message and requires a new approach and new forms (see Matthew 9:16–17; Mark 2:21–22; Luke 5:36–38).

Proclamation of the Message

Jesus described the proclamation of truth during the present age in the Parable of the Sower (Matthew

13:3–9, 18–23; Mark 4:1–9, 13–20; Luke 8:4–15). In each of the synoptic Gospels He interpreted the parable, leaving no doubt as to its meaning. According to the parable, the seed of the good news of the kingdom is sown on four kinds of soils, representing responses of hearers to the Word: by the wayside, among stones, among thorns, and on good ground. In the first instance the seed is snatched away by Satan; in the second, trials and tribulations of life tend to snuff out what interest may have been kindled; in the third, the cares and temptations of life choke out the Word; in the last, the seed bears much fruit. The parable indicates the results that will come from sowing the seed, and it illustrates the fact that a majority of people do not, for one reason or another, receive the truth of God unto salvation.

Growth of the Truth (Kingdom) in the World

Two parables illustrate the growth of the kingdom of God in the world: the Seed Growing Secretly (Mark 4:26–29) and the Mustard Seed (Matthew 13:31–32; Mark 4:30–32; Luke 13:18–19). Though the mustard seed is small, its growth into a large bush is rapid—attaining a height of fifteen feet or more in Palestine.[2] Like the mustard seed, the kingdom of heaven rose rapidly from an insignificant beginning, with an unremarkable band of Jesus' followers, to unusually large proportions. In interpreting this parable, many emphasize a perversion of the divine design for the kingdom by pointing to the birds lodging in the branches of the tree. Since birds represent satanic power elsewhere in Matthew 13, they are also taken to indicate evil here, and to point to corruption in the organized church today. The Parable of Seed Growing Secretly describes the imperceptible growth of the kingdom in the world as the work of God moves forward to the day of reckoning.

Corruption of the Message and Work of God

While it may not be the purpose of the Mustard Seed Parable to describe a perversion of the truth, two parables are sometimes taken as demonstrating this fact: the Leaven (Matthew 13:33; Luke 13:20–21), and the Wheat and Tares (Matthew 13:24–30, 36–43). Since leaven in Scripture standardly speaks of evil (Exodus 12:15; Leviticus 2:11; 6:17; 10:12; Matthew 16:6; Mark 8:15; 1 Corinthians 5:6–8; Galatians 5:9), some argue that such must be the case in this parable. They conclude that it refers to the corruption of the doctrine of the kingdom by false doctrine. But Jesus compared the kingdom not to leaven but to what happens *when* leaven (yeast) is put into the ingredients that will make bread. A ferment, a dynamic, disturbing resistless process takes place—from which nothing can escape. The process is irreversible. So the parable suggests that the sowing of the Word will produce a new kingdom by a quiet, irresistible working from within. In the case of the wheat and tares, however, the meaning is clear because of our Lord's interpretation. Satan counterfeits the Gospel with his own brand of religion and mere professors and real possessors of the truth grow up together in Christendom, to be separated at the judgment.

2. Parables Concerning Salvation and Forgiveness of Sin

Since the primary purpose of the Son of Man was "to seek and to save that which was lost" (Luke 19:10), we would expect to find the largest number of parables in the category of salvation and forgiveness of sins. Perhaps the best known of this classification are the parables of Luke 15: the Lost Sheep; the Lost Coin; and the Prodigal Son. These were aimed at the scribes and Pharisees, who criticized Jesus for His association with tax collectors and sinners (15:1–2) and who sought to justify themselves before men (16:15). Apparently Jesus likened the ninety nine sheep, the nine coins, and the elder brother to the Pharisees, who considered themselves spiritually safe because they rigorously kept the Law. We should not, however, be led into the erroneous idea that the Pharisees really were regenerated. The point is that on these hypocrites the Lord focused little attention, for His ministry was mainly to those who recognized their need of a Savior—the tax collectors and sinners, likened here to the hundredth sheep, the lost coin, and the prodigal son. Over one of these who repents there is more joy in heaven than over the ninety nine who consider themselves righteous before God (Luke 15:7).

Related to the message of Luke 15 is the Parable of the Pharisee and tax collector (Luke 18:9–14, KJV). In verse 9, Jesus made it clear whom He addressed: "And he spoke this parable unto certain which trusted in themselves that they were righteous, and despised others." In the following verses the Pharisee stands self-confident in his self-righteousness, but the tax collector recognizes his sinfulness and asks for divine favor (grace). Verse 13 is incorrectly translated in the King James Version. Instead of asking for mercy, he asked God to be propitious to him. The sinner no longer needs to beg God to be propitious (well disposed) toward him because God is propitious as a result of the work of Christ on the Cross (1 John 2:2). The point of the parable, however, is that the tax collector was justified because he came in humility, recognizing his sin and resting on divine provision (grace).

Another parable which compares the attitude of the scribes and Pharisees and tax collectors and sinners is that of the Two Sons Called to Work (Matthew 21:28–32). The one son represents the tax collectors and harlots, who at first had no sympathy for John the Baptist's message, but later repented and believed. The other son represents the chief priests and elders, who as religious men professed an initial interest in John but did not receive his message in their hearts. Of course the former receive the blessing of salvation. The true son of God is the one who obeys Him—meets His requirements—not the one who merely makes a verbal profession of doing so.

Two parables that illustrate the value of believers for whom Christ made the supreme sacrifice are the Hid Treasure and the Pearl of Great Price (Matthew 13:44–46). Some falsely use these parables as a text for an evangelistic message in which sinners are exhorted to give up and to sell everything to find the pearl or treasure: salvation. That is not the gospel. The gospel is the grace of God making provision for sinners and seeking them in their sin.

The field in these parables represents the world, as it does in the first two parables of Matthew 13. The man who gave up all to buy the field and its treasure, and the merchant who bought the pearl, can be none other than Christ, who made the supreme sacrifice to pay the sin debt of the whole world. Within the world are those who believe on Him—treasure and pearl. Some see the treasure as representative of Israel and the pearl as the Church. Others view the treasure as individual believers and the pearl as believers collectively. It is difficult to identify the treasure and pearl clearly, but the main point of the parables seems clear: Christ would purchase for Himself a special treasure made up of both Jews and Gentiles.

Another pair of parables somewhat related in message are the Marriage of the King's Son (Matthew 22:1–14) and the Great Supper (Luke 14:16–24). The former is a parable in two parts which tells first of the Jews who refuse the king's invitation, resulting in God's turning from the Jew to the Gentiles; second, it tells of some who dare to come before the king in their own way. They are willing enough to come to God but do not want to meet His conditions. They do not have the wedding garment—His robe of righteousness. For such there is no hope of acceptance.

The Parable of the Great Supper differs somewhat from that of the marriage. At the supper, there is no indication of hostility to Christ or His servants, but pure indifference. Here three groups are involved: those who at first received the invitation and refused;

the poor, maimed, halt, and blind; and those among the highways and hedges. It would appear that the first group represents the scribes and Pharisees; the second and third groups (which respond) represent the tax collectors, sinners, and Gentiles.

Another pair of parables that speak of salvation and of God's judgment for failure to receive His grace are the Barren Fig Tree (Luke 13:6–9, KJV) and the Strait Gate and Shut Door (Luke 13:23–30). The fig tree parable is a continuation of the message of verse 5, "Except you repent, you shall all likewise perish." The fig tree (representing Israel or any individual soul) had been barren for three years and could not now be expected to bear—according to the usual performance of the fig. Even though Israel did not show any signs of repentance, God manifests a willingness to give her another chance. The parable teaches both the longsuffering and the severity of God.

In the Parable of the Strait Gate and Shut Door, Jesus warns of the danger of being excluded from the kingdom of God. He urges His hearers to "strain every nerve to enter" the kingdom (v. 24) while there is yet opportunity. After it is too late, many will seek to enter and will not be able to do so. Knowing Christ after the flesh will not be enough; they must have a personal commitment to Him. Moreover, in the future day when the judgment is over, the Gentiles will possess an important place in the kingdom, contrary to the expectation of the Jews.

A last pair of related parables pertaining to salvation are the Door of the Sheep (John 10:1–10) and the Good Shepherd (John 10:11–18, 25–30). Jesus had just healed a man born blind. As was frequently the case after one of His miracles, the Pharisees stirred up trouble. In fact, the leaders among the Jews had decided that if any man should confess Christ, he would be put out of the synagogue, which was a terrible stigma for a Jew to bear. They fulfilled their threat in this case. Then, in response to the Pharisees' question as to whether they were blind, Jesus delivered the Parable on the Door of the Sheep. In it He sought to show that He was the way into the new economy. The one who entered the fold and became a member of the flock found salvation through the person of Christ.

As a member of the flock he shall do service ("shall go in and out") and find sustenance ("find pasture"). Those who refused to come by way of the door (such as the Pharisees) and sought salvation by means of their own righteousness are classed as thieves and robbers. They are outside the fold. These religious leaders, who thought they had excommunicated the man born blind, found themselves in *their* spiritual blindness shut out of the fold.

Then Jesus went on to proclaim Himself as the Good Shepherd—in authority over the flock and the new order. Moreover, as Good Shepherd, He would lay down His life for His sheep. On the basis of this supreme sacrifice, He would also choose sheep from among the Gentiles, and both Jews and Gentiles would be one *flock* (v. 16, *fold* in the KJV is an incorrect translation). The flock might be housed in many folds, but they all belonged to the same flock. His shepherdhood also included watching, tender care, and keeping of the flock.

On more than one occasion Jesus made it clear that there was no middle ground between acceptance and rejection of the Savior—between the saved and lost condition. In at least one parable this point is well illustrated. A certain evil spirit left a man; later finding the man without sufficient moral defense, it entered his life with seven more wicked spirits (Matthew 12:43–45; Luke 11:24–26). It is not enough merely to live a good life—to be negative about evil. One must be full of good and must possess positive righteousness, available through Christ alone.

In the foregoing parable, the individual's difficulty came from evil spirits that entered him. In another parable, man's source of difficulty or defilement is described as coming from within (Matthew 15:10–11, 15–20; Mark 7:14–23). Not only does the individual have to combat the work of evil spirits but also his fallen nature within, for his heart is desperately wicked and the source of all kinds of defilement.

After delivering the Parable of the Unclean Spirit that Returned, Jesus dealt with those who asked of Him a sign. To them He answered with the Parable of the Inward Light (Matthew 6:22–23; Luke 11:34–36). With the eye the physical body is lighted. The soul too has an eye, and those whose spiritual sight has not been darkened by impenitence have no need of a sign. Their soul is full of light because of spiritual developments occurring within them when they belong to the Savior.

Under the figure of Two Roads (Matthew 7:13–

14), Jesus pictured the alternate moral courses open to human beings in this life. The one appeals to the natural inclinations of the fallen nature, and the destination is spiritual death. The other, the spiritual way, appears restrictive and difficult, but its destination is spiritual life. Travelers must choose which highway they wish to travel.

Christ, in another parable (Matthew 7:24–27; Luke 6:46–49), portrayed the Two Builders. One wisely built his life and character on a faith rooted in Christ; the other foolishly tried to build a life and character without being effectively established in Christ. The solid foundation of the former stood when tested by the storms of life; the latter crumpled on the shifting sands of unbelief when the storms of judgment clouded the horizon.

3. Parables Concerning the Treatment of Christ

In the process of providing salvation, Christ suffered greatly at the hands of His opponents and was rejected by them. At least two parables deal with this theme: the Wicked Husbandmen (Matthew 21:33–41; Mark 12:1–9; Luke 20:9–16), and the Rejected Stone (Matthew 21:42–46; Mark 12:10–11; Luke 20:7–19). In all three gospels these two parables appear in sequence. In the first parable, He likened His enemies to vinedressers who failed to fulfill their responsibility of keeping the vineyard (Israel) for their landlord (God). In fact, they maltreated the servants (prophets) of the landlord when they came with messages from their master. Finally, they even slew the son (Jesus Christ) of the landlord; for this God would destroy them.

In the second parable the Pharisees appear as builders who cast away a certain stone (Christ) as unfit for the structure they were building. But this stone became head of the corner and also became a powerful weapon in the hand of God for destroying opponents of the Messiah. Progression appears in this sequence of parables: the first ends with the death of Christ; the second proclaims His triumph.

4. Parables Concerning Fellowship with God

Those who have, in faith, appropriated the work of Christ and experienced the new birth have the privilege of fellowship with the Father and the Son. Jesus expressed this in several parables. Two, on prayer, are closely related: the Importunate Friend (Luke 11:5–8) and the Unjust Judge (Luke 18:1–8). Both demonstrate that God will hear His children, but that prayer should be persistent. But these two parables differ slightly. The former shows prayer is never out of season; the latter that it is sure to bring blessing and not a curse. The second parable is almost stronger than the first in making the point that if an unjust judge would yield to a persistent and unknown widow, how much more will a just God be ready to reward His own who constantly cry to Him.

Certainly the work of Christ on the Cross in settling the sin problem should stir fires of adoration and gratitude in our hearts. While Jesus dined with Simon the Pharisee, an uninvited woman of the street came in and began to weep at Jesus' feet and wipe His feet

with her hair and anoint them with ointment in gratitude for forgiveness of sins.[3] Simon began to wonder
why Jesus would accept this attention from such a
disreputable character, to which the Master replied
with the Parable of the Two Debtors (Luke 7:41–43).
In it a creditor voided the debts of two debtors. The
one owed a large sum and the other a small sum.
Christ indicated that the one who owed the larger
amount would be more grateful. The point of the
parable seems to be that the gratitude of sinners depends on *their estimate* of the amount remitted to
them.

Another parable that demonstrates the blessed relationship of Christ with His disciples is that of the Bride
and Bridegroom (Mark 2:19–20; Luke 5:34–35). The
scribes and Pharisees criticized Jesus' disciples because
they did not fast as did the Pharisees and the disciples
of John the Baptist. Jesus replied that when the bridegroom is present, the children of the bridechamber
have no occasion for fasting. When the bridegroom is
taken away, they will fast. Obviously He referred to
His joyous relationship with His disciples and His
coming departure.

The most beautiful of this group is the Parable of
the Vine and the Branches (John 15:1–11). Here the
primary message concerns the ministry of Christ to
and through His disciples, and the conditions for fruit
bearing. The true vine is Christ Himself—the source
of all spiritual life and blessing. The true branches
are regenerated souls united to Christ, and therefore
members of His body and designed to bring forth
fruit. The vine supplies nourishment to the branches

so that they might be fruitful. Of themselves the branches can do nothing. They abide in the vine and permit the life-giving properties of the vine to flow through them. The branches are then characterized by fruitfulness (vv. 2, 8); joyfulness (v. 11); and effectual prayer (v. 7). As pruning causes greater fruitfulness in the plant world, the corrective hand of God accomplishes a similar purpose in the spiritual realm. (The question as to who are the unfruitful branches is controversial and beyond the purpose of this book.)

While the Parable of the Vine and the Branches describes spiritual nourishment and blessing for the disciple, God's promises do not stop there. He has also committed Himself to supply temporal needs. Nestled in one of the extended passages on temporal supply is the Parable of the Rich Fool (Luke 12:16–21, KJV). In it a rich farmer was consumed with a passion to amass worldly goods, but after building many barns and filling them up, he died. Here Jesus taught that abundant life does not depend on wealth, and that life itself cannot be secured by wealth. In connection with this parable He uttered a warning and a promise. The former appears in verse 15: "Take heed, and beware of covetousness: for a man's life consists not in the abundance of the things which he possesses"; and the latter in verse 31: "Seek ye first the kingdom of God; and all these things shall be added unto you."

5. Parables Concerning Witness or Discipleship

Fellowship with God should culminate in discipleship. Several parables embody this theme. In the first place, discipleship demands complete self renunciation. Becoming a disciple of Jesus Christ is at least as serious as any other costly or dangerous undertaking. Just as a man who prepares to build a tower first counts the cost to determine whether he can finish it (Luke 14:28–30), and as a king estimates his military resources before he goes into battle (Luke 14:31–32), so the disciple of Christ should count the cost of discipleship and prepare himself to live a life of complete self renunciation. This does not mean he must turn into a self-effacing vegetable; it involves giving over the right to control one's own life to God. Actually, the disciple might be a fearless warrior for the truth, a successful entrepreneur, or a world leader in the arts and sciences.

A disciple without a true devotion to Christ and its accompaniment of exemplary living is like salt which has lost its savor (Matthew 5:13; Mark 9:50; Luke 14:33–35). In that condition it is good for absolutely nothing. Effective Christians, like good salt, have a preservative or corruption-arresting, seasoning, and cleansing effect on society. Moreover, as salt creates thirst, so believers should create a thirst for God among their associates.

Closely related to the salt parable is the Lighted Lamp (Matthew 5:15; Mark 4:21; Luke 8:16–17; 11:33). The former parable emphasizes the character of the Christian; the latter, the diffusion of his testimony. The light of the gospel will dispel the darkness of sin.

If disciples desire the most effective testimony, they must engage in self-judgment. Whatever in our walk or service exposes the soul to the danger of unholy feelings, or causes us to be a stumbling block to others, should be forsaken at all cost. Such is the message of the parable on offending members (Matthew 5:29–30; Mark 9:43, 45, 47). In fact, no sacrifice is too great if it promotes a correct spiritual condition and a good testimony on the part of the believer.

6. Parables Concerning Relations with Others

As disciples of Christ carry on their ministry in the world, they are counseled about their relation to others. In response to Peter's question about how many times one should forgive another, Jesus delivered the Parable of the Unmerciful Servant (Matthew 18:23–35). In it, a creditor remitted a large debt owed him; this debtor in turn, as creditor, failed to remit a lesser debt owed him but threw his debtor into prison. When the first creditor heard about it, he retaliated in like fashion. Jesus dealt here with the hatefulness of an unforgiving spirit and conveyed the idea that if God forgave us so much, we should be willing to forgive all who sin against us.

A very familiar parable on human relationships is the Good Samaritan (Luke 10:30–37). A man robbed on the Jericho road was ignored by a priest and a Levite and cared for by a Samaritan. To answer the question, "Who is my neighbor?", Jesus shows that neighborliness is not related merely to proximity, but involves helping the needy with whom we come in contact. The priest and Levite were both as close to the wounded man as the Samaritan, but he "became neighbor" (v. 36, literal translation) and had compassion on the needy one. Jesus said, "Go, and do likewise" (v. 37), i.e., have a spirit of divine concern and altruism, be a neighbor to the one who has no natural claim upon you.

7. Parables Concerning Rewards

Faithful disciples of the Lord may expect rewards for their service. On one occasion Peter asked Jesus what would be the disciples' reward for all their sacrifices. Jesus replied with tremendous promises (Matthew 19:28–29). These were followed, however, with a *but,* and after the *but* came the Parable of the Laborers in the Vineyard (Matthew 20:1–16). In it a certain householder hired laborers early in the morning, at the third hour, the sixth hour, the ninth hour, and the eleventh hour—ultimately giving the same pay to all.

When murmuring arose over this seeming unfairness, he reminded those who served longest that he had a right to do as he wished about remuneration, as long as he kept his bargain with the workers. The message of the parable is this: While God keeps His promises to those who serve Him, He alone can judge what is just. Moreover, God is sovereign and will retain His rights in the matter of rewards. He will reward the work done, but He will reward according to His sovereign will. No one has a right to demand rewards for service to God. Since Christ declared, "Without Me you can do nothing" (John 15:5), all our successes are achieved by His strength. Then, any reward must be bestowed solely on the basis of God's grace—not because of our merit.

It is up to us to be faithful in serving God, leaving the distribution of rewards to Him. In His grace and generosity He will do what is right. The parable may also be stretched to suggest that those who enter His service late in the Christian era may expect the same rewards as those who followed Christ at the beginning. Or the interpretation may suggest that the gift of salvation will be the same for those who put their faith in Christ early in life and for whose who do so near the end of their days on earth.

A similar parable of service appears in Luke 17:7–10. Here the Lord points out that when servants do what they are ordered to do, masters do not thank (or reward) those servants. Likewise, servants of God, when they have fulfilled the commands of God, will recognize they have merely done their duty. The main thrust of the parable is that a servant of God can make no *just claim* for having done more than was due.

8. Parables Concerning the Return of Christ

Rewards for service will be distributed when Christ returns for His own. Six parables deal with the theme of His return. Of course, many parables deal with judgment in connection with the return of Christ, but these are reserved for the next section. Those with primary emphasis on His return are considered here. In Luke 12:35–38 Jesus teaches the duty of loyal vigilance concerning His return. Just as servants should be prepared to meet their master at whatever hour a wedding feast breaks up and he returns home, so believers are to be ready for Christ's return at any time.

Under another figure of speech—the breaking in of a thief—He presents a similar message (Luke 12:39–

40; Matthew 24:43–44). The householder is exhorted to constant watchfulness, lest while he sleeps the Lord will come as a thief in the night. The coming of a thief in the night refers to unexpected events (see 1 Thessalonians 5:2; 2 Peter 3:10; Revelation 3:3; 16:15), and the reader should not be disturbed by a comparison of the Lord's return with something unpleasant.

To underscore the importance of watchfulness, Jesus changes the figure—this time to a servant in the house awaiting the return of his master (Matthew 24:45–51; Luke 12:42–46). While there may have been some uncertainty as to whether or not a thief would break in, there is no uncertainty that the master will return. There is a temptation, though, to grow careless as he delays his coming day after day. Gradually the purifying effects of the Lord's return wear off, and the servant even turns to abusing his brethren. For such, judgment is certain. It would appear from verse 51 that if one pursues this careless course and winds up a confirmed worldling at Christ's coming, that would be an indication he was never really a believer and he deserves eternal condemnation. Yet one more parable belonging in this group—the householder and the porter (Mark 13:34–37)—exhorts watchfulness in view of the return of Christ, and is so self-explanatory that it requires no comment here.

Our Lord further underscores the importance of preparedness for His coming and for the next life in the Parable of the Unrighteous Steward (Luke 16:1–13). This steward, accused of unsatisfactory handling of his master's goods and about to be fired, decided on a course of action to win new friends who would

SOME PARABLES OF JESUS CHRIST			
Parable	*Matthew*	*Mark*	*Luke*
1. Lamp Under a Basket	5:14–16	4:21, 22	8:16, 17 11:33–36
2. A Wise Man Builds on Rock and a Foolish Man Builds on Sand	7:24–27		6:47–49
3. Unshrunk (New) Cloth on an Old Garment	9:16	2:21	5:36
4. New Wine in Old Wineskins	9:17	2:22	5:37, 38
5. The Sower	13:3–23	4:2–20	8:4–15
6. The Tares (Weeds)	13:24–30		
7. The Mustard Seed	13:31, 32	4:30–32	13:18, 19
8. The Leaven	13:33		13:20, 21
9. The Hidden Treasure	13:44		
10. The Pearl of Great Price	13:45, 46		
11. The Dragnet	13:47–50		
12. The Lost Sheep	18:12–14		15:3–7
13. The Unforgiving Servant	18:23–35		
14. The Workers in the Vineyard	20:1–16		
15. The Two Sons	21:28–32		
16. The Wicked Vinedressers	21:33–45	12:1–12	20:9–19
17. The Wedding Feast	22:2–14		
18. The Fig Tree	24:32–44	13:28–32	21:29–33
19. The Wise and Foolish Virgins	25:1–13		
20. The Talents	25:14–30		

PARABLES OF JESUS—*Cont'd*			
Parable	*Matthew*	*Mark*	*Luke*
21. The Growing Seed		4:26–29	
22. The Absent Householder		13:33–37	
23. The Creditor and Two Debtors			7:41–43
24. The Good Samaritan			10:30–37
25. A Friend in Need			11:5–13
26. The Rich Fool			12:16–21
27. The Faithful Servant and the Evil Servant			12:35–40
28. Faithful and Wise Steward			12:42–48
29. The Barren Fig Tree			13:6–9
30. The Great Supper			14:16–24
31. Building a Tower and a King Making War			14:25–35
32. The Lost Coin			15:8–10
33. The Lost Son			15:11–32
34. The Unjust Steward			16:1–13
35. The Rich Man and Lazarus			16:19–31
36. Unprofitable Servants			17:7–10
37. The Persistent Widow			18:1–8
38. The Pharisee and the Tax Collector			18:9–14
39. The Minas (Pounds)			19:11–27

help him when he was out of a job. He called in all of his master's creditors and reduced the amounts they owed to him. For this he won commendation from his master; and Jesus seems to commend him too.

Many have difficulty in interpreting this parable, largely because of trying to interpret unimportant details. The fundamental problem arises, however, in the fact that Jesus seems to commend dishonesty. But a closer look shows that He is trying to teach His disciples that even the unrighteous men of their generation use present opportunities to prepare for the future. They could take a lesson from unbelievers in this respect, and by being faithful stewards now they could give a good account at the end of their service.

While in the previous parables Christ exhorted watchfulness in view of His return, because the time for that was uncertain, He did give signs indicating the nearness of that return. In the Parable of the Sprouting Fig Tree (Matthew 24:32–35; Mark 13:28–31; Luke 21:29–33), He teaches that as the budding of the fig tree indicates the coming of summer, so certain conditions were sure signs of His second coming. The context of each parable demonstrates that these signs include earthquakes, famines, pestilence, the rise of false christs, wars, and especially the Great Tribulation, during which Daniel's "abomination of desolation" will appear (Matthew 24:15; Mark 13:14). After this Tribulation Christ will return. It should be added that the pretribulation rapture of the saints is not under discussion in the Gospels, with the probable exception of John 14:1–3.

9. Parables Concerning Judgment

When Jesus returns at the end of the Tribulation, there will be a judgment of all people then living. The Parable of the Fishnet (Matthew 13:47–50) speaks of this judgment in general terms. In it a net is cast into the sea, gathering all sorts of things. When full, it is towed to shore, the contents sorted, and the bad cast away. This judgment does not come at the end of the *world* (Matthew 13:49 is incorrectly translated in some versions), but at the end or consummation of the *age*. It is therefore not to be confused with the Great White Throne judgment.

Generally speaking, the judgments listed in Matthew come when Christ returns at the end of the Tribulation and conclude with the ushering in of the kingdom or Millennium. This is most clearly seen in Matthew 25:34, where those declared righteous enter the kingdom. At the premillennial judgment, the wicked will be cast into punishment; and the righteous will remain on earth, going into the Millennium. Since this order of events is intimated in such passages as Matthew 13:49 and 13:41–43, it would seem they definitely have to do with the posttribulation judgment.

Three other parables pertain to the posttribulation judgment of Christ. Two of these are similar, but apparently not identical: the Ten Pounds (Luke 19:11–27) and the Ten Talents (Matthew 25:14–30). The differences are numerous; a few of them follow:

a) In Luke, Jesus is journeying to Jerusalem; in Matthew, He has entered Jerusalem triumphantly and speaks from the Mount of Olives.

b) In Luke, He speaks to a mixed group; in Matthew, to the disciples.
c) In Luke, the pounds are distributed equally; in Matthew, the talents are distributed unequally.
d) In Luke, the unprofitable servant is deprived of his pound; in Matthew, he is severely punished.
e) In Luke, a nobleman goes to seek a crown; in Matthew, a householder leaves home for a time.
f) In Luke, the rewards are proportionate to what the individual has gained; in Matthew, they are the same.

In short, it appears that these are two different parables rather than two accounts of the same one.

Since the Parable of the Pounds immediately precedes the triumphal entry into Jerusalem, when Jesus was first hailed as King and then crucified, its interpretation seems to be related to those events. The nobleman going into a far country to seek a kingdom must be none other than our Lord Himself. His servants would then be the disciples or other believers, and the citizens who hated Him would be Christ-rejecters. The latter are to be slain (cast into the place of condemnation) at His coming. The disciples are to be rewarded according to their service during His absence. This parable is a warning to Jews about opposition to Him; to the disciples it is an exhortation to patient waiting and active service for Christ until His return. By entrusting sums of money to each of his household servants, he seeks to test their faithfulness. For their faithfulness they are not given something to sit down and enjoy, but a greater sphere of ministry.

Certainly it is true that as we take advantage of our opportunitites to serve the Lord, more will open to us; if we neglect those that come our way, we will soon be without even those.

Like the Parable of the Pounds, the Parable of the Talents demonstrates the importance of faithfulness in the light of Christ's return. Here a man (Christ) traveling into a far country distributes his goods unequally among his servants (instead of giving to each an equal amount as in the previous parable). Upon his return, he judges these servants on the basis of how well they have used their gifts. The faithful receive rewards, but the unfaithful are severely punished. Perhaps there is an indication in verse 30 that faithlessness indicates a lack of regenerating experience. Therefore faithless ones are cast into perdition.

Another parable of judgment, one which has been the subject of much debate, is that of the Ten Virgins (Matthew 25:1–13). It is obvious that Jesus here taught the importance of watchfulness, in the light of His return, but several questions remain. Who are the virgins? On what basis are they judged? When does this judgment occur? What is its significance?

The following is offered as a tentative interpretation. The parable describes the judgment of Israel. The ten virgins refer to the professing remnant of Israel after the Church has been taken up by the rapture. The five wise virgins represent the believing remnant; the foolish, the unbelieving who profess to be looking for Messiah's coming in power. The marriage of the bridegroom to the bride has already taken place in heaven, and the parable alludes to the wedding feast which takes place on earth. The bridegroom's coming is the return of the Lord in glory at the end of the Tribulation. Entrance into the marriage feast corresponds to entrance into the kingdom of heaven on earth (the Millennium).

That this interpretation is reasonably correct may be defended from several standpoints. First, consider the context. The Olivet Discourse (Matthew 24—25) tells of the Tribulation, Christ's coming at the end of it, and the judgment to follow, after which the blessed will enter the kingdom. The parables of these chapters illustrate the main course of events. Matthew 24:27–51 describes what will happen at the end of the Tribulation. Matthew 25:1 begins with "then." So at the time of His coming after the Tribulation, the judgment of the ten virgins will occur.

Second, from the standpoint of Jewish imagery, it must be recognized that the bridegroom has gone to get his bride. The virgins are to join the procession on the way back to the bridegroom's house and are waiting at some intermediate place. To call Christ the bridegroom and the virgins the Church, as some do, completely confuses the customary Oriental procedure. Some manuscripts add the words "and the bride" at the end of Matthew 25:1. While those readings are inferior and incorrect, they at least indicate the interpretation held by some in the early Church. This event takes place after the rapture.

Third, the judgment of the virgins cannot have anything to do with the rapture because in the clear references to the rapture, believers are caught up to meet the Lord in the air. At that time there is no judgment scene of Matthew 25:31 ff., Gentiles are judged on the basis of their treatment of "my brethren" (more than likely Christ's brethren after the flesh—Jews), and there is no other mention in this passage of their judgment, what would be more likely than to find in this parable a premillennial judgment of the Jews? The five wise virgins (representing regenerate Jews) then enter the millennium along with righteous Gentiles vindicated in the judgment of Matthew 25.

A last parable on judgment has to do with individual judgment, which occurs when a person departs his earthly life: the Rich Man and Lazarus (Luke 16:19–31). While many prefer to call this a parable, others object and treat it as an historical incident. In either case the message is not greatly changed. Moreover, it seems unwise to base an idea of contact between the saved and unsaved in the next life on this one reference. For the significance of this passage, we need to remember the context. Preceding it is the parable of the unjust steward, which seeks to show the benefits that follow a wise use of present advantages. The rich man, instead of taking advantage of opportunities to do good on earth, made wealth his highest good. His riches became a stumbling block to a virile faith in God and a life of blessing to others. He forfeited his chance to lay up treasure in heaven.

Lazarus, however, maintained a faith in God during his years on earth; for this he was rewarded in the next life. This passage is obviously designed to squelch the Pharisees (whom He is addressing), who were always asking for a sign. The rich man, now in torment, first asks for relief for himself. Failing in that, he asks that

Lazarus return from the dead to warn his brothers. Such a sign might more effectively lead to their repentance. The answer is "No!" Men have all they need for a knowledge of the truth—the preaching of Moses and the prophets. Resurrection from the dead will be no more successful. After all, Saul did not repent when he saw Samuel at Endor; the Pharisees retained their hardness of heart after the resurrection of Lazarus at Bethany; and they would later try to explain away the resurrection of Jesus Christ.

Signs enough they had. Let them listen to the clear preaching of the Word. Plummer comments, "Wonders may impress a worldly mind for the moment; but only a will freely submitting itself to moral control can avail to change the heart."[4]

NOTES

1. Archibald M. Hunter, *Interpreting the Parables* (Philadelphia: Westminster, 1960), p. 14.

2. Palestinian mustard seed is black and small like our petunia seed.

3. Apparently the woman had been converted shortly before this occasion because Luke 7:48 translated literally would be, "Your sins are forgiven." So there is no question here of salvation by works. Her adoration is an evidence of her faith. Moreover, Jesus said in verse 50, "Your faith has saved you."

4. Alfred Plummer, *A Critical and Exegetical Commentary on the Gospel According to Saint Luke* (Edinburgh: T. & T. Clark, 1913), p. 396.

SEVEN

The Miracles of Christ

Nature of the Miraculous

SINCE the term *miracle* is popularly applied to un-usual events, even by those who profess not to believe in the supernatural, it is not always easy to give the word its true biblical significance. Probably the simplest definition is C. S. Lewis': "An interference with Nature by supernatural power."[1] Also, a definition by Machen is helpful: "A miracle is an event in the external world that is wrought by the immediate power of God."[2] By this he means that a divine work is miraculous when God "uses no means but puts forth His creative power as He put it forth when He first made all things of nothing."[3]

In other words, we may say that a miracle occurs when God steps in to do something beyond what could be accomplished according to the laws of nature as we understand them, and what actually may be in violation of them. Moreover, it is beyond the powers of human beings and all of their intellectual or scientific ability. To be sure, God reveals His power or speaks in a general way at all times and to all the world through the laws or processes of nature (natural revelation, Romans 1:20). But in miracles He speaks to particular individuals with a specific message to which He calls them to give heed.

Key Terms

Four Greek words appear in the Gospels to describe the supernatural works of Jesus: *teras* (translated *won-*

der) speaks of their extraordinary character; *sēmeion (sign)* symbolizes heavenly truths and indicates Christ's immediate connection with a higher spiritual world; *dunamis (power)* describes an exercise of divine power and demonstrates the fact that higher forces have entered into and are working in this lower world of ours; *ergon (work)* refers to miraculous deeds which Christ came to do. The first three of these terms appear together in Acts 2:22, KJV: "Jesus of Nazareth, a man approved of God among you by miracles [*dunamesin*] and wonders [*terasin*], and signs [*sēmeiois*], which God did by him in the midst of you as you yourselves also know."[4]

The Purpose of Miracles

Jesus sought to meet specific needs of individuals with His wonderful works. But they were not isolated events in the life of a remarkable person; they were related to a divine purpose. Nor are miracles scattered helter-skelter throughout the Bible. Four periods in biblical history are especially characterized by them: the days of Moses, Elijah and Elisha, Daniel, and Christ and the early Church. In each case, miracles serve to accredit the message and the messenger of God at critical periods of the Hebrew-Christian tradition.

During Jesus' ministry, He used miracles to demonstrate His deity, to prove that He was sent from God, to support His Messiahship, to lead His followers to saving faith, to give evidence of an inner spiritual rejuvenation (as in the case of the healing of the paralytic, Mark 2:10–11), and as an instructional aid to help prepare His disciples for the ministry they were to perform (e.g., Mark 8:16–21). And, of course, the miracles of the incarnation, the resurrection, and the ascension are essential to the divine provision of salvation for mankind.

The Plausibility of Miracles

People in our scientific age frequently have difficulty accepting the miraculous. From our earliest days at school we are impressed with natural law—with the constancy or uniformity of operations in the universe. As we grow older and begin to develop a world view for ourselves, a conflict arises between this outlook on nature and the supernatural. How shall we resolve the problem? Can we accept the miraculous?

Miracles and "Laws" of Nature

Let us look at the laws of nature themselves. What are they? Do they preclude the possibility of miracles? As to the character of the laws of nature, Boettner observes, "They are not themselves forces in nature, but are merely general statements of the way in which these forces act so far as we have been able to observe them. They are not powers which rule all nature and force obedience to themselves, but rather mere abstractions which have no concrete existence in the external world."[5] In the same vein, C. S. Lewis concludes:

> We are in the habit of talking as if they caused events to happen; but they have never caused any event at all. . . . They produce no events: they

state the pattern to which every event—if only it can be induced to happen—must conform, just as the rules of arithmetic state the pattern to which all transactions with money must conform—if only you can get hold of any money. Thus in one sense the laws of nature cover the whole field of space and time; in another, what they leave out is precisely the whole real universe—the incessant torrent of actual events which makes up true history. That must come from somewhere else. To think the laws can produce it is like thinking that you can create real money by simply doing sums.[6]

It should be clear, then, that the laws of nature are merely observations of uniformity or constancy in nature. They are not forces which initiate action. They describe the way nature behaves—when its course is not affected by a superior power.

On the human plane, there is constant introduction of new factors or forces to interfere with the normal (untampered) course of nature. For example, chemicals mixed in certain quantities may produce a drug beneficial to human beings. If another force, such as heat or another chemical, is introduced, the result may be an explosion—or a deadly poison. Thus human beings are constantly performing "miracles" as they interfere with nature. Thousands of their inventions violate the laws of nature. Is God less than His creatures?

Lewis concludes:

The more certain we are of the law the more clearly we know that if new factors have been introduced the result will vary accordingly. What we do not know, as physicists, is whether supernatural power might be one of the new factors . . . Miracle is, from the point of view of the scientist, a form of doctoring, tampering, (if you like) cheating. It introduces a new factor into the situation, namely supernatural force, which the scientist had not reckoned on.[7]

How Science and Religion Relate

There need not be any basic conflict between science and religion. "Science . . . has for the most part now clearly seen that to seek to *describe* an order in nature does not imply the denial of a ground of nature."[8] Increasingly there is a tendency to recognize that science is one thing and religion another. Science seeks to describe phenomena and to develop new inventions in the physical world. In short, it seeks to answer the question, "How?" Religion seeks to describe phenomena and broaden horizons in the spiritual world. It seeks the reasons behind the phenomena. In short, it tries to answer the question, "Why?"

That this tension can be reconciled is clear from the fact that a number of outstanding scientists today are thoroughgoing supernaturalists—believers in miracles. The difficulty comes when human interpreters

proceed upon the hypothesis that miracles are impossible. Thus a nontheistic world view is made the criterion of history. Instead of examining the world to obtain a world view, the unbelievers use their world view to construct the history of the world. And the history they construct is self-contradictory.[9]

More Openness to the Miraculous

Let us not be too antiquated in our defense of the miraculous. It is easy to set up straw men in our apologetic for the faith. For some time there has been a tendency to abandon the extreme position in the denial of miracles. At the turn of the century, Adolf Harnack, a great liberal, could write, "Much that was formerly rejected has been reestablished on a close investigation, and in the light of comprehensive experience. Who in these days, for example, could make such short work of the miraculous cures in the Gospels as was the custom of scholars formerly?"[10] Since his day a greater trend in this direction has set in. This does not mean that the world is being converted to conservative Christianity; but a belief in the miraculous is much more intellectually respectable than it used to be, especially with the advent of so-called New Age thinking. We may conclude, then, that a belief in the miraculous is plausible in our day.

Miracles Important to Christian Faith

Without the miraculous dimension, Christianity would have no message, no solace for our age. A Jesus who is merely a martyr for the truth, a prince of philanthropists, a paragon of ethical teachers, could offer humanity only a threadbare idealism. The only answer to the choppy seas of life is a Savior who can say, "Peace, be still." The only hope for victory over satanic power is through the One whom the demons recognize and obey. The only hope for the body in this life and the next lies in the One who is Lord of life and death. The only hope for the soul rests in the One who died for our sins and rose again and ever lives to make intercession for us.

How to Study Miracles

The miracles of our Lord are easily passed over as interesting and dramatic phenomena, but a careful investigation provides valuable information to the Bible student. Here are several ways to approach them

Classify the Miracles

For instance, they may be organized according to whether they display Christ's power over nature, demons, sickness and disease, or physical deformity.

Study Them as Teaching Tools

What point did Jesus make in connection with a miracle?

Note Their Apologetic Value

They are evidence of Christ's deity. In almost every instance, the wonders Jesus performed were humanly impossible.

Think about Their Relation to the Purpose of the Writer

How does a given miracle contribute to the picture of Jesus he tries to present? Why is the miracle located where it is? How is it interesting in connection with its context?

What Do They Reveal about the Person of Christ?

Some of the facts we glean concern His power, compassion, love, attitude toward Judaism, toward government, and toward respect of persons.

Note Jesus' Method or Procedure
When Performing Miracles

For instance, He *spoke* to the three whom He raised from the dead. He *touched* a leper.

What Do They Reveal about
the Recipient of a Miracle?

What is his economic or social position, religious outlook, his gratitude? What about the effect on him physically, psychologically, spiritually?

Note the Relative Need of
the Beneficiaries of Miracles

Visualize the Drama of the Occasion

Develop a sanctified imagination. For instance, imagine Jairus nervously fidgeting in the background as Jesus initially ignores his request and turns to deal with the woman who had touched the hem of His garment. No doubt the thought flashed through Jairus' mind that his daughter might not have died if the Master had made greater haste.

Jesus' Miracles

The Gospels record thirty-five separate miracles performed by Jesus. Of these Matthew mentions 20;

Mark, 18; Luke 20; and John, 7. Obviously, however, these are not all the miracles of our Lord. Matthew, for instance, alludes to twelve occasions when Jesus performed a number of wonderful works (4:23–24; 8:16; 9:35; 10:1, 8; 11:4–5; 11:20–24; 12:15; 14:14; 14:36; 15:30; 19:2; 21:14). Apparently the gospel writers selected from the large number that the Lord performed. There are many possible ways of arranging the miracles, depending on the purpose of the commentator. Perhaps it will be helpful here to chart them in the order of their occurrence. Then they can be easily related to the chronological narrative of chapter 8.

Individual Consideration of Jesus' Miracles

Miracle 1: Turning Water into Wine (John 2:1–11)

After Jesus' baptism by John the Baptist, He returned to Galilee. Arriving in Cana, He and His disciples and His mother went to a wedding reception. Apparently the number of unexpected guests drained the supply of wine; possibly preparations had been inadequate. At any rate the wine was soon exhausted. Jesus' mother, to meet a need and perhaps thinking that here was a chance for her to show off her Son or to give Him an opportunity to make good on the publicity of John the Baptist, told Him about the situation. In so doing, she probably made an implied request that He help solve the problem, but Jesus voiced a gentle rebuke: "Woman, what have I to do with you? My hour is not yet come" (John 2:4, KJV).

Undoubtedly, Jesus wished here to put a difference between His divine program and His mother's earthly considerations, implying that He would reveal Himself at the proper time. Apparently Mary read an implied yes in Jesus' approach, however, for she gave orders to the servants to render Him whatever assistance He required. Jesus did meet the need, turning water into wine, and "thus revealed his glory" and helped to establish the faith of His disciples (cf. John 16:30, 31). Jesus' presence on this occasion indicates that He came to sanctify all of human life—to consecrate its times of joy as well as its times of sorrow. Further, by His presence He beautified marriage and gave dignity and honor to the Christian family. This miracle symbolized that He came to dispense the true "wine that makes glad the heart of man" (Psalm 104:15).

Miracle 2: Healing a Nobleman's Son at Cana (John 4:46–54)

Returning to Galilee after His early Judean ministry, Jesus again entered Cana (about a year after his first miracle). There He met a nobleman whose son was at the point of death (John 4:46–54). From the Greek, we probably should conclude that the man was a royal official of Herod Antipas, ruler of Galilee and Perea. The nature of the nobleman's plea indicated that he had faith in Jesus' ability to heal his son if the Master were present in person. Since the child was too sick to be moved, the nobleman asked Jesus to go to Capernaum to heal him. But Jesus tested the man's faith further, healing by "remote control" and expecting

THE MIRACLES OF JESUS CHRIST

Miracle	Matthew	Mark	Luke	John
1. Turning Water into Wine				2:1–11
2. Healing a Nobleman's Son at Cana				4:46–54
3. Healing a Lame Man at the Pool of Bethesda				5:1–9
4. Providing First Miraculous Catch of Fish			5:1–11	
5. Delivering a Synagogue Demoniac		1:23–28	4:31–36	
6. Healing Peter's Mother-in-Law	8:14–17	1:29–31	4:38–39	
7. Cleansing a Leper	8:2–4	1:40–45	5:12–16	
8. Healing a Paralytic	9:2–8	2:3–15	5:18–26	
9. Healing a Man with a Withered Hand	12:9–14	3:1–5	6:6–11	
10. Healing a Centurion's Servant	8:5–13		7:1–10	
11. Raising a Widow's Son			7:11–17	
12. Healing a Blind and Dumb Demoniac	12:22		11:14	

THE MIRACLES OF JESUS—*Cont'd*				
Miracle	*Matthew*	*Mark*	*Luke*	*John*
13. Stilling a Storm	8:18, 23–27	4:35–41	8:22–25	
14. Delivering the Gadarene Demoniacs	8:28–34	5:1–20	8:26–39	
15. Healing a Woman with an Issue of Blood	9:20–22	5:25–34	8:43–48	
16. Raising Jairus' Daughter	9:18–19, 23–26	5:22–24, 35–43	8:41–42, 49–56	
17. Healing Two Blind Men	9:27–31			
18. Delivering a Dumb Demoniac	9:32–33			
19. Feeding the 5,000	14:14–21	6:35–44	9:12–17	6:4–13
20. Walking on the Water	14:24–33	6:45–52		6:16–21
21. Delivering a Syrophoeni- cian's Daughter	15:21–28	7:24–30		
22. Healing a Deaf Mute in Decapolis		7:31–37		
23. Feeding 4,000	15:32–39	8:1–9		
24. Healing a Blind Man at Bethsaida		8:22–26		
25. Delivering a Demon- Possessed Boy	17:14–18	9:14–29	9:38–43	

THE MIRACLES OF JESUS—*Cont'd*

Miracle	Matthew	Mark	Luke	John
26. Finding the Tribute Money	17:24–27			
27. Healing a Man Born Blind				9:1–7
28. Healing a Crippled Woman on the Sabbath			13:10–17	
29. Healing a Man with Dropsy			14:1–6	
30. Raising of Lazareth				11:17–44
31. Cleansing Ten Lepers			17:11–19	
32. Healing Blind Bartimaeus	20:29–34	10:46–52	18:35–43	
33. Cursing the Fig Tree	21:18–19	11:12–14		
34. Restoring Malchus' Ear			22:49–51	18:10
35. Providing Second Miraculous Catch of Fish				21:1–14

him to accept the fact. The royal official did, and, as he returned home, his servants came to tell him that the child was dramatically improving. Comparing notes, they discovered the boy had taken a turn for the better at the precise time when Jesus uttered the healing words. Here, as in many other instances, the evidential value of Christ's miracles is presented. He spoke of His works as signs to lead their witnesses to saving faith (John 4:48); after the miracle, the nobleman's whole household believed (v. 53).

Miracle 3: Healing a Lame Man at the Pool of Bethesda (John 5:1-9)

Some months later, Jesus went to Jerusalem to participate in an unnamed feast, possibly the feast of the Passover (John 5:1). While there, He went to the Pool of Bethesda, where there were hot springs. Engaging an invalid in conversation, Jesus discovered that he had been lame for thirty eight years and that he had waited there for a long time to get into the pool at its highest point of potency. Unable to get into the pool himself, and without the aid of others to put him into the waters, he had waited in vain for healing. Then the Master spoke the words of healing, and the man was then able to walk.[11] It is significant that of all the "great many disabled people" lying by the pool, Jesus focused on only one who was also ready for healing of soul. Thus a physical healing was a means to spiritual regeneration and an opportunity for Jesus to assert a claim to deity.

Miracle 4: Providing First Miraculous Catch of Fish (Luke 5:1-11)

Apparently Jesus' disciples had returned to their normal occupations after an initial period of service with the Master, for He called them a second time at the beginning of His Galilean ministry—this time asking them to make a clean break with their secular employment and follow Him full time. Clearly these disciples had had abundant preparation for such a response. They had served with the Master in Galilee and Judea and had seen Him turn water into wine and heal the nobleman's son in Cana and restore the lame man at the Pool of Bethesda. Moreover, it appears that the mother of James and John, Salome, was the sister of the Virgin Mary (compare Mark 15:40 and John 19:25); therefore James and John were Jesus' cousins. Today, we should not berate our listeners if lack of preparation makes them unwilling to take a major step of discipleship; rather, we should instead prepare them for such a step. It is interesting that Jesus called busy men to be His coworkers. Conceivably, men diligent in secular pursuits would also prove to be diligent in religious duties. As Jesus came upon the four fishermen on this particular morning, they were quite discouraged. They had worked all night and caught nothing; now they were washing out their nets.

Jesus' first request was to use Simon's boat for a pulpit to preach to the crowd on the shore. Then He instructed the fishermen to let down their nets again. This time they caught so many fish that the two ships (belonging to Simon, Andrew, James, and John) began to sink. Peter, as spokesman for the four, recognized the miracle as an evidence of the Master's divine power and origin and said, "Depart from me, for I am a sinful man, O Lord" (Luke 5:8). By this incident the four fishermen gained further preparation for a life of total discipleship to the Lord.

Miracle 5: Delivering a Synagogue Demoniac
(Mark 1:23-28; Luke 4:31-36)

Following His rejection at Nazareth, Jesus moved His headquarters to Capernaum. Soon afterward He encountered a demon possessed man in the synagogue on the Sabbath day (Mark 1:23-28; Luke 4:31-36). The demons in the man immediately took the defensive, recognizing the superiority of Jesus.[12] The Master then rebuked them and delivered the man from his enslavement. Two important observations may be gathered from this miracle: (1) Jesus had power over the supernatural demons as well as over the natural sphere; (2) the demons here, as elsewhere, recognized Jesus for who He was, even though men often did not.

Miracle 6: Healing Peter's Mother-in-Law
(Matthew 8:14-17; Mark 1:29-31; Luke 4:38-39)

After the sabbath service was over, the apostolic group went to Peter's house, probably for dinner. Sadness hung over the home because Peter's mother-in-law was ill with a fever, but Jesus healed her and immediately she began to serve the guests (Matthew 8:14-17; Mark 1:29-31; Luke 4:38-39). In this miracle Jesus demonstrated His concern for the needs of His disciples (then and now) as well as for the troubled multitudes. This was one of the few instances in which Jesus performed a miracle when the case was not impossible from a human standpoint. Conceivably the woman could have recovered from her fever in process of time. The special feature of this situation, however, is that she arose *immediately* and resumed her household tasks. There was no period of recuperation.

Miracle 7: Cleansing a Leper (Matthew 8:2–4; Mark 1:40–45; Luke 5:12–16)

Shortly afterwards Jesus and His disciples began a preaching tour of Galilee. On the way, they met a leper who begged for healing (Matthew 8:2–4; Mark 1:40–45; Luke 5:12–16). The faith of the leper was exemplary, for he did not say, "If you can," but, "If you will," make me clean. The action of the Savior was remarkable, for He touched the untouchable. The command of the Savior was significant, for He told the leper to report to the priest for ceremonial cleansing; in this He demonstrated His respect for the Mosaic Law. The priest must have been amazed. When in Israel had there been such a remarkable occurrence? Jesus further ordered the leper not to spread abroad the news of what had happened to him. Apparently the Master wanted to spare Himself the trouble of curious crowds interested only in His wonderful works.

Miracle 8: Healing a Paralytic (Matthew 9:2–8; Mark 2:3–15; Luke 5:18–26)

After Jesus' return to Capernaum from this preaching tour, the townspeople heard of His arrival and crowded around His residence.[13] Four friends of a paralytic made a brave attempt to get their helpless charge to the Master, but they failed because the crowd was so dense. Undaunted, they climbed up on the roof, pulled up the tiles, and lowered the helpless man into Jesus' presence. Jesus pronounced the sins of the man forgiven; then, noticing that some of the scribes thought He was guilty of blasphemy, He ordered the paralytic to rise, take up his bed, and return home. The outward healing was intended as an evidence of inward cleansing and as evidence that He, the Son of Man, had power to forgive sins. Noteworthy in the study of this miracle is the persistent faith of the friends of the crippled man to get him to Jesus, Jesus' ability to read the minds of men, and His claim to be the Son of Man and to forgive sins (Matthew 9:2–8; Mark 2:3–12; Luke 5:18–26).

Miracle 9: Healing a Man with a Withered Hand (Matthew 12:9-14; Mark 3:1-5; Luke 6:6-11)

It is remarkable how many of His gracious works Jesus performed on the Sabbath. On one occasion He declared Himself to be Lord of the Sabbath, and apparently He felt that a good way to honor the Father on the Sabbath was to release men from their unhappy lot in life.[14] During His early Galilean ministry, He healed a man with a withered hand on the Sabbath (Matthew 12:9–14; Mark 3:1–5; Luke 6:6–11). For the leaders of the Jews, this was a test case, because they wanted to accuse Him of breaking the Sabbath laws. He recognized this and, moved with righteous indignation at the hardness of their hearts, He healed the man. The reaction of the Pharisees was to seek counsel of the Herodians to find a way to destroy Jesus. Jesus' breaking of the Pharisees' traditions and putting them to shame before all the people so infuriated them that they could even join league with the

Herodians, the Romanizing party in the land, for Jesus' power threatened them both.

Miracle 10: Healing a Centurion's Servant (Matthew 8:5–13; Luke 7:1–10)

During His second preaching tour of Galilee, Jesus stopped briefly in Capernaum. There He found a stir among the elders of the Jews because the Roman centurion (evidently a proselyte) who built their synagogue had appealed to them to heal his servant. They turned to Jesus for help (Matthew 8:5–13; Luke 7:1). Jesus honored their request and started out for the centurion's house. Before He arrived, a message came from the officer saying he was not worthy of a visit from Jesus, and that if Jesus would just say the word, the servant would be healed. Jesus marveled at such faith and restored the servant. This was the first miracle Jesus performed on a Gentile (or on behalf of a Gentile). As with the healing of the nobleman's son at Cana, Jesus performed it at a distance, but this time the suggestion for such a method came from the petitioner rather than the Master.

Miracle 11: Raising a Widow's Son (Luke 7:11–17)

The next day Jesus and His disciples journeyed to Nain. Approaching the city gate, they came upon a funeral procession. The corpse was the only son of a widow. In New Testament Palestine, without social security or old age benefits of other types, a childless widow was often reduced to poverty. Jesus was moved with compassion for the woman. Stopping the procession by touching the bier, Jesus addressed the corpse and raised him from the dead. Then, instead of claiming the resurrected one as a disciple, the Lord restored him to his mother, for whose sake he had been brought to life (Luke 7:11–17).

Miracle 12: Healing a Blind and Dumb Demoniac (Matthew 12:22; Luke 11:14)

Later in the second Galilean tour, there was brought to Jesus a demon possessed man who was blind and dumb (Matthew 12:22; Luke 1:14). Conceivably no exorcist could heal such a one because communication with him would be virtually impossible. But one case was no more difficult for Jesus than another. The Master healed him. The result: awe and wonder by the common people and opposition by the Pharisees. Their explanation of such an amazing phenomenon was that the prince of demons had enabled Jesus to cast out one of the lesser demons. This discussion gave rise to the pronouncement about the unpardonable sin.

Miracle 13: Stilling a Storm (Matthew 8:18, 23–27; Mark 4:35–41; Luke 8:22–25)

After delivering the Parable of the Sower and other kingdom parables, Jesus dismissed the multitude, entered a boat, and began to cross the Sea of Galilee. Utterly exhausted, He fell asleep in the stern. Soon a violent squall roared down from the hills of Galilee. The boat began to fill with water, and the disciples grew panic stricken. The storm must have been much worse than usual or these seasoned fishermen would not have been terrified. They woke Him, crying, "Do you not care that we perish?"

He rebuked their lack of faith. But first He rebuked the elements, "and the wind ceased, and there was a great calm." Both the wind and its effects subsided immediately. Winds sometimes do suddenly cease, but waves remain choppy for sometime afterward. In this instance the sea also became as glass immediately. The disciples were filled with godly fear. Here was a kind of supernatural power that was new to them (Matthew 8:18, 23–27; Mark 4:35–41; Luke 8:22–25). Exorcism of demons they knew, and accounts of raising from the dead they had read in the Old Testament; but they had never known of a prophet with this kind of power.

Miracle 14: Delivering the Gadarene Demoniacs (Matthew 8:28-34; Mark 5:1-20; Luke 8:26-39)

Reaching the other side, they disembarked in the territory of the Gadarenes. There they met a violent and naked demoniac (according to Matthew 8:28, two demoniacs)[15] who lived in the tombs, probably the caves that were used for burial purposes by nearby townspeople. As in the case of other deliverances of demon possessed individuals, the demons recognized Jesus as the Son of God. An added feature is significant. The demons asked Jesus, "Have you come here to torment us before the time?" Though not omniscient, the demons possessed great knowledge, recognizing Jesus as Messiah and Son of God, but the crowds, the leaders of the Jews, and even the disciples had a hard time coming to such a conclusion; they even had some idea of the time of their judgment.

The big question often raised in connection with this miracle concerns Jesus' ethics in permitting the demons to enter swine when He knew the result would be great loss of property for the villagers. Plummer offers two suggestions as a tentative solution:

> (1) A visible effect of the departure of the demons was necessary to convince the demoniacs and their neighbors of the completeness of the cure. Brutes and private property may be sacrificed where the sanity and lives of persons are concerned. (2) The keepers of the swine were Jews who were breaking the Jewish law, which was binding on them, and perhaps on the whole district.[16]

Of course it is evident from the text that Jesus merely permitted the demons to enter the pigs. Then when demonic power came upon the animals they went wild and destroyed themselves. Scripture does not say that either Jesus or the demons drove the pigs into the water. Instead of raising a question of Jesus' ethics at this point, it is just as valid to suggest that the demons brought about this destruction of property in order to stir up the ill will of the community against Jesus and prevent Him from ministering in their midst.

The Gadarenes, terrified over what further catastrophe might befall them if this Galilean wonder worker remained among them, begged Him to leave their territory. Traveling to the western shore of the Sea of

Galilee, the apostolic company again faced a needy multitude. Especially importunate was Jairus, a ruler of the synagogue, who begged that Jesus come to his home and heal his daughter, who lay at the point of death. The Master responded immediately, but as He walked to Jairus' home, a crowd gathered around Him.

Miracle 15: Healing a Woman with an Issue of Blood (Matthew 9:20–22; Mark 5:25–34; Luke 8:43–48)

In the midst was a woman who had suffered some sort of bloody discharge for twelve years. She had spent all her money on doctors and had endured much as they experimented on her in an effort to effect a cure. In her great need she went to Jesus. Being levitically unclean, she approached Him from the rear with the superstitious belief that there was healing power even in His garments. Touching Him, she was immediately cured.[17] Jesus stopped and demanded to know who had touched Him. No doubt He did so for the good of the woman and to present the miracle to the multitude. At length she confessed and Jesus pronounced His blessing on her (Matthew 9:20–22; Mark 5:25–34; Luke 8:43–48).

Miracle 16: Raising Jairus' Daughter (Matthew 9:18–19, 23–26; Mark 5:22–24, 35–43; Luke 8:41–42, 49–56)

Meanwhile, Jairus was impatiently waiting for Jesus' interview with the woman to end. No sooner did it end than one of his servants came with the report that his daughter was dead. No doubt he felt that if the woman had not delayed Jesus, his daughter might have been spared. But Jesus reassured Jairus. Arriving at the ruler's house, He excluded all the mourners and entered with the parents, Peter, James, and John. As He earlier raised the widow's son from the dead, and as He later was to do with Lazarus, Jesus simply *commanded,* "Maid, arise." Immediately she did so and took nourishment.

Some, in an effort to minimize Jesus' power, have strongly emphasized His comment that the girl was only sleeping. By way of an answer, we must note that, first, the miraculous element is still present. Jesus healed the girl. Second, this figure of speech is often used for death in the New Testament. Jesus' statement that she was not dead but merely sleeping probably indicated the temporary nature of her decease. Third the evangelist notes that she was dead (Luke 8:53).

Miracle 17: Healing Two
Blind Men (Matthew 9:27–31)

Shortly afterwards, Jesus healed two blind men, who apparently had heard of the resurrection of Jairus' daughter (Matthew 9:27–31). Whether the men recognized Jesus as the Messiah or simply alluded to His parentage in addressing Him as the Son of David is open to question. Probably the former is true. To associate the kingdom of heaven with the Davidic dynasty took a real act of faith when the Herodian dynasty was in power and when the Maccabean line had gained such a hold on the hearts of the people for their exploits in reestablishing the freedom of the Jews during the intertestamental period.

At any rate, He touched their eyes and healed them, charging them not to advertise the matter. Perhaps it should be stated once more that the Master frequently issued this command to prevent crowds interested merely in their physical welfare from mobbing Him and hindering His greater spiritual ministry. From the account of this miracle a searching question leaps at us. Is much of our lack of success in Christian circles today due to lack of faith? How much could the Lord do for us if He faced us with the same condition as He did these blind men, "According to your faith be it unto you"?

Miracle 18: Delivering a Dumb Demoniac (Matthew 9:32–33)

A chain reaction had set in. The raising of Jairus' daughter led to the healing of the blind men. The report of the healing of the blind men led to the deliverance of a dumb man possessed with a devil. His friends brought him to Jesus with glorious results: the demon left and the man spoke. The crowds marveled but the Pharisees again claimed that the Lord exorcised the demons by satanic power (Matthew 9:32–33).

Miracle 19: Feeding the 5,000 (Matthew 14:14–21; Mark 6:35–44; Luke 9:12–17; John 6:4–13)

Later in the middle period of Jesus' Galilean ministry, He sent the disciples out in pairs to preach and heal. When they returned, He took them aside for rest and instruction in an uninhabited place near Bethsaida. But still a crowd followed them. At the end of the day the disciples wanted to send the tired and hungry multitude away, but Jesus had compassion on them and inquired how much food was available. Andrew reported that a lad had a lunch of five loaves and two fish. Jesus ordered that the 5,000 men (plus women and children) be arranged in companies of fifty. Then He offered the blessing, broke the loaves and fish, and gave them to His disciples to distribute. After everyone had eaten enough, twelve baskets of scraps remained.

This is the only one of Jesus' miracles that was reported by all four Gospel writers (Matthew 14:14–21; Mark 6:35–44; Luke 9:12–17; John 6:4–13). What significance is to be attached to such a fact is open to question. Certainly it points to Jesus as the Bread of Life and as the Source of supply for all our needs.

Miracle 20: Walking on the Water
(Matthew 14:24–33; Mark 6:45–52;
John 6:16–21)

When the crowd had had enough to eat, Jesus sent them away. He also directed the disciples to go to the other (west) side of the Sea of Galilee, while He went up into a mountain to pray. As they crossed over, a storm arose and the disciples found themselves in difficulty. It is significant that the apostles were in trouble while in the center of God's will. Often Christian workers interpret their difficulties as evidence that they are out of the Lord's will and are therefore being disciplined. Certainly that is not always the case.

Jesus was aware of the difficulties of His followers and came to them, walking on the water. Such an appearance in the middle of the night terrified the disciples, but the Master identified Himself. Peter, testing Him, said, if He was really the Lord, He should command him to walk on the water too. This the Lord did, and Peter was all right as long as he kept his eyes on the Lord. But when he began to think about the storm, he started to sink. Jesus pulled Peter into the boat and stilled the squall. Actually this is a triple miracle: Jesus walked on water, Peter walked on water, and the storm was stilled (Matthew 14:24–33; Mark 6:45–52; John 6:16–21). Among the lessons of this miracle is the truth that as long as believers look to Jesus in the storms of life, they may tread underfoot the turbulent surgings that confront them. When they fix their attention on the stormy winds and waters, they begin to sink.

Miracle 21: Delivering a Syrophoenician's Daughter (Matthew 15:21–28; Mark 7:24–30)

During the later period of the Galilean ministry, Jesus moved north briefly to the Phoenician border. There He met a Phoenician woman whose daughter was demon possessed. In parabolic speech the Lord told her that His ministry was to the house of Israel; but she assumed a position of great humility, willing to accept any "leftover" grace that He might have for a Gentile. Jesus honored her importunity and humility and healed her daughter. This is the second recorded miracle on behalf of a Gentile. Like the healing of the centurion's servant, it was performed at a distance. Jesus never saw the Phoenician woman's daughter, who remained at home while her mother sought help for her (Matthew 15:21–28; Mark 7:24–30).

Miracle 22: Healing a Deaf Mute in Decapolis (Mark 7:31–37)

Next Jesus moved southeast into the region of Decapolis, where a deaf mute was brought to Him. On this occasion the Lord made more elaborate preparations for healing than was frequently the case. Jesus put His fingers in the man's ears. Then He put spittle on the man's tongue, and looking to heaven commanded, "Be opened." Immediately the man's hearing was restored and his speech made plain (Mark 7:31–37).

There must be special meaning in the various ways Jesus effected healing, and if we could recreate the circumstances of each cure we would understand these variations better. Why should He heal one in the crowd and another outside the city, why should He speak a word of immediate restoration to one and send another to wash in the Pool of Siloam? In this case the reason for the method of healing can be guessed. The symbolic actions of putting His fingers into the man's ears and spitting and touching his tongue would awaken faith and expectation in one with whom it was otherwise impossible to communicate. Also, by "looking up to heaven" Jesus claimed divine help and an acknowledgment of His oneness with the Father.

Miracle 23: Feeding 4,000 (Matthew 15:32–39; Mark 8:1–9)

While Jesus was still on the eastern side of the Sea of Galilee, the feeding of the 4,000 occurred. The people had been following Him for three days, virtually without food; and He could not send them away hungry. The disciples apparently had not learned their lesson from the feeding of the 5,000. Again they wondered how they would feed the multitude. But Jesus multiplied the available seven loaves and a few fish and fed 4,000 men, plus women and children. In comparison with the feeding of the 5,000, we see that this time the need was more desperate, the provisions were slightly different, the number of men was fewer, though the total may not have been, and fewer baskets of leftovers remained. In the case of feeding the 5,000, however, the basket size was small; here it was the large hamper size (Matthew 15:32–39; Mark 8:1–9).

Miracle 24: Healing a Blind Man at Bethsaida (Mark 8:22–26)

Crossing to the western shore of the Sea of Galilee once more, Jesus landed near Magdala and then moved north to Bethsaida, where a blind man was brought to Him for healing. Jesus took the man outside the town. Then He put spittle on his eyes, after which the man saw indistinctly. Jesus then touched his eyes again and he saw clearly. Since after the first stage of healing the patient reported that men appeared as trees, we may conclude that he remembered what trees and men looked like and therefore was not born blind.

This case is one of few progressive cures recorded in the gospels. In this case, as well as in many others, Jesus performs a miracle on one who has been *brought* to Him. Others had faith to believe that the Master would accomplish a work of grace in their friend. Certainly this points up the necessity for us to bring others to Jesus today. They are helplessly bound with the shackles of sin and do not come of their own accord.

Miracle 25: *Delivering a Demon-Possessed Boy* (Matthew 17:14–18; Mark 9:14–29; Luke 9:38–43)

As the Lord came down from the Mount of Transfiguration with Peter, James and John, He met the rest of the disciples and a man who was greatly disturbed over his demon possessed son. His disturbance was increased because he had brought the boy to the disciples and they had been unable to heal him. Jesus assured the father that all things were possible to him who believes, to which the father replied, "Lord, I believe; help my unbelief." Then Jesus commanded the evil spirit to come out of the boy, which it did. But in leaving, it so severely abused the boy that he appeared to be dead. Performing another miracle, Jesus restored him to full health.

In the ensuing discussion between Jesus and His disciples, we find a double significance of this account. First they asked, "Why could *we* not cast it out?" Perhaps their failure lay in looking more to their own abilities than to divine resources. Second, Jesus pointed out, "This kind does not go out except by prayer and fasting," indicating that there are degrees of power among the demons, and some require greater divine power to defeat them (Matthew 17:14–18; Mark 9:14–29; Luke 9:38–43).

Miracle 26: Finding the Tribute Money (Matthew 17:24–27)

Returning to Capernaum from the transfiguration, Jesus was faced with the tax collectors—apparently Jews who sought the annual half-shekel head tax for the temple treasury. They got to Peter first and asked if his master paid tribute. To this Peter replied "Yes," indicating that Jesus had been in the habit of paying the temple tax. When he went back to headquarters to bring the matter to Jesus' attention, the Master in His omniscience read Peter's thoughts.

In the ensuing conversation, Jesus implied that He did not need to pay tax to the temple of His Father (He was greater than the temple and Himself the true temple, John 2:21); however, He would pay the tax to avoid offense. If He refused to pay at this stage of His ministry, He would be misunderstood as an insubordinate, a law breaker. His enemies would have another occasion to condemn Him. Therefore He sent Peter to catch a fish in which the disciple would find a coin equal to a shekel, which would pay the tax for both of them (Matthew 17:24–27).

Miracle 27: Healing a Man Born Blind (John 9:1–7)

Near the beginning of His later Judean ministry, Jesus had a head-on collision with the Pharisees in the temple, which resulted in their effort to kill Him. But He escaped, and as He left the temple, He saw a beggar blind from birth. Presently His disciples began to discuss whether the sin of this man or his parents was responsible for his blindness. As to how a child could sin before birth and suffer the consequences in life, Plummer notes a Jewish view that it was possible for an unborn babe to have emotions and that these might be sinful.[18] Jesus replied with a third alternative: that this blindness occurred for the greater glory of God. In other words, they should not, like Job's friends, assume a necessary connection between sin and calamity.

Some will question the goodness of God in permitting a man to suffer for so many years just so Jesus could be glorified by performing a miracle. That is a rather crude way to put the matter. Perhaps we should say: "God allowed this suffering and performed the miracle so that, from the testimony of the wonderful work, the grace of God might become operative in the lives of many others." Viewed from such a standpoint, the suffering does not seem heartless or unfair.

Deciding to use means, Jesus made clay with spittle and anointed the man's eyes and sent him to wash[19] in the pool of Siloam. Passing the test of his faith, the man saw and went home to tell his family. After Jesus departed, the healed man ran into trouble because the Pharisees tried to turn him against Jesus. After considerable cross examination, they excommunicated him from the synagogue because he appeared to be a disciple of Christ. Jesus found him in his dejected state and encouraged his faith in the Son of God (John 9:1–38).

Miracle 28: Healing a Crippled Woman on the Sabbath (Luke 13:10–17)

Not long after Jesus' first meeting with Mary and Martha, He healed a woman in a synagogue on the Sabbath day. She had been bent over and crippled for eighteen years. The Lord took the initiative in the matter, called her to Him, put His hands on her and pronounced her healed. Immediately the ruler of the synagogue lost his temper because Jesus healed on the Sabbath, for which he received a spirited lecture on hypocrisy. His opponents were shamed into silence, and the people praised God for His wonderful works (Luke 13:10–17).

Miracle 29: Healing a Man with Dropsy (Luke 14:1–6)

One or more Sabbaths later, the Lord was taking a meal in a Pharisee's home. One of the guests was afflicted with dropsy, and Jesus healed him. This time the Master took the offensive, pointing out that when something happened to one of their animals on the Sabbath, the Pharisees took care of it. By inference, He states there is nothing wrong with alleviating human suffering on the Sabbath (Luke 14:1–6).

Miracle 30: Raising of Lazarus (John 11:17–44)

While Jesus was ministering in Perea a few weeks before His crucifixion, He received an urgent message from Mary and Martha of Bethany to come and heal

Lazarus, who was ill. But the Master did not come at once, seeming to wait deliberately until the death of Lazarus, so God would have the greater glory. When He approached the edge of town, anxious Martha came rushing to scold Him for not coming sooner because Lazarus was now dead. In her state of mind Jesus' assurances concerning resurrection were of little avail, and she went dashing off to get Mary, who had remained at home. When Mary met Him, her tender remonstrances caused Jesus to cry. He proceeded without further delay to the tomb and ordered the stone to be removed. Then, as in the case of the other raisings from the dead, He called to the dead person. Lazarus came forth bound in grave clothes, which Jesus commanded to be removed.

While Jesus would perform miracles, He expected human beings to do their part. At Cana they were ordered to fill the waterpots with water; the man born blind was told to wash in the pool of Siloam; in this instance the onlookers were expected to remove the stone and loose the burial bands. As on many other occasions, Jesus was a divider of men. Many believed on Him because of this miracle, but the Pharisees became more vehemently opposed (John 11:17–46).

Miracle 31: Cleansing Ten Lepers (Luke 17:11–19)

As Jesus made His last journey to Jerusalem, He circled around through Samaria. Entering a village, He met ten lepers who cried to Him for mercy. According to the gospel record, He did not pronounce healing or promise it but told them to show themselves to the priest in order that he might pronounce them clean, implying that He would heal them. As they went in faith to the priest, they discovered they were being healed. Imagine their delight as they saw the effects of their leprosy fading away! But only one returned to express his gratitude to Jesus (Luke 17:11–19). We have here an indication that many of those whom Jesus healed never developed any great faith in Him or became His followers.

Miracle 32: Healing Blind Bartimaeus
(Matthew 20:29–34; Mark 10:46–52;
Luke 18:35–43)

Shortly before His triumphal entry into Jerusalem, Jesus healed two blind men near Jericho. The variation in the three accounts requires some discussion (Matthew 20:29–34; Mark 10:46–52; Luke 18:35–43). Because Matthew speaks of two blind men who were healed as Jesus left Jericho, and Mark and Luke speak of one blind man, Bartimaeus, being healed as He came to Jericho, many have thought that these were two separate miracles or two irreconcilable accounts of the same one. Since nearly all elements are the same in the three accounts, I feel that only one miracle is represented. As to the difficulties, they are easily removed. From modern archaeological discovery, we now know that in Jesus' day there were two Jerichos— an Old Testament Jericho and a New Testament Jericho a mile or two apart.

Matthew may be describing the incident from the standpoint of Jesus having left the one, and the other two gospel writers from the standpoint of Jesus entering the other. As for the number of persons involved, we may conclude that there were two, Bartimaeus and another. Bartimaeus was more vocal and the spokesman for both.

Miracle 33: *Cursing the Fig Tree* (Matthew 21:18–19; Mark 11:12–14)

On Monday morning of Passion Week, as Jesus and His disciples walked from Bethany to Jerusalem, they observed an unfruitful fig tree, which Jesus cursed. On the following day it was completely dried up. Many have raised the question as to why Jesus would have expected to find figs on the tree and why He should have cursed the tree when He did not find figs, since it was not the season for figs (Matthew 21:18–19; Mark 11:12–14). Several answers have been given:

1. Normally the fruit precedes the leaves; so if leaves were on the tree out of season, fruit should be there too.
2. Fig trees which retain their leaves through the winter usually have figs also.
3. Before the fruit appears, it is preceded by a growth called *taqsh;* Jesus did not observe any *taqsh* and therefore cursed the tree.
4. This action symbolized how it would fare with a person or the Hebrew people when God came looking for the fruit of righteousness and found nothing but leaves of boastful and empty profession.

Another question asked in connection with this miracle is why should Jesus have treated the tree as a moral agent, punishing it as if its unfruitfulness involved guilt? Obviously this is a symbolic miracle. Trench gives a fair summary of the significance:

> It was condemned, not so much for having no fruit, as that, not having fruit, it clothed itself abundantly with leaves, with the foliage which, according to the natural order of the tree's development, gave pledge and promise that fruit should be found on it, if sought. And this will then exactly answer to the sin of Israel, which under this tree was symbolized—that sin being not so much that it was without fruit as that it boasted of so much. The true fruit of that people, as of any people before the Incarnation, would have been to admit that it had no fruit, that without Christ, without the Incarnate Son of God, it could do nothing; to have presented itself before God bare and naked and empty altogether. But this was exactly what Israel refused to do.[20]

Miracle 34: Restoring Malchus' Ear (Luke 22:49-51; John 18:10)

In the Garden of Gethsemane an armed band led by Judas came to capture Jesus and take Him away for trial and death. Peter, leaping to the defense of his Lord, drew his sword and cut off the ear of Malchus, servant to the high priest. Jesus condemned the action, stating that He could command twelve legions of angels to defend Him if He wished, but now His time had come, and the prophecies of His suffering and death must be fulfilled (Matthew 26:53–54).

Jesus then restored Malchus' ear (Luke 22:49–51; cf. John 18:10).

Miracle 35: *Providing Second Miraculous Catch of Fish (John 21:1-14)*

After the resurrection, seven of the disciples went fishing in the Sea of Galilee. Working all night, they caught nothing. In the morning Jesus (whose identity was not at first discerned) stood on the shore and asked them about their success. When they admitted their failure, He told them to cast their net on the other side of the boat. Soon the net bulged with fish. Then they recognized that it was Jesus. Peter immediately jumped into the water and swam to shore. When the boat and the net were brought to land, Jesus served them bread and fish around a camp-fire—welcome indeed to damp, tired, and hungry men. After the meal, Jesus had a private conversation with Peter, in which He reinstated him to his apostolic responsibilities. As after the first miraculous catch of fish (Luke 5:1–11), so here Jesus issued a call to discipleship (John 21:1–22).

NOTES

1. C. S. Lewis, *Miracles* (New York: Macmillan, 1947), p. 15.

2. J. Gresham Machen. *The Christian View of Man* (New York: Macmillan, 1937), p. 117.

3. *Ibid.*

4. W. Graham Scroggie, *A Guide to the Gospels* (London: Pickering & Inglis, 1948), pp. 203–4.

5. Loraine Boettner, *Studies in Theology* (Grand Rapids: Eerdmans, 1947), p. 61.

6. Lewis, p. 71.

7. *Ibid.,* pp. 70–71.

8. C. J. Wright, *Miracle in History and in Modern Thought* (New York: Henry Holt & Co., 1930), p. 178.

9. Gordon H. Clark, "The Resurrection," *Christianity Today,* April 15, 1957, p. 19.

10. Adolf Harnack, *Christianity and History,* p. 63, quoted in W. Sanday, *Outlines of the Life of Christ* (New York: Scribners, 1905), p. 101.

11. The best manuscripts omit the words "waiting for the moving of the water. For an angel went down at a certain season into the pool, and troubled the water: Whosoever then first after the troubling of the water stepped in was made whole of whatsoever disease he had" (John 5:3–4). Seemingly there was nothing in the original about any supernatural moving of the water: that was a popular superstition. It is common knowledge today that when thermal waters bubble up, set in motion by gases, they then have the greatest healing power.

12. There must have been more than one, because they said, "What have *we* to do with you?" (Mark 1:24).

13. Possibly the headquarters of the disciples in Capernaum was a house belonging to Simon Peter and the home of his family while the group was away on preaching tours. Certainly he was a man of some means, since he had been in business for himself. And as head of the apostolic group, what would be more natural than for him to entertain them in his home on occasion? It is not necessary to conclude that all twelve of them stayed at his home, however, because James, John, Levi, and others may have had sufficient means to maintain homes in or near Capernaum.

14. Jesus' sabbath activity was not a breach of the Law

of Moses but of the Pharisees' interpretation of it. Perhaps Jesus wished to condemn their whole system of legal righteousness in His opposition to their interpretation of the fourth commandment. Jesus did not, however, make a regular practice of healing on the Sabbath.

15. There is no contradiction, necessarily, between the three Gospels as to whether there were one or two demoniacs. Probably one was more vocal than the other. At any rate the demonic power likely would have had the same reaction in either case, and it was the demons who spoke (for comparison see Matthew 8:28–34; Mark 5:1–20; Luke 8:26–39). It is significant that Jesus regarded demoniacs not as merely demented but as subjects of an alien spiritual power. He addressed the evil spirits as distinct from the man.

16. Alfred Plummer, *A Critical and Exegetical Commentary on the Gospel According to St. Luke* (Edinburgh: T. & T. Clark, 1913), p. 228.

17. There is no need to inject into this account the superstitious belief that there actually was healing power in Christ's clothing. In His omniscience He no doubt knew the woman's intent and identity. His question of who touched Him, then, was not for the purpose of seeking information.

18. Alfred Plummer, *The Gospel According to St. John* (Cambridge: Cambridge U., 1882), p. 204.

19. Probably this was not to be an entire bath. The Greek word used here is commonly employed in connection with washing parts of the body.

20. Richard C. Trench, *Notes on the Miracles of our Lord* (Westwood, N.J.: Revell, n. d.), pp. 348–49.

EIGHT

The Narrative
of the Life of Christ

Thirty Years of Preparation

AFTER Augustus became master of the Roman world, he launched numerous projects aimed at tidying up that world and giving it greater stability and prosperity. One of those efforts was an imperial census, involving enrollment and payment of a poll tax. When Augustus's orders for the census reached Palestine, Joseph of Nazareth and his espoused wife Mary trudged down to Bethlehem (their ancestral home) to meet the Roman requirements. There Christ was born (Luke 2:1–7). In exactly what year, is another question.

When Christ Was Born

When Dionysius established the basis of our present calendar in 525, he equated the Roman year 754 A.U.C. (*ab urbe condita*, "from the foundation of the city," i.e., Rome) with A.D. 1. But evidence shows that that conclusion was wrong. In the first place, we now know that Herod died in March or April of 750 A.U.C. (4 B.C.); Christ was born up to a couple of years before the king's death. Second, there is evidence from the census to consider. Finegan concludes that a likely time for that event was 6 or 5 B.C.[1] Hoehner essentially agrees, dating the census between 6 and

4 B.C.[2] Hoehner also discusses numerous problems connected with the question of the census.

Third, John 2:20 provides a criterion to peg the date of Christ's birth. At the time of this discussion recorded in John, Herod's temple had been under construction 46 years, and Christ was slightly over 30 years of age (Luke 3:23). Since Herod began the temple in 733 A.U.C., we add 46 to find the date referred to in the John 2 passage: 779 A.U.C. Subtract Christ's age at the time, 30, and we get 749 A.U.C or 5 B.C. for the date of His birth. Since He was a little over 30, and since the temple may have been in building slightly over 46 years, the date of Christ's birth could possibly be pushed back to 6 B.C. In conclusion, then, these three lines of evidence seem to lead to a date of 5 or 6 B.C. for the birth of Christ.[3] Hoehner argues that a December date for the Nativity is acceptable.[4]

Born of a Virgin

Whatever may be the exact date of Jesus' birth, there is no uncertainty in the New Testament about His virginal conception. While it is true that the Greek word translated *virgin* in Matthew 1:23 and Luke 1:27 also may be translated *a young woman,* the context clearly demonstrates that the meaning *virgin* is intended.[5] Note particularly Mary's testimony in Luke 1:35; the angel's declaration in the following verse that Christ was conceived by the Holy Spirit; that the "of whom" in Matthew 1:16 is in the feminine in the Greek; the consternation of Joseph in Matthew 1:18 ff; and the angel's assurance to him that the child to be born had been conceived by the Holy Spirit. In this connection Sweet offers a helpful comment:

> It was charged—and the slander which was very early in origin and circumstantial in character obtained an extraordinary hold upon the hostile Jewish mind—that Jesus was the illegitimate offspring of Mary. The Gospel of Matthew meets that slander by giving a bird's-eye view of the movement of the history from Abraham to the Messiah in the form of a genealogy of Joseph, who in the light of all the facts concerning the origin of Jesus marries Mary and gives her the protection of his stainless name and royal lineage. The extraordinary boldness and brilliancy of this apologetic method ought not to be overlooked. The formal charge that Jesus is the son of Mary, not of Joseph, is admitted—the slander involved is refuted by bringing Joseph forward as a witness for Mary. Nothing could have been more natural for a man fearless in the confidence of truth; nothing could have been more impossible for one insecure in his hold upon the facts.[6]

Shepherds and Magi

The shepherds tending their flocks near Bethlehem were the first to hear the good news of the birth of Christ. If the suggestion that these shepherds kept the sheep destined for temple sacrifices be true, it is only fitting that they should have the first report of a Savior's birth. Here was One born to be the perfect sacrifice—to end the whole sacrificial system instituted by Moses. Dramatic indeed was the angelic announcement to the shepherds (Luke 2:8–14).

While the shepherds adored their Savior in the Bethlehem stable, certain wise men (magi, perhaps astrologers) in the East made preparations for a journey to Palestine. How they discovered that the star which they saw announced the birth of a King of the Jews, we do not know. These Magi were probably court advisors, similar to those found in Nebuchadnezzar's palace in Daniel's time. They must have come from somewhere in Mesopotamia, and probably traveled a distance of 500 or 600 miles by camel to find the newborn King.

When they arrived, Jesus was no longer in the manger but had been moved to a house in Bethlehem (Matthew 2:11). While the wise men journeyed, Jesus' circumcision occurred (on the eighth day), He was named (Luke 2:21), and Mary's purification according to the Law of Moses was accomplished (forty days for a male child). At the time of the latter, the Holy Child was presented in the temple and the customary sacrifice offered on His behalf. When Simeon and Anna saw Him there, the Spirit of God showed them that this was the Messiah for whom Israel and the Gentiles waited (Luke 2:25–38).

When the wise men arrived in Jerusalem, they naturally went to the court of Herod for information concerning the new King of Israel. This request no doubt disturbed the power hungry and insecure Herod. But rather than dismiss the whole matter, he used the wise men to do a bit of sleuthing for him. Learning from the chief priests and scribes that a ruler of Israel should be born in Bethlehem, he sent the wise men there with the command that they return to tell him all the details—in order that he might worship the new King too.

But Herod was foiled because, warned by God, the wise men went home another way. Probably the following night Joseph too was warned in a dream to flee with his family into Egypt to escape the wrath of Herod, who wanted to kill the baby Jesus. More than a day or two could hardly have elapsed between Herod's interview with the wise men and the flight of the Holy Family, because Bethlehem was only about six miles from Jerusalem. Herod then decided on a more drastic course—the slaying of all infants of Bethlehem under two years of age. Perhaps then he could breathe more easily again. But his prey had escaped. The Holy Family remained in Egypt until after Herod's death, and then they returned to Nazareth, where Joseph set up his carpenter shop (Matthew 2:1–23).

His Childhood

Of Jesus' childhood practically nothing is known. From Luke 2:51 we conclude that He was obedient and well-behaved. There is no hint that attributes of His deity were obvious during childhood. After all, He humbled Himself in the incarnation. Having assumed a body of limitation, His glory rarely became evident, especially in earlier life.

The curtain of silence parted just once during His childhood years, when Jesus was twelve. On one of the family's annual trips to the Passover at Jerusalem, He became so engrossed in theological discussion with doctors of the Law in the temple that He failed to join

His parents and relatives when departure time arrived. Discovering His disappearance, Mary and Joseph returned to Jerusalem, finally locating Him in the temple. The theologians were astonished at His knowledge; Mary and Joseph scolded Him for failing to join the company bound for Nazareth; Jesus evidenced a consciousness of His mission, "Did you not know that I was bound to be in my Father's house?" (Luke 2:49, REB). If this pilgrimage was an annual affair (Luke 2:41), we may assume that Jesus frequently engaged in discussions with the Pharisees and Sadducees in the capital and came to know firsthand their hypocrisy and externalism—those faults He was later to condemn so effectively.

Opening Events of Christ's Ministry

After eighteen years of silence (Luke 2:51–52), the curtain rises again on the drama of the life of Christ. From the wings comes a rough man of the wilderness—John the Baptist.

John and the Baptism of Jesus

Clothed in a coarse garment woven of camel's hair and maintaining himself on a diet of locusts and wild honey, he makes a strange herald for the King of kings. Yet, with all of his rusticity, John is an effective minister of God. Filled with the Spirit from birth (Luke 1:14–16), he fearlessly proclaims the baptism of repentance for the remission of sins and the coming of the kingdom of heaven; and he humbly fades to the background when Christ appears on the scene. In fact,

MARY, JOSEPH AND JESUS FLEE TO EGYPT

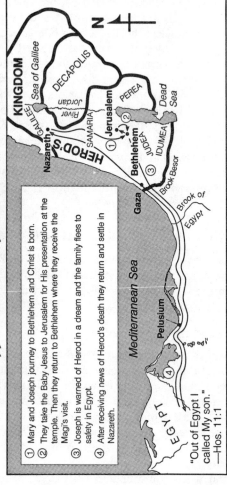

① Mary and Joseph journey to Bethlehem and Christ is born.

② They take the Baby Jesus to Jerusalem for His presentation at the temple. Then they return to Bethlehem where they receive the Magi's visit.

③ Joseph is warned of Herod in a dream and the family flees to safety in Egypt.

④ After receiving news of Herod's death they return and settle in Nazareth.

"Out of Egypt I called My son."
—Hos. 11:1

John's main purpose is to serve as the forerunner of Christ, as Isaiah prophesied (40:3; cf. Matthew 3:3; Mark 1:2–3; Luke 3:4–5).

While John prepared the way *for* the coming of Christ, there was yet further need for the preparation *of* Christ. This was accomplished by the baptism and temptation.

Meaning of Christ's Baptism

One day as John was baptizing in the Jordan, Jesus asked that John baptize Him too. After some profession of humility, John agreed to do so. Exactly what significance is to be attached to Jesus' baptism has been the subject of much discussion. Certainly this was not a testimony of a salvation experience or a symbol of purification, because He was sinless. Though it has been argued that by this act Christ was identifying Himself with sinful humanity, His real act of becoming sin for us occurred on the cross.

It has also been suggested that here we have the inauguration of Christ to His priestly ministry. Yet, in a sense, His work as God's true High Priest did not begin until the offering of His sacrifice on Calvary. Perhaps the most satisfactory explanation is that Christ's baptism marks His inauguration into His prophetic office. In the New Testament, prophetic ministry has to do more with preaching the truth than with predicting the future. Surely the baptism marks the inauguration of Jesus Christ to His public ministry, whatever else it involves. Moreover, the baptism was followed by divine approval: "You are my beloved Son; in You I am well pleased" (Luke 3:22). Here was the divine investiture; now His official life was to begin. Jesus had just turned thirty (Luke 3:23).

The Temptation of Christ

It would appear from indications in the Gospels that the temptation of Christ took place immediately after His baptism. It also seems clear that the temptation lasted for forty days, and that the threefold temptation recorded in the Gospels occurred at the end of that time (Matthew 4:2–3; Mark 1:13; Luke 4:2). The temptation was definitely on the divine agenda for Christ's life, because the Holy Spirit led (*drove,* Mark 1:12) Him into the wilderness that Satan might tempt Him there.

Without doubt, Satan aimed his temptation at the humanity of Christ. Since He had fasted for forty days, our Lord's physical needs were acute; why not preserve Himself by turning stones into bread? Why not avoid the agony of the cross and immediately enjoy the homage of the kingdoms of this world by worshiping Satan? For Christ these temptations were real: He could turn stones into bread; He could command the aid of angels; He would welcome, from the human standpoint, an avoidance of the cross.

Significance of Christ's Temptation

In the temptation encounter, Satan was trying to get Christ to declare His independence from God and go His own way. If Christ had succumbed at any of these points, His voluntary humiliation or human limitation would have been violated, to say nothing of wrecking God's plan of salvation and invalidating Old

Testament prophecies. Apart from the importance of Christ's victory to the plan of salvation and the doctrine of the inspiration of Scripture, it is significant to the believer in at least three other respects.

First, Christ, as our sinless High Priest, has been tempted in all points that we are (Hebrews 4:15), and so can be fully sympathetic with us.[7] Second, as we compare the success of the last Adam (Jesus) when tempted by Satan with the failure of the first Adam under temptation, it is clear Christ came to restore that which the race lost in the fall of Adam. Third, we can learn from His temptation that it is possible to have victory in the same way: by the Word of God ("It is written," was His reply). That is our defense against the onslaughts of the evil one in our day, too.

First Disciples, First Miracles

Events now moved with great rapidity. Just before Jesus returned from the wilderness, John faced representatives from the priests, Levites, and Pharisees, who questioned him concerning his identity. He made it clear that he was merely a herald announcing the coming of the Christ. The following day Jesus returned from the wilderness and came into the area where John was ministering (John 1:29). Immediately John proclaimed Him to be the Lamb of God and the Son of God. The next day (John 1:35), John the Baptist and two of his disciples met Jesus, and the disciples—Andrew and (doubtless) John,[8] the son of Zebedee—followed Jesus. Andrew brought along his brother Simon; John probably brought James afterward. On the day after that (John 1:43) Jesus called

Philip, who persuaded Nathanael to follow the Master.

On the third day (John 2:1),[9] Jesus arrived at Cana of Galilee, where he performed His first miracle of turning water into wine (John 2:1—12). Of this miracle Stalker comments:

> It was a manifestation of His glory intended specially for His new disciples, who, we are told, thenceforward believed on Him, which means, no doubt, that they were fully convinced that He was the Messiah. It was intended also to strike the keynote of His ministry as altogether different from the Baptist's. John was an ascetic hermit, who fled from the abodes of men and called his hearers out into the wilderness. But Jesus had glad tidings to bring to men's hearts; He was to mingle in their common life, and produce a happy revolution in their circumstances, which would be like the turning of the water of their life into wine.[10]

At the termination of the feast, Jesus, His mother,[11] His brothers and disciples stayed at Capernaum for a few days before He journeyed to Jerusalem to attend the Passover. It does not seem that Jesus engaged in any public ministry between the miracle at Cana and His trip to Jerusalem. Probably He spent the time instructing His disciples.

Early Judean Ministry
(about a year)

Pilgrims poured into Jerusalem from all parts of Jewry to attend the feast of the Passover. Jesus was counted among the devout. Perhaps He joined a band of Capernaum pilgrims destined for the Holy City. Seemingly His disciples accompanied Him; certainly they attended the feast (John 2:17, 23). The band probably took the trans-Jordanic route, skirting Samaria. Devout Jews commonly avoided Samaria, and it appears from John 4:4 that Jesus did not customarily go through Samaria.

Jerusalem at Passover

Upon arrival in Jerusalem, Jesus and His disciples went to the temple. There the Lord, incensed over the desecration and defilement of His holy house, drove out the merchants, who made a fat profit selling sacrificial animals, and the moneychangers, who were becoming rich by exchanging the coins of many lands for the sacred shekel, which was required of worshipers as a sort of head tax (John 2:13–22).

While none of the Jewish rulers seems to have acknowledged Jesus' Messiahship, many of the common people did so as He performed numerous miracles in the city (John 2:23). And one of the Pharisees, Nicodemus, sought Him out by night to learn more fully the way of truth (John 3:1–21). Whether he came under cover of darkness because of fear, or because this was the only way he could have adequate opportunity to converse with the Master, is beside the point. The fact is, he did come; and he was impressed that Jesus' message and ministry were accredited with miracles. But to him, Jesus was a teacher who could help him be a better moral man, a better subject of the kingdom. Immediately the Master declared that

EVENTS IN CHRIST'S MINISTRY

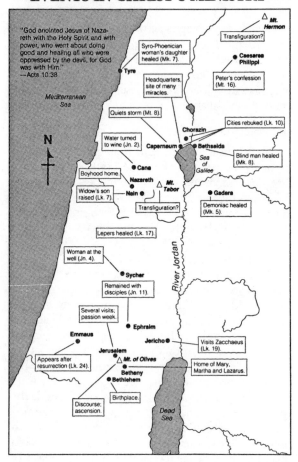

"God anointed Jesus of Nazareth with the Holy Spirit and with power, who went about doing good and healing all who were oppressed by the devil, for God was with Him."
—Acts 10:38

Mediterranean Sea

△ Mt. Hermon

Transfiguration?

● Caesarea Philippi

Peter's confession (Mt. 16).

Syro-Phoenician woman's daughter healed (Mk. 7).

● Tyre

Headquarters, site of many miracles.

N

Quiets storm (Mt. 8).

Water turned to wine (Jn. 2).

Chorazin

Cities rebuked (Lk. 10).

Capernaum ● ● Bethsaida

Sea of Galilee

Blind man healed (Mk. 8).

Boyhood home.

● Cana

Nazareth

△ Mt. Tabor

Widow's son raised (Lk. 7).

● Nain

Transfiguration?

● Gadera

Demoniac healed (Mk. 5).

Lepers healed (Lk. 17).

Woman at the well (Jn. 4).

● Sychar

River Jordan

Remained with disciples (Jn. 11).

Several visits; passion week.

● Ephraim

● Emmaus

Jericho ●

Visits Zacchaeus (Lk. 19).

Jerusalem

△ Mt. of Olives

Appears after resurrection (Lk. 24).

● Bethany

● Bethlehem

Home of Mary, Martha and Lazarus.

Birthplace.

Discourse; ascension.

Dead Sea

without the new birth he could not even *enter* the kingdom of God. This new birth is a spiritual birth based on absolute trust in the Son of God.

Ministry in Judea

Soon afterward, Jesus left Jerusalem to minister in the outlying villages of Judea (John 3:22). During this period some converts were baptized, though Jesus Himself did not do it but committed that ministry to His disciples (John 4:2). At this point in Jesus' ministry, He apparently did not perform any miracles, preach in synagogues, call new disciples, or endeavor in a general way to organize a new movement. All these efforts came more specifically after John the Baptist's ministry concluded. Some would say of this period that Jesus was merely feeling His way. Others, taking a more supernaturalistic approach, believe He was making an appeal to the people to recognize Him as the Messiah. They were being tested as the leaders of the Jews had been in Jerusalem.

During Jesus' village ministry in Judea, John the Baptist entered the picture once more. John and Jesus carried on their ministries not far apart (John 3:25–36), and some of John's disciples became alarmed because their leader's influence was waning in favor of Jesus. But they failed either to discourage the Baptist or arouse envy on his part. He reasserted his loyalty to the Messiah and recognized that he would soon fade out of the picture. Said John of Jesus: "He must increase, but I must decrease" (John 3:30).

Ministry in Samaria and Galilee

Shortly after this incident, Jesus determined to return to Galilee (John 4:1–3). The reason is a matter of some debate. It seems likely that Jesus chose to avoid continued conflict between His disciples and those of John, or He felt the need for a more extended preparation for His ministry on the part of John; so He withdrew and left the field to His forerunner.

On the way back to Galilee, Jesus went through Samaria, stopping on the way to minister to the spiritual needs of the Samaritan woman at Jacob's well (John 4). The discourse included a revelation of Himself as the Messiah, a statement on the nature of God, an observation on true worship, and a description of the satisfying nature of the water of life He offered. After His successful encounter with the Samaritan woman, Jesus realized a substantial harvest of souls in that area as a result of her testimony. When He returned to Galilee and entered Cana, a nobleman from Capernaum begged Him to come and heal his son. Jesus healed the child at a distance, and the nobleman had the faith to accept the Master's pronouncement and returned home to discover that all was well (John 4:46–54).

Back to Jerusalem

Probably Jesus remained in seclusion for some months after this event and then went to one of the Jewish feasts in Jerusalem (John 5:1; possibly the Passover). On this occasion He healed a lame man by the pool of Bethesda. While in Jerusalem, Jesus again faced the rulers of the Jews, who this time tried to kill Him. When they had sought some accreditation of His message before, He told them, "Destroy this temple, and in three days I will raise it up" (John 2:19). On this occasion He was more specific and pointed to a four-fold witness to Himself: John the Baptist, His works, the Father, and the Scriptures (John 5:33–47).

About this time, John, who had moved his base of operation from Judea into Perea or Galilee (both controlled by Herod Antipas), was imprisoned. Jesus traveled north to begin his Galilean ministry (Matthew 4:12; Mark 1:14).

The Gospel writers pass over the whole first year of Jesus' ministry in virtual silence. In fact, were it not for the Gospel of John, we would be almost totally unaware of the detail concerning the early Judean ministry presented above. Why Matthew, Mark, and Luke omit this material is not easy to determine.

The Galilean Ministry: Early Period (from imprisonment of John the Baptist to choosing of the twelve; about four months)

Our Lord spent most of His earthly life in the province of Galilee. He lived there until He reached thirty years of age, and later performed about twenty months of His little-more-than-three-year public ministry in the area. So for most of His life He was hardly twenty miles from the Sea of Galilee. In Christ's day, Galilee was quite cosmopolitan. Many Gentiles lived there and important trade routes ran through it.

Therefore, Christ found a freer spirit and a greater receptiveness in Galilee than in Judea. Also, the cosmopolitanism of Galilee and the location of Greco-Roman centers in Decapolis, on the eastern side of the Sea of Galilee, contributed to the disciples' knowledge of Greek and their ability to write in that language during the early days of the Church.

Return to Nazareth and Rejection

The imprisonment of John the Baptist seemed to serve as a signal for Jesus to begin His public ministry in earnest. He no longer faced any competition with the Baptist's work, and the preparation for the Messiah was completed. Soon after returning to Galilee, Jesus went to His hometown of Nazareth to proclaim His Messiahship. His opportunity came when He was asked to read and comment on the Scripture during a synagogue service. Reading from Isaiah 61:1–2, He declared that the prophecy concerning the anointed one who would preach the gospel to the poor and minister to their spiritual needs was now being fulfilled before their eyes. At first they listened gladly; but when the implications of His claims became more obvious, they lost their temper and sought to toss Him over a cliff near the town (Luke 4:16–30).

Ministry in Capernaum

After His rejection at Nazareth, Jesus went to Capernaum. To carry on a most effective ministry, He needed helpers. Earlier, Simon and Andrew, James and John had shared His ministry, but they had returned to their fishing. Now He called them to make a clean break with their old occupation and become fishers of men (Matthew 4:18–22; Mark 1:16–20; Luke 5:11). Before calling them to a life of complete devotion to Him, however, He demonstrated anew His identity by means of a miraculous catch of fish (Luke 5:1–10).

Presently the disciples had opportunity to observe the great power and authority of their Lord. In the Capernaum synagogue He taught with authority as He explained the doctrines of the faith; this contrasted with the approach of the Pharisees, who preferred rather to quote other Jewish teachers. He commanded with authority as He ordered the demon to come out of the demoniac in the same synagogue (Mark 1:21–28; Luke 4:31–37). Later that day, the Sabbath, He healed Peter's mother-in-law, who was afflicted with a fever (Matthew 8:14–17; Mark 1:29–31; Luke 4:38–41). When the Sabbath was over, He healed a multitude of other Capernaum folk outside Peter's home (Mark 1:32–34).

The First Galilean Tour: Great Success

On the following day, Jesus and His disciples began a tour of Galilean towns (Matthew 4:23–25; Mark 1:35–39; Luke 4:42–44). Along the way they met a leper, an untouchable, whom Jesus touched and healed (Matthew 8:2–4; Mark 1:40–45; Luke 5:12–16). Wishing to avoid crowds of the merely curious or seekers of physical healing alone, Jesus charged him not to spread the news abroad. But the blessing was too good for the leper to keep to himself. As a result, the Lord was mobbed whenever He went into a town,

GALILEAN MINISTRY

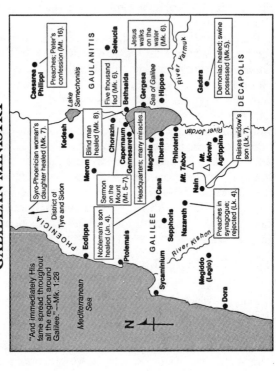

"And immediately His fame spread throughout all the region around Galilee."—Mk. 1:28

Syro-Phoenician woman's daughter healed (Mk. 7).

District of Tyre and Sidon

Preaches; Peter's confession (Mt. 16).

Blind man healed (Mk. 8).

Five thousand fed (Mk. 6).

Jesus walks on the water (Mk. 6).

Demoniac healed; swine possessed (Mk. 5).

Nobleman's son healed (Jn. 4).

Sermon on the Mount (Mt. 5–7).

Headquarters; many miracles.

Raises widow's son (Lk. 7).

Preaches in synagogue; rejected (Lk. 4).

PHOENICIA

Mediterranean Sea

Ecdippa

Ptolemais

Sycaminium

Megiddo (Legio)

Dora

GALILEE

Sepphoris

Nazareth

Cana

River Kishon

Nain

Mt. Tabor

Mt. Moreh

Agrippina

Philoteria

Tiberias

Magdala

Gennesaret

Capernaum

Chorazin

Merom

Kedesh

Lake Semechonitis

Ceesarea Philippi

GAULANITIS

Seleucia

Bethsaida

Sea of Galilee

Gergesa

Hippos

River Yarmuk

Gadera

DECAPOLIS

River Jordan

N

so He had to resort to teaching in rural places, where great crowds came to hear Him. Returning to Capernaum from a preaching tour in Galilee, Jesus again faced the throngs. On one occasion, when seekers pressed closely upon Him as He ministered within a house, four friends of a man sick with palsy opened the roof above Jesus and lowered the man into the Master's presence for healing (Matthew 9:1-8; Mark 2:1-12; Luke 5:17-26).

Growing Criticism

A short time later, while Jesus was walking near the Sea of Galilee, He encountered a tax collector by the name of Levi sitting in his customs house. In the ensuing conversation, Levi, later called Matthew, was converted and responded to Jesus' call to follow Him. In honor of his newfound Master, Levi gave a banquet in his house. During the meal some of the scribes and Pharisees present began to gripe. First, they criticized Jesus for eating with tax collectors and sinners, to which He answered that He "came not to call the righteous, but sinners to repentance." Second, they asked why His disciples did not fast, as the disciples of John the Baptist and the Pharisees did. To this He replied, "Why should the children of the bride-chamber fast when the bridegroom is with them?" Moreover, He pointed out that He was introducing a new order, with new approaches and worship forms (Matthew 9:9-17; Mark 2:13-22; Luke 5:27-39, KJV).

Shortly afterward, while Jesus and His disciples were passing through some wheat fields on the Sabbath,

His disciples picked a little of the wheat. The Pharisees immediately challenged Him for breaking the Sabbath. But Jesus countered with the biblical account of how David in his need had eaten the sacred bread in the tabernacle. From this illustration we may gather that the disciples were in great need, therefore they could not be accused of breaking the spirit of the Sabbath regulations. Certainly they were not guilty of harvesting. Besides, Jesus declared that He was Lord of the Sabbath. This was quite an assertion to throw in the teeth of the Pharisees, who alone claimed to have the official interpretation of regulations governing the Sabbath (Matthew 12:1–8; Mark 2:23–28; Luke 6:1–5). Apparently on the same day, Jesus met a man with a withered hand in the synagogue and healed him, whereupon the Pharisees grew furious and tried to hatch a plot with the Herodians to destroy Him (Matthew 12:9–14; Mark 3:1–6; Luke 6:6–11).

The Galilean Ministry: Middle Period (from choosing the twelve to withdrawal into northern Galilee; about ten months)

While the leaders of the Jews conspired against Jesus, the common people heard Him gladly. His fame became so great that crowds gathered from many parts of Palestine: Galilee, Judea, Idumea, trans-Jordan, and Phoenicia. So zealous were the diseased and disabled to touch Him, to be healed, that He was in danger of being crushed by the mob. Therefore, Jesus taught from a boat on the Sea of Galilee (Matthew 12:15–21; Mark 3:7–12).

Choosing and Training the Twelve

Now the need for helpers became more acute. So Jesus, going up on a mountainside, spent the night in prayer about this (Luke 6:12). In the morning He selected from among the larger group of disciples currently following Him a total of twelve who were to have a special relationship with Him. On what basis the Master made His selection we are not told. They included, however, seven who had served Him before on numerous occasions: Peter, James, John, Andrew, Philip, Nathanael (Bartholomew), and Levi (Matthew); with an added five: Thomas, James the son of Alphaeus, Thaddaeus, Simon the Cananean, and Judas Iscariot. He chose them that they might "be with Him and that He might send them out to preach, and to have power to heal sicknesses and to cast out demons" (Mark 3:14–15). Not only were the disciples to be present witnesses but also founders of the Church.

Having chosen the disciples, Jesus proceeded to instruct them with the great Sermon on the Mount (Matthew 5–7). That the sermon was delivered at this point in His ministry is clear from Matthew 4:25 and Luke 6:17. In both references, the same cosmopolitan crowd present when He selected His disciples was nearby while He instructed the disciples. The Sermon on the Mount covers a wide range of subjects relating to Christian experience[12] and everyday life. At the beginning, Jesus lists in the Beatitudes some of the graces that should characterize the life of a believer; this parallels to some extent the fruit of the Spirit of Galatians

5:22–23. Then He teaches about Christian witness, the manner and importance of prayer, and the full provision of the Father for the daily needs of His own. Among other things, Jesus also deepens the application of the Law to apply to the motives and attitudes. He also denounces mere externalism in religion, condemns the easy breaking of the marriage tie, and enunciates the Golden Rule as a guide for successful social relations.

The Second Galilean Tour

The period of instruction over, Jesus began His second preaching tour of Galilee. Entering Capernaum, He found a stir among the elders because the Roman centurion who had built their synagogue appealed to them to heal his sick servant. Since they had no such miracle working power, the elders turned to Jesus for help. He honored their request and especially the great faith of the centurion (Matthew 8:5–13; Luke 7:1–10).

John's Question

The next day, Jesus and His disciples journeyed to Nain, where the Lord raised a widow's son from the dead (Luke 7:11–17).[13] This and other activities of Jesus brought about an inquiry from John the Baptist: "Are You the Coming One, or do we look for another?" This question poses problems. Did John, who had so unequivocally declared that Jesus was the Lamb of God, now have a lapse of faith? Had months in prison affected his mental and spiritual perception? Or did he ask this to give Jesus another opportunity to assert His Messiahship to John's disciples or the surrounding crowds? Possibly John evidenced impatience rather than doubt at this point. His question may be urging Jesus to demonstrate the full power of His Messiahship now—power which the raising of the widow's son revealed He possessed. Possibly he was encouraging Jesus to set up His Messianic kingdom. Jesus' answer was to have John's messengers go tell him the good works they had seen and that the gospel was being preached. That was His present work: acts of mercy rather than judgment and administration (Matthew 11:2–19; Luke 7:18–35).

But the fact that Jesus' ministry consisted primarily of acts of mercy did not eliminate all judgment from His declarations. Because of the poor response in Chorazin, Bethsaida, and Capernaum, He pronounced woes on them (Matthew 11:20–24). Apparently these towns declined and disappeared not long after Christ's day, and the sites of all three remain uninhabited to the present. However, even in judgment God remembers mercy. Shortly after this denunciation Christ uttered one of His most tender invitations, "Come to Me, all you who labor and are heavy laden, and I will give you rest" (Matthew 11:28).

Stiffening Resistance

About this time a certain Pharisee named Simon invited Jesus to dinner. During the entertainment, an uninvited woman of the street came in and expressed her love and gratitude to Him by wiping His feet with her hair and anointing them with ointment (Luke

7:36–50). Criticized for accepting her devotion, Jesus
reminded Simon that those who place a high value on
their forgiveness are most grateful; Simon had been
negligent in performing some of the common courte-
sies on His behalf.

Somewhere during this second tour of Galilee, Jesus
engaged in a day of teaching. Near the beginning of
the day, scribes from Jerusalem accused Him of performing His miracles by the power of Satan instead of
the Holy Spirit. This, He said, was the unpardonable
sin (Matthew 12:22–37; Mark 3:22–30). Shortly afterward, as He taught the multitude, His mother and
brothers sent for Him. This request brought His pronouncement regarding a new spiritual kinship in the
family of God: "For whosoever shall do the will of
God, the same is my brother, and my sister, and
mother" (Matthew 12:46–50; Mark 3:31–35; Luke
8:19–21, KJV).

Key Teachings about the Kingdom

Then Jesus went out of the house and sat by the
seaside, where He delivered the famous kingdom parables (Matthew 13:1–53; Mark 4:1–34; Luke 8:4–
18.)[14] In these parables, Jesus taught that as the truth
was preached (as the seed was sown), much of it would
fall on unreceptive hearts; but some would bear fruit
unto eternal life. As this group of believers (the kingdom) became established in the world, a mixture of
mere professors (tares) would drift in; these would be
sorted out at the judgment. While this new religious
movement would have a small beginning (as a grain of

mustard seed), it would grow to immense proportions, and its advance would create a tremendous ferment in society (parable of leaven). The parables of the hid treasure and the pearl demonstrate the value of believers to the Lord, who paid the supreme sacrifice to purchase them for Himself. The parable of the dragnet indicates a judgment to come at the end of the age.

More Miracles

At the end of this day of teaching came a day or two of miracles. That night as Jesus crossed the Sea of Galilee with His disciples, a terrible storm arose—it must have been a bad one to frighten these seasoned fishermen. He stilled the storm and rebuked their lack of faith (Matthew 8:18, 23–27; Mark 4:35–41; Luke 8:22–25). When they reached shore they met two Gadarene demoniacs from whom Jesus cast demons. When the Master had granted the demons' request to enter a nearby herd of swine, the whole herd ran into the sea. Therefore, Jesus and His disciples were driven out of the area; so they returned to the Galilean side of the sea (Matthew 8:28–34; Mark 5:1–20; Luke 8:26–39). When they reached the other side, Jesus healed a woman with an incurable issue of blood and raised the daughter of Jairus from the dead (Matthew 9:18–26; Mark 5:21–43; Luke 8:40–56). Shortly thereafter, He healed two blind men and a dumb demoniac who had apparently heard of the resurrection of Jairus' daughter (Matthew 9:27–34).

Another Return to Nazareth and Rejection

Next Jesus returned to His hometown, Nazareth, to give them another opportunity to receive the truth. Again they could not accept Him. They knew Jesus as a man only; they remembered His relatives. For them the great gulf between a knowledge of Him as man and a recognition of Him as God was too great. At least they did not attempt to kill Him this time (Matthew 13:54–56; Mark 6:1–6; cf. Luke 4:16–30).

The Third Galilean Tour: Disciples' Mission

Rejected at Nazareth, Jesus embarked on His third Galilean tour (Matthew 9:35; Mark 6:6). This time, however, He sent His disciples out to shoulder part of the burden. Journeying in pairs, they preached repentance and performed miracles (Matthew 9:36–11:1; Mark 6:7–13; Luke 9:1–6). They had been observers long enough; it was time for them to serve their apprenticeship.

At the close of this tour, Jesus received news of the murder of John the Baptist and so withdrew to a wilderness retreat for rest and reflection (Matthew 14:1–13; Mark 6:14–32; Luke 9:7–10). No doubt this stunning news served as a pointed object lesson to the disciples to demonstrate the cost of discipleship.

But the apostolic group was not to slip away for a vacation so easily. Some recognized them as they departed and spread the word around. People came from all the surrounding towns. Jesus had compassion on them and ministered to them. Day turned to evening and there was no food for the crowds. The disciples wanted to send them all home; Jesus answered with a miracle. With five loaves and two fish He fed 5,000 men, besides women and children (Matthew 14:15–21; Mark 6:33–44; Luke 9:11–17; John 6:1–13).

Then He sent the disciples away to the other side of the Sea of Galilee, and He slipped off to a mountainside to pray. From His vantage point, the Master observed His disciples in trouble in the midst of heavy seas; so He came to them walking on the water. At first they did not recognize Him. Peter, in order to make sure, asked Jesus to demonstrate His identity by bidding him come to Jesus on the water. This the Master did, and Peter walked on the water for some distance until his faith failed. Then Jesus entered the boat, the winds ceased, and they crossed over in safety (Matthew 14:24–33; Mark 6:47–52; John 6:16–21).

When they arrived in Gennesaret (on the western side of the Sea of Galilee; apparently the feeding of the 5,000 occurred on the eastern side), the crowds gathered again and Jesus healed many (Matthew 14:34–36; Mark 6:53–56). Probably on the same day, Jesus delivered His great address on the bread of life (John 6:22–59). During the ministry in Gennesaret, some of the Pharisees came to find fault. They were successful, for Jesus' disciples failed to observe the customary ceremonial washings before eating. Chances are they were so busy with the ministry that they did not have time for the niceties of life. One can just see the glare in Jesus' eye as He reminded the Pharisees that they had actually destroyed the true meaning and message of much of the Scripture with their traditions (Matthew 15:1–20; Mark 7:1–23).

The Galilean Ministry: Later Period
(from journey into northern Galilee to departure for Jerusalem; about six months)

After singeing the beards of the Pharisees with His rebuke, Jesus traveled north to the border of Phoenicia. There a Gentile woman sought His help in delivering her demon possessed daughter (Matthew 15:21–28; Mark 7:24–30). Granting her request, He moved southeast to the region of Decapolis, where He healed a deaf mute and an unspecified number of other afflicted individuals (Matthew 15:29–31; Mark 7:31–37).[15] As usual, the crowds came flocking and the Master had an even more serious situation on His hands than when He fed the 5,000. The people had been following Him for three days, virtually without food, and He could not send them away hungry.

More Miracles and Disciples' Training

The disciples apparently had not learned their lesson from the feeding of the 5,000. Again they wondered how they would feed the multitude. But Jesus multiplied the available seven loaves and a few fish and fed the 4,000, plus women and children. As before there were several baskets of leftovers (Matthew 15:32–38; Mark 8:1–9). Having fed the multitude Jesus sent them away, and He and His disciples took ship for the western side of the Sea of Galilee, landing near Magdala. Soon the Pharisees and Sadducees came seeking a sign from heaven, in order to tempt Him. But Jesus did not cater to their hardened hearts; so He turned them away empty handed (Matthew 15:39–

16:4; Mark 8:10–12). Soon after this, He moved north to Bethsaida, where He healed a blind man (Mark 8:22–26). To those who have faith the wonders of God are always present.

Peter's Great Confession

The next several recorded events of the later period of the Galilean ministry deal primarily with relations between Jesus and His disciples. These events occurred in the region of Caesarea Philippi, where the apostolic group went after the healing at Bethsaida. First Jesus elicited from Peter the great confession ("You are the Christ, the Son of the living God," Matthew 16:16). Apparently Peter acted as spokesman for the group. To this, Jesus responded with an announcement of His coming sufferings, death, and resurrection. Peter took no delight in such a program; he probably wanted a Messianic kingdom without a suffering Messiah. Jesus recognized the satanic implications of Peter's opposition and rebuked him.

The Transfiguration

Then the Master assured the disciples that the kingdom of God would indeed come with power at His second coming. In order to give the disciples a glimpse of that future kingdom and to provide encouragement for them and for Himself during trying days ahead, Jesus took Peter, James, and John up on a mountain where the transfiguration of Jesus occurred.

Many observations could be made about the persons present at the transfiguration. For instance, Moses may represent the Law, and Elijah the Prophets;

to Him, all the Law and Prophets witness (Luke 24:27; Acts 28:23). The work of the Law and Prophets was anticipatory and temporary. Christ's work marked fulfillment and a finalization of their anticipations. (God has in these last days revealed Himself through His Son, Hebrews 1:1.) Second, there was something unusual about the death of each: God buried Moses, He translated Elijah, and He caused Christ to bear the sin of mankind and raised Him from the dead.

Peter wanted to build shelters on the mountain and remain in the midst of all this glory. But Christ denied the privilege. Mountaintop experiences are not given merely that they may be enjoyed; they are preparations for the valleys. Soon the appearances faded away, and Jesus and His disciples descended to the everyday challenges of life. Almost immediately they were met by a crowd and reproached by a man with a demon possessed son, whom the other disciples had been unable to cure. Jesus healed the boy, and He immediately departed with His disciples into Galilee. Along the way, He taught them a second time concerning His coming suffering, death, and resurrection. (For all these events see Matthew 16:13–17:23; Mark 8:27–9:32; Luke 9:18–45.)

Back to Capernaum

When Jesus and His disciples returned to Capernaum, tax collectors—apparently Jews who sought the annual half-shekel head tax for the Temple treasury—approached Simon Peter about Jesus' payment of the tax. Jesus sent Simon to catch a fish and cut it open and there find a shekel to pay for both of them (Matthew 17:24–27). While this was going on at their place of residence,[16] the other disciples were arguing over which of them was to be the greatest in the kingdom. The Master rebuked them by setting a child in their midst (possibly one of Peter's) and giving them a lesson on humility as a mark of true greatness (Matthew 18:1–5; Mark 9:33–37; Luke 9:46–48).

During these final days in Capernaum, the Lord also taught on the seriousness of being a stumbling block and on forgiveness (Matthew 18:6–35; Mark 9:38–50; Luke 9:49–50). When it came time for the feast of Tabernacles, Jesus' brothers encouraged Him to take His disciples and go to Judea to demonstrate His works there. But knowing that if He were openly to move into Judea with His disciples He would be killed, He sent His brothers on ahead and remained in Galilee (John 7:1–9).

The Later Judean Ministry
(about three months)

After the rest of the family left, Jesus wended His way south also—but secretly (Matthew 19:1–2; Mark 10:1; John 7:10). He went through Samaria again but did not meet the same kind of reception as He had before. As His disciples went into one of the villages to announce His coming, they were given a cold shoulder. James and John wanted to call down fire from heaven to destroy the town, but Jesus rebuked them and pointed out that the Son of Man had come to save men's lives, not to destroy them (Luke 9:51–

56). A little later the party met two men who professed to be the Lord's disciples, but they put their family obligations first. To them Jesus presented the cost of true discipleship: "No one, having put his hand to the plow, and looking back, is fit for the kingdom of God" (Luke 9:62).

To Jerusalem for Tabernacles: Opposition Hardens

Meanwhile, Jesus' brothers arrived at the feast of Tabernacles without Him. Many of the common people began to inquire about Him and to discuss Him in secret because they were afraid of the rulers of the Jews. Finally, about the middle of the feast He came to the temple and began to preach. His audience was divided in their opinions; some believed and some did not. The Pharisees and chief priests sent men to kidnap Him; but when they heard His message and saw His demeanor, they were powerless to do so.

But the Pharisees had not yet emptied their bag of tricks. They found a woman caught in the very act of adultery and brought her to Jesus, saying that the Mosaic Law demanded she be stoned, and asked what He would recommend. His answer: "He that is without sin among you, let him first cast a stone at her" (John 8:7, KJV). Soon her crowd of accusers drifted away.

After the feast, Jesus and the Pharisees continued to parry verbal blows. In the course of the discussion, Jesus delivered His famous sermons on the light of the world and spiritual freedom. At the end of the second, the Pharisees picked up stones to kill Him; but He escaped from their midst. As He did so, He saw a man blind from birth and healed him. Again the Pharisees criticized; and when they saw that the healed man had become a disciple of Jesus, they excommunicated him from the synagogue.

As the Lord conversed with His new convert about spiritual blindness, some of the Pharisees overheard and asked if they were blind. They asked for it; so He gave them another lecture, this time on the Good Shepherd, in which He spoke about His identity and work and the means of salvation. Also, He pointed out that entrance to the fold was only through Himself, the Shepherd. The Pharisees had excommunicated the man born blind who had become one of Jesus' disciples and threatened to cut off others who would follow Him. Now they found themselves excluded from the faith for their failure to come by way of Christ. (For the narrative of the last paragraphs see John 7:10—10:21.)

Ministry Near Jerusalem

At this point, Jesus seems to have left Jerusalem to minister nearby. This ministry, it appears, occurred at a time between the feast of Tabernacles and the feast of Dedication—between John 10:21 and 22. Luke 10:1—13:21 details the events of this period in Jesus' life. First, the ministry of the seventy is mentioned. These He sent out by twos to announce to towns which Jesus intended to visit that the kingdom of God was come. They were then to act as heralds of the coming Christ and to report to Him which cities had received their message. It cannot be determined with certainty when Jesus sent out the seventy (perhaps before He left Galilee), but apparently they brought their report to Him in Judea. Where they went is also open to question. Since there is no record of any extended ministry in Judea or Samaria at this time, and since He presently went to Perea for a term of ministry there, we may conclude that they went to the latter.

Also during this period, Jesus met a certain lawyer who inquired what he should do to obtain eternal life. The Master answered by asking what the Law had to say about the subject, to which the lawyer replied, "You shall love the Lord your God with all your heart, and with all your soul and with all your strength, and with all your mind; and your neighbor as yourself" (Luke 10:27, KJV). Jesus then said, "This do, and you shall live" (v. 28). When the lawyer questioned who was his neighbor, Jesus replied with the parable of the Good Samaritan.

Shortly thereafter, Jesus was the guest of Martha and Mary, the former being distressed with her household tasks while Mary sat at His feet to hear His blessed teachings. Luke 11 contains Jesus' subsequent teachings to His disciples on prayer and a record of further controversy with the Pharisees. Luke 12 outlines some of His public teachings delivered during this period. Luke 13 records the healing of a crippled woman on the Sabbath, with our Lord's defense.

Back to Jerusalem

The time of the feast of Dedication[17] having come, Jesus went up to Jerusalem again (John 10:22 ff.). As

He was walking in the temple some of the Jews again asked Him if He were the Christ. He answered by speaking about the value of His works as evidence of His identity and His essential oneness with the Father. Again His claims proved to be too much for the Jews. They sought to capture Him, but He escaped.

The Perean Ministry
(about three months)

After His rejection at the feast of Dedication, Jesus journeyed to Bethabara, a site fifteen miles south of the Sea of Galilee where John had baptized Him. There He enjoyed a successful ministry (John 10:40–42). Ultimately He journeyed toward Jerusalem again (through Perea), teaching on the way. Among His teachings was an answer to a query whether only a few should be saved (Luke 13:22–30), and a reply to a warning against Herod Antipas (Luke 13:31–35). In the former instance He stressed the importance of the individual's making sure he was saved; in the latter, He declared in essence that His purposes would be carried out *on schedule*. Somewhere en route, a Pharisee asked the Lord to take dinner with him on the Sabbath. A man sick with dropsy was there and Jesus healed him. Later in the meal Jesus spoke the Parable of the Great Supper, which describes the failure of the Jewish leaders to receive the truth and the need for extending the invitation to tax collectors, sinners, and Gentiles (Luke 14:1–24).

On another occasion during this journey, He preached to the multitudes concerning the cost of discipleship (Luke 14:25–35). Shortly thereafter, the Pharisees criticized Jesus because He received sinners and ate with them. In reply, Jesus told the three famous parables of Luke 15: the lost sheep, the lost coin, and the prodigal son. In all three, Jesus made the point that He was most interested in ministering to those who were lost *and who knew it*. He also took occasion to tell two parables to the disciples emphasizing the importance of utilizing present opportunities to prepare for the future life (Luke 16). Moreover, He taught them the importance of avoiding giving offense to others, of forgiveness, and of faith (Luke 17:1–10).

While Jesus was still traveling south through Perea, He received an urgent message from Mary and Martha in Bethany to come and heal Lazarus, who was sick. Jesus seemed almost deliberately to delay His going to Bethany in order that God might gain greater glory. When He arrived in Bethany, Lazarus was dead. The sisters reproached Him for delaying so long. Jesus commanded the mourners to remove the stone from the grave, and He called Lazarus back to life. The testimony of the miracle was great: "Then many of the Jews . . . believed in him" (John 11:45). But the Jewish rulers grew even more resolute in their determination to destroy Jesus and "from that day forth they took counsel together for to put him to death" (John 11:53, KJV). So Jesus and His disciples moved north to Ephraim on the border of Judea.

Eventually He returned to Jerusalem by a rather circuitous route through Samaria and Galilee, then south through Perea. Meeting ten lepers on the way, He heard their cries for mercy and healed them (Luke

17:11–19). About the same time, He spoke to His disciples concerning His second coming (Luke 17:22–37) and told them two parables on prayer—emphasizing importunity and humility in prayer (Luke 18:1–14).

As the group entered Perea just north of the Dead Sea, Jesus continued teaching. To the Pharisees He asserted the tightness of the marriage knot (Matthew 19:1–12; Mark 10:1–12); to the disciples He underlined the importance of having faith as little children to enter the kingdom of God (Matthew 19:13–15; Mark 10:13–16; Luke 18:15–17); to the rich young ruler He declared that building up treasure on earth must take second place to building up treasure in heaven (Matthew 19:16—20:16; Mark 10:17–31; Luke 18:18–30).

Turning to the disciples again (as they went into Judea), He spoke to them again of His passion (Matthew 20:17–19; Mark 10:32–34; Luke 18:31–34) and rebuked the selfish ambition of James and John who desired the chief places in the kingdom (Matthew 20:20–28; Mark 10:35–45). Outside of Jericho Jesus healed blind Bartimaeus (Matthew 20:29–34; Mark 10:46–52; Luke 18:35–43), and near the same town the conversion of Zacchaeus took place (Luke 19:1–10). On the heels of Zacchaeus' conversion, Jesus spoke the parable of the pounds (Luke 19:11–27). At about that point the group reached Bethany (six days before the Passover according to John 12:1), which was to serve as Jesus' headquarters during the passion week (John 11:55—12:1, 9–11).

The Passion Week

The week for which Christ was born had arrived. Whether one holds that Christ's primary purpose in coming was to set up His Kingdom or to die for the sins of humanity, he will find his viewpoint supported during the Passion Week. As the Messiah, Christ was to be *both* king and a suffering servant. During these days He offered Himself as king, was initially accepted, then rejected and crucified. But His kingship will become a reality too—when He comes again. In the following outline of the Passion Week, the traditional reckoning is followed; but for that reason it is not necessarily correct at every point.[18]

Sunday

On Sunday morning, Jesus and His disciples journeyed from Bethany to Jerusalem (Matthew 21:1–9; Mark 11:1–10; Luke 19:29–40; John 12:12–19). As they climbed over the Mount of Olives, Jesus sent two disciples to find an ass's colt on which He might ride into Jerusalem. On the brow of the mount, Jesus stopped to lament over Jerusalem for her rejection of Him, and predicted her destruction (Luke 9:41–44). Meanwhile, a rumor spread that He was coming; and a crowd with palm branches in their hands gathered to greet Him.

As He entered the city, they spread their cloaks and the palm branches in His path and shouted, "Hosanna: blessed is the King of Israel who comes in the name of the Lord" (John 12:13, KJV). Apparently this crowd had been greatly impressed by the resurrection of Lazarus (John 12:17). The Pharisees sniveled, "The world is gone after him." But their day would come. During the ensuing hours the Lord must have enjoyed the favor of the multitudes. No doubt He also ministered to them. At the end of the day, Jesus returned to Bethany to spend the night (Mark 11:11).

Monday

On Monday, Jesus' prestige and authority retained the previous day's peak. On the way from Bethany, He saw a fig tree with leaves but no fruit, and He cursed the tree. The following day, when He and His disciples passed by, it was completely dried up (Matthew 21:18–22; Mark 11:12–14, 20–26).

When the Master arrived in the temple, He was angry a second time over the commercialization of Jewish worship. Again He called a halt to the buying and selling and money changing.[19] Afterward, the blind and lame sought Him out in the temple and He healed them. Some of the children cried, "Hosanna to the son of David." All of this was too much for the scribes and chief priests, who again sought a way to destroy Jesus, but He departed peaceably to Bethany that night (Matthew 21:12–17; Mark 11:15–19; Luke 19:45–48).

Tuesday

On Tuesday, as He taught in the temple, Jesus first clashed head on with the chief priests, scribes, and elders who challenged His authority to teach. He told them He would reveal the source of His authority if they would tell Him whether John's baptism was from heaven or men. They were afraid to answer; a reply in either direction would throw them open to criticism. Then he lashed them with parables, which in general described their rejection of Him and their ultimate judgment. They got the point; but they were unable to retaliate for fear of the people, who recognized Him as a prophet (Matthew 21:23—22:14; Mark 11:27—12:12; Luke 20:1–19).

CHRIST'S TRIAL AND CRUCIFIXION— SITES IN JERUSALEM

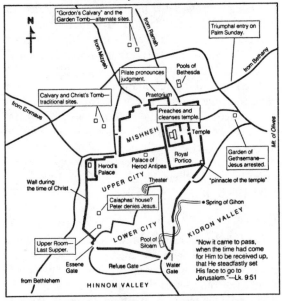

"Gordon's Calvary" and the Garden Tomb—alternate sites.

Triumphal entry on Palm Sunday.

from Ramah

from Mizpeh

Pilate pronounces judgment.

Pools of Bethesda

from Bethany

Calvary and Christ's Tomb—traditional sites.

from Emmaus

Praetorium

Preaches and cleanses temple.

MISHNEH

Temple

Mt. of Olives

Palace of Herod Antipas

Royal Portico

Garden of Gethsemane—Jesus arrested.

Herod's Palace

"pinnacle of the temple"

Wall during the time of Christ

UPPER CITY

Theater

Caiaphas' house? Peter denies Jesus.

Spring of Gihon

LOWER CITY

KIDRON VALLEY

Upper Room—Last Supper.

Pool of Siloam

Essene Gate

Refuse Gate

Water Gate

"Now it came to pass, when the time had come for Him to be received up, that He steadfastly set His face to go to Jerusalem."—Lk. 9:51

from Bethlehem

HINNOM VALLEY

Next He faced the Herodians and the Pharisees, who tried to trip Him up with the question of whether or not it was lawful to give tribute to Caesar. He answered with the famous words, "Render therefore unto Caesar the things which are Caesar's; and unto God the things that are God's" (Matthew 22:21, KJV). Then the Sadducees, who did not believe in the resurrection, came with a question about the resurrection, saying, "Seven brothers, in turn, all married the same woman; none left any children. Which one can claim her as wife in the resurrection?" In brief, He replied that men will not be interested in the affairs of this life during the life to come (see Matthew 22:23–33; Mark 12:18–27; Luke 20:27–40).

Then the Pharisees tried another ruse, asking the Lord which was the greatest commandment. This, too, He answered effectively: "You shall love the Lord your God with all your heart, and with all your soul, and with all your mind. This is the first and great commandment. And the second is like unto it, you shall love your neighbor as yourself" (Matthew 22:37–39, KJV). Then Jesus asked a question concerning His identity and put all His opponents to silence (Matthew 22:41–46; Mark 12:35–37).

Having regained the offensive, Jesus denounced the Pharisees. He pointed up the legalism which they imposed on Jewry, their love of religious show, their desire for prestige and authority, their hypocrisy, and their emphasis on externals—on form, on the letter of the Law rather than devotion to God. His description leaves little unsaid (Matthew 23:1–39; Mark 12:38–40; Luke 20:45–47). Immediately after this invective, by way of contrast Jesus commended a widow for her sacrificial giving (Mark 12:41–44; Luke 21:1–4). Then several Greeks came to talk with Jesus; in conversing with them, He described His imminent death (John 12:20–36). Later He commented on His rejection by the Jews (John 12:37–50).

Then Jesus and His disciples left the temple. As they did, His disciples referred to the magnificence of the structure, to which He replied with a prophecy of its destruction. Later, on the Mount of Olives, they asked Him when this destruction would occur and what would be the sign of His coming and of the end of the age. He answered with the great Olivet Discourse (Matthew 24—25; Mark 13:1–37; Luke 21:5–38). In brief, this tells about the Tribulation, the latter part of which will be more severe than the first. At the end of the Tribulation, He will return and judge all who are then living. Those declared righteous enter His kingdom, while those judged unrighteous are sent into everlasting punishment. At the close of this address, Jesus predicted His betrayal and death as coming in a couple of days (Matthew 26:1–5; Mark 14:1–2; Luke 22:1–2).

Tuesday Night

That night Simon of Bethany gave a supper in honor of Jesus. During, or after, the meal Mary, sister of Martha and Lazarus, anointed the Master's head and feet with a costly ointment and then wiped His feet with her hair. Greedy Judas took issue with such a *wasteful* practice, professing an interest in the poor; but Jesus squelched him saying that she did this in preparation for His burial, and that the poor would remain with them always, but He would not. If Mary caught the significance of Christ's Passion announcements, she appears to have been the only one who did. In this connection, it is interesting to note that Mary did not go with the other women to the tomb to embalm Him on the resurrection morning (Matthew 26:6–13; Mark 14:3–9; John 12:1–9). That same night Judas Iscariot made a deal with the chief priests to betray Jesus for thirty pieces of silver (Matthew 26:14–16; Mark 14:10–11; Luke 22:3–6).

No events are described as taking place on Wednesday. If Jesus and His disciples rested, they did wisely. The staggering physical and emotional strains of the next two or three days would shake even the strongest constitutions.

Thursday Night

During the day on Thursday Jesus' disciples prepared the Passover, and as night fell He sat down to eat the Paschal Meal with them (Matthew 26:17–20; Mark 14:12–17; Luke 22:7–16). During the meal the Master washed the disciples' feet, predicted His betrayal and departure, revealed that Judas would betray Him, and foretold Peter's triple denial (Matthew 26:21–35; Mark 14:18–31; Luke 22:21–38; John 13). Meanwhile Jesus instituted the Lord's Supper (Matthew 26:26–29; Mark 14:22–25; Luke 22:17–20; cf. 1 Corinthians 11:23–26). After the gloomy forecast of John 13, the Master's encouragement in John 14 was certainly welcomed. He promised to prepare a place in heaven for them, to come back

for them, and meanwhile to send the Holy Spirit
to comfort and teach them. Following a benediction
(John 14:27–31), the group arose and made their way
to the Garden of Gethsemane.

On the way, Jesus spoke of the importance of fellowship with God, warned of persecution for the believer, underlined the coming ministry of the Holy
Spirit on their behalf and in relation to unbelievers,
and reviewed His coming death, resurrection, and second advent (John 15–16). About this time, Jesus uttered His great high priestly prayer (John 17). Arriving
at the garden, He told the disciples to wait for Him at
a certain spot while He went on a little farther and
prayed. Exhausted, they fell asleep. Three times He
came to awaken them, but they could not stay awake.
As He awoke them for the third time, Judas entered
the garden with an armed band to capture Jesus. As
Judas betrayed Jesus with a kiss, Peter intervened and
cut off the ear of Malchus, servant of the High Priest;
but Jesus restored it (Matthew 26:36–56; Mark
14:32–52; Luke 22:39–53; John 18:1–12).

Friday Morning

By this time it was probably midnight. Very early
on Friday the guard took Jesus to Annas, father-in-law
of Caiaphas, current high priest, for a preliminary hearing (John 18:12–14, 19–23). Annas then sent Him to
Caiaphas, before whom the guard mocked and struck
Him. While Jesus was in the High Priest's audience
room, Peter denied Him for the third time and the
cock crowed, as the Lord had predicted. Daybreak had
arrived and the Sanhedrin could now officially convene

to prosecute the hated Galilean. They judged Him guilty and took Him to Pilate for the first of three Roman hearings. Meanwhile, Judas, sick of betraying Jesus, returned in remorse to the chief priests and elders, threw the thirty pieces of silver on the temple floor, and rushed out to commit suicide.

Pilate, about as unconcerned over problems of Jewish religion as Roman officials in the day of Paul would prove to be, found nothing worthy of condemnation in Jesus. When he learned Jesus was from Galilee, he turned Him over to Herod Antipas, ruler of Galilee, who happened to be in Jerusalem at the time. Herod simply mocked Him, dressed Him in a beautiful robe, and sent Him back to Pilate. Pilate again wanted to release Jesus; but ultimately, after making three attempts to have Jesus released, he yielded to the pressure of the mob[20] to crucify[21] Him, releasing Barabbas (who had been convicted of murder and sedition) in place of Jesus. Then Pilate scourged Jesus, and the soldiers placed a crown of thorns on His head. Robing Him in purple, they hailed Him King of the Jews. Then they put His own clothes back on Him, hit Him on the head with a reed, driving in the thorns, spat upon Him, and bowed in mock worship. Next they forced Him to carry His own cross, but along the road, they forced Simon, a Cyrenian, to carry it the rest of the way.

Some woman followed Him, weeping; but He told them to weep rather for themselves because of coming judgment on Jerusalem. Arriving at Golgotha, Jesus was crucified between two thieves. As they nailed Him to the Cross, He prayed for forgiveness for those who bore guilt in this whole nefarious business. Then they offered Him wine mingled with myrrh, which He refused. This drink would have had a stupifying effect, and soldiers offered it to facilitate their handling of condemned persons. But Jesus refused to drink, wishing to have all His faculties unclouded as He assumed His task of bearing the sins of the whole world. Meanwhile an inscription was placed above Jesus' Cross, which *in toto* probably read, "This is Jesus of Nazareth, the King of the Jews."

The soldiers who stood guard at the foot of His Cross cast lots for His clothing. While He hung on the Cross the crowds ridiculed Him. Even the two thieves joined in, but later one of them repented and was converted. In the midst of all this, Jesus looked down and saw His mother and John standing together. He committed her to the beloved disciple's care. Then darkness covered the earth for three hours while Jesus suffered in silence. Afterward He received a drink, cried, "It is finished,"[22] commended His spirit to the Father, and died. The veil of the temple was rent, the earth quaked, graves were opened, many saints arose from the dead, and the centurion declared that He was the Son of God.

Friday Afternoon

In the afternoon the chief priests asked Pilate to have the bodies taken down before sunset, because the next day was the Sabbath. Jesus was dead, but His side was pierced with a sword just to make sure; the legs of the criminals were broken to hasten death. Then Joseph of Arimathea and Nicodemus went to Pilate to obtain the body of Jesus for burial, preparing it as the wealthy would and putting it in Joseph's tomb near Golgotha.[23] During the Sabbath the Sanhedrin persuaded Pilate to seal the sepulcher and post a guard, lest His disciples steal the body of their Master (for references on the trial and crucifixion of Jesus, see Matthew 26:57–27:66; Mark 14:53–15:47; Luke 22:54–23:56; John 18:24–19:42).

The Resurrection and Post-Resurrection Ministry

Four Denials of Christ's Resurrection

Antisupernaturalists have developed numerous theories to explain away the historical resurrection of Jesus Christ.

The Swoon Theory

Some have suggested a swoon theory: that Jesus did not really die, but merely lapsed into a temporary coma or swooned as a result of His physical sufferings. He merely recovered then and did not rise from the dead. But unconsciousness from Friday to Sunday would not have allowed a healthy appearance on His part; neither would it have left Him with the vigor and vitality reflected in His subsequent rapid movements and direction of the affairs of His disciples. And would not the piercing of His side and the tremendous loss of blood lead to death? Also, if Jesus merely swooned, He must have been the same, bodily, after the resurrection as before, which was not the case.

Again, if He did not rise from the dead, our Lord permitted the Gospel message to be founded on a hoax, which is entirely contrary to His nature and approach. Moreover, the salvation of humanity could only be obtained by the death of a sacrificial victim; a swoon would be meaningless. And if Jesus merely swooned, He must have died at some later time and disappeared from history. Of this there is no hint in Scripture or even in legend. This theory has been generally rejected even by modern liberal thinkers.

The Theft Theory

A second non-Christian view of the resurrection is the stolen body theory, which generally teaches that the disciples stole the body and then preached the resurrection. Viewed from the standpoint of the intervention of either friend or foe, this theory seems impossible. Would Jesus' enemies do the very thing most likely to spread the story of His resurrection? And wouldn't they have produced His body when the disciples did preach resurrection? If Jesus' friends had wished to steal the body, could they? There was the stone, the seal, and the guard. Would they have taken time to unwind the bands of embalming cloth from His body and leave them in the tomb (John 20:6–7)? If successful, would they have preached the resurrection with such convincing power? This falsehood would always have been a burden on their consciences, and there would have been the dread that one of their number might betray the secret. Certainly it is established from the Scripture and history that the disciples were convinced of the resurrection of Jesus Christ.

The Vision Theory

A third theory of the resurrection is the vision theory. But if it be admitted, as some do, that Jesus really appeared to His disciples in visions, the door has been opened to the miraculous and why not just as well admit a real resurrection, as the Scripture indicates? Others, however, say that Mary Magdalene, an excitable woman,[24] had a vision of the resurrected Lord, and the disciples eagerly embraced the idea and passed it on, also imagining that they saw visions of Him. The whole business of the resurrection is made to be merely a product of the subconscious. Here again some questions are in order. If a product of the psychological makeup of the individual, a vision is merely a transference to supposed reality of what has already taken possession of the mind; there is an excited expectation that the idea will somehow become a reality.

But did Mary or the other women expect Him to arise? Did they not go to the tomb to anoint or embalm Him? Did not Mary mistake Jesus for the gardener? Didn't the disciples at first refuse to believe Mary when she told them of the resurrection? Also, is it not true that in a vision appearance the one viewed is shrouded in glory? Jesus in every instance appeared as a normal man. Aren't visions usually fleeting things? Jesus spoke at length to numbers of disciples at one time. When individuals have visions which are a product of the mind, do they stand up to their visions and say, "I don't believe it," as Thomas did?

The Spiritual-Only Theory

Fourth, many treat the resurrection in a spiritual sense. Christ became spiritually alive in the disciples' hearts. They were possessed by His spirit. And today, when individuals have an experience of faith, Christ becomes alive in them. So the resurrection is constantly taking place. It is true that the spirit of Christ took possession of the disciples after the ascension and that the Spirit comes to indwell the hearts of believers today when they receive Christ by faith. But the resurrection of Christ was to the early disciples an objective reality—upon which was *based* a spiritual experience. The subjective spiritual experience was not a substitution for the objective reality.[25]

Evidence for the Resurrection

In connection with the foregoing antisupernatural theories of the resurrection, some evidence for the resurrection has been presented. More is in order.

Christ's Anticipation

First of all, there is Christ's own anticipation of the resurrection—and His words in red-letter editions of the New Testament are often given special value. On numerous occasions He anticipated His death, burial, and resurrection. Especially pointed is His assertion in John 2:19, 21–22; "Destroy this temple, and in three days I will raise it up . . . But he spoke of the temple of his body."

The Appearances of the Resurrected Christ

Second, there are the resurrection appearances. The chronology of the resurrection narrative seems to be as follows. At dawn there was an earthquake. An angel of the Lord came down and rolled away the stone from the sepulcher and sat on it. The soldiers, terrified, were transfixed for the moment and then returned to the city to be bribed by the priests and elders to report that the disciples had stolen the body. Then Mary Magdalene and the other women came to anoint Jesus. Finding the stone removed, they assumed that the body had been removed by the Jews. Mary ran to find Peter and John and tell them. Meanwhile the other women entered the tomb and the angels told them of the resurrection and commanded them to tell the disciples.

Soon Peter and John arrived at the tomb to confirm that the body was gone, and they soon left. Mary lingered behind weeping, and Jesus appeared to her first (Mark 16:9–11; John 20:11–18). Second, He appeared to the other women (Matthew 28:9–10); third, to the two disciples on the way to Emmaus (Mark 16:12–13; Luke 24:13–32); fourth, to Peter (Luke 24:33–35; cf. 1 Corinthians 15:5); fifth, to ten Apostles in a house (Mark 16:14; Luke 24:33–43; John 20:19–25). All of these appearances seem to have taken place on Resurrection Sunday. On the following Sunday, He appeared to the eleven in a house, Thomas being present (John 20:26–31).

Later, in Galilee, He met seven apostles by the Sea of Galilee, at which time there was a miraculous catch of fish (John 21:1–14); He interviewed Peter (John 21:15–25) and appeared to 500 disciples (Matthew 28:16–20; Mark 16:15–18; 1 Corinthians 15:6). Probably He also appeared to James, His brother, at

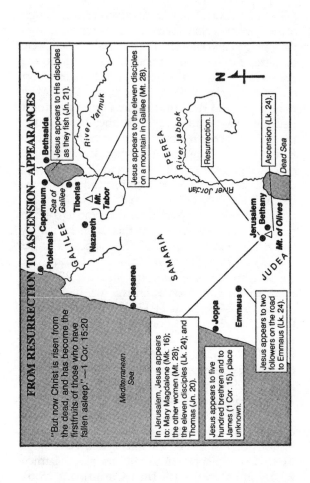

FROM RESURRECTION TO ASCENSION—APPEARANCES

"But now Christ is risen from the dead, and has become the firstfruits of those who have fallen asleep." —1 Cor. 15:20

Jesus appears to His disciples as they fish (Jn. 21).

Jesus appears to the eleven disciples on a mountain in Galilee (Mt. 28).

Resurrection.

Ascension (Lk. 24).

In Jerusalem, Jesus appears to: Mary Magdalene (Mk. 16); the other women (Mt. 28); the eleven disciples (Lk. 24); and Thomas (Jn. 20).

Jesus appears to five hundred brethren and to James (1 Cor. 15), place unknown.

Jesus appears to two followers on the road to Emmaus (Lk. 24).

Bethsaida

Capernaum

Sea of Galilee

Tiberias

Mt. Tabor

Nazareth

GALILEE

Ptolemais

Caesarea

SAMARIA

Joppa

Emmaus

JUDEA Mt. of Olives

Jerusalem

Bethany

PEREA

River Yarmuk

River Jabbok

River Jordan

Dead Sea

Mediterranean Sea

N

this time because the family would have been living in Galilee (1 Corinthians 15:7). Returning to Jerusalem, He met with the eleven on the Mount of Olives (Luke 24:44–49) and later with a large group as He gave His last commission and ascended (Mark 16:19–20; Luke 24:50–53; Acts 1:3–12). Certainly the disciples were competent witnesses to the resurrection. They would not have been fooled; they knew Him well.

The Utter Change in the Disciples

We must also note the change in the disciples after the resurrection and ascension, the observance of the first day of the week as the Lord's Day, and the fact of the Christian Church as evidences for the resurrection. A satisfactory alternative explanation to the resurrection as the basis of these historical facts has not been forthcoming. A desupernaturalized Jesus could not have made the impact on His generation that He did, and His followers acting in His name could not have made the significant impact on their generation that they did. A desupernaturalized Jesus is no Jesus at all. It is the supernatural that makes Him unique. There have been other great and good men with remarkable systems of ethics, but there has been only one God-man that has broken into history.

The Significance of the Resurrection

A consideration of the resurrection would not be complete without a word concerning its significance.

• It is a proof of Christ's person. He could hardly be reckoned as the God-man if He remained in the grave.

- It is essential to our salvation. Were He to remain in the grave, He would have no more significance as the founder of our faith than Mohammed or Buddha. The resurrection marked a completed salvation; Romans 4:25 might better be translated, "who . . . was raised *on account of* our justification." There was no longer any need for Him to remain in the tomb; He had paid sin's penalty.
- The resurrection is essential to Christ's present work of intercession, advocacy, and preparing a place for us.
- It is essential to His future work of the resurrection of humanity, His judgments, and His reign on David's throne.
- It is an evidence of the inspiration of Scripture. The resurrection is the fulfillment of many prophecies and as such gives support to the whole doctrine of inspiration.
- His last appearance was connected with our mission. In a sense, His was now accomplished, and He wants us to take up where He left off.

NOTES

1. Jack Finegan, *Handbook of Biblical Chronology* (Princeton: Princeton U., 1964), p. 238.

2. Harold W. Hoehner, *Chronological Aspects of the Life of Christ* (Grand Rapids: Zondervan, 1977), p. 23.

3. For further discussion, see W. P. Armstrong, "Chronology of the New Testament," in *International Standard Bible Encyclopaedia,* 2d ed., 1:644–47; William M. Ramsay, *Was Christ Born at Bethlehem?* (London: Hodder & Stoughton, 1898), pp. 117–251; George A. Bar-

ton, *Archaeology and the Bible,* 7th ed. (Philadelphia: Amer. S.S. Union, 1937), pp. 553–58; and Jack Finegan, *Handbook of Biblical Chronology,* pp. 215–85.

4. Hoehner, p. 26.

5. For discussion of the divine-human nature of Jesus' person, see chapter 4.

6. Louis M. Sweet, "The Genealogy of Jesus Christ," in *International Standard Bible Encyclopaedia,* 2d ed., 2:1196–97.

7. No doubt He was tempted on many other issues during the days previous to the temptation period and later on during His ministry.

8. John is probably referring to himself here with his customary humility.

9. To what "the third day" refers is a matter of dispute. Most feel that it refers to the third day after His departure to Galilee. The feast, then, probably took place about a week after Jesus met John as He returned from the wilderness testing.

10. James Stalker, *The Life of Jesus Christ* (Westwood, N.J.: Revell, 1891), p. 52.

11. Since Joseph is not mentioned in this account or in any subsequent events in the life of Christ, we may presume that he was no longer living.

12. It should be remembered that this sermon was delivered to disciples, who were all at least professed believers. Judas was the only one who turned out to be an unbeliever later. Certainly this was not a discourse on good works which, if performed, would issue in eternal life, as many preach today. Salvation is by faith, not works.

13. Certain women, including Mary Magdalene, Joanna, and Susanna, also accompanied Jesus on this tour. Whether they were with Him from the outset or joined the party later is uncertain (Luke 8:1–3).

14. For a fuller discussion, see chapter 6.

15. It must be kept in mind that the Gospels narrate only a selected number of miracles—for that matter only selected events of all types—from the public ministry of Christ.

16. Perhaps this was the home of Jesus' mother, or a home base maintained by the disciples, or the home of Simon Peter.

17. The feast of Dedication celebrated the rededication of the temple by the Maccabeans, after its desecration by Antiochus Epiphanes; both events occurred before the middle of the second century B.C. The feast was held on the twenty fifth of Kislev (December). Other feasts mentioned in this narration of the life of Christ are the Passover and the feast of Tabernacles. The former commemorated the exodus of the Jews from Egypt in the days of Moses and was celebrated on the fifteenth to the twenty second of Nisan (April). The latter was a harvest festival held on the fifteenth to the twenty second of Tishri (corresponding to parts of our September and October).

18. For a discussion of the arguments in favor of a Wednesday, Thursday, or Friday crucifixion, see Hoehner, pp. 65–74. Bibliography on the subject appears on those pages. Hoehner concludes that the Friday view is most acceptable.

19. See under Annas, chapter 9.

20. Perhaps the mobs of Jerusalem were merely fickle, changing from praise to hate in the four or five days since the triumphal entry. Perhaps they were disillusioned because Jesus did not set up His Messianic kingdom as they expected. Perhaps this was not the same crowd that welcomed Him so gladly on Sunday.

21. Why the method of crucifixion was chosen has been variously explained. Some say that this mode came to mind because it had already been prescribed for Barabbas. Others note that it was the usual mode of punish-

ment for sedition. Yet others suggest that the leaders of the Jews suggested it because it was a Roman form of punishment, and they could more easily throw the responsibility for Jesus' death on the Romans in this way.

22. Primarily, "It is finished" refers to Christ's bearing the curse of man's sin. But it also may refer in a more general way to Christ's suffering, to His bodily limitation and humiliation.

23. The location of Golgotha is one of the unsettled problems of biblical archaeology. Many have been enamored with the idea of "Gordon's Calvary," but it is a comparatively recent identification, having been made during the latter part of the nineteenth century. While the acceptance of the traditional site of the Church of the Holy Sepulcher is faced with problems, a large percentage, if not a large majority of archaeologists believe that it is still the best possibility. One of the problems about accepting the site of the Church of the Holy Sepulcher concerns the location of the city wall in Jesus' day. It has now been determined that the site was indeed outside the wall in Jesus' day, and there is therefore no strong reason for rejecting it. Other sites around Jerusalem have been suggested.

24. There is no basis in fact for assuming that Mary was a nervous, excitable woman, given to "seeing things" because of the after effects of her demon possession. She was completely and gloriously healed by the Lord and appears as a tower of strength, standing during the Passion Week when most of the disciples buckled.

25. For further discussion, see William Milligan, *The Resurrection of Our Lord* (London: Macmillan, 1890); Merrill C. Tenney, *The Reality of the Resurrection* (Chicago: Moody, 1972); Grant R. Osborne, *The Resurrection Narra-*

tives (Grand Rapids: Baker, 1984); Terry L. Miethe, ed., *Did Jesus Rise from the Dead?* (San Francisco: Harper & Row, 1987); Normal L. Geisler, *The Battle for the Resurrection* (Nashville: Thomas Nelson, 1989).

NINE

Significant Personalities in the Life of Christ

DURING the narration of Christ's earthly life, there is frequent mention of individuals with whom He came in contact or who were related to Him. Now we have an opportunity to become better acquainted with them. We shall not discuss all persons mentioned, only those with whom Jesus personally came in contact. Most prominent, of course, are His coworkers—the disciples.

His Coworkers

Before we look at the disciples individually, we can infer several general observations from information provided in the Gospels and early church tradition. First, the twelve are called both disciples and apostles, the former signifying *learners* and the latter *sent ones*. Neither term is restricted to them, but both are used of them in a special sense. Second, all of the disciples were Galileans, except Judas, who was probably a Judean. Third, as to occupation, Peter, Andrew, James, and John were fishermen. Possibly Nathanael and Thomas were too (John 21:2). Matthew was a tax collector. Of the rest nothing is known. Fourth, three wrote books of the Bible: Matthew, a Gospel; Peter, two epistles, in addition to influencing Mark in the writing of his Gospel; and John, a Gospel, three epistles, and Revelation.

Fifth, the New Testament contains four lists of the apostles: Matthew 10:2–4; Mark 3:16–19; Luke 6:14–16; Acts 1:13, 26. In these, Simon Peter always appears in first place, Philip always in fifth, James (son of Alphaeus) always in ninth, and Judas last. Sixth, as to their death, Scripture and tradition indicate that ten suffered martyrdom (four by crucifixion), one committed suicide, and two died a natural death. The New Testament is specific about only two: James, the son of Zebedee, was beheaded by Herod Agrippa I in A.D. 44 (Acts 12:1–2); Judas committed suicide (Matthew 27:3–5; Acts 1:16–20) just before the death of Christ.

Andrew

Someone has characterized Andrew as a "successful nonentity." He was not in the limelight or a dynamic personality like Peter, James, and John. Yet he was of great importance to the Christian movement. It was he who brought Peter to the Lord. He was prominent at the feeding of the five thousand, knowing the lad who had the five loaves and two fish (John 6:8–9). He was also the one who brought the request of the inquiring Greeks to Jesus at the time of the Passover (John 12:20–36). He was characterized by spiritual perception, common sense, and a general demeanor which led others to appeal to him when in difficulty.

Andrew was a fisherman of Bethsaida of Galilee, the brother of Simon; his father's name was John (John 1:42, 44; 21:15–17). Greatly interested in spiritual things, he had traveled to Bethabara (or Bethany) beyond Jordan to hear John the Baptist, and became his disciple. When Jesus appeared on the scene, Andrew was the first to become His disciple. Immediately he brought Peter to the Master (John 1:40–41). Andrew probably accompanied Jesus as He returned to Galilee and was therefore present at the first miracle at Cana (John 2:2), and later at the Passover in Jerusalem (John 2:13), during Christ's early Judean ministry (John 3), and in Samaria (John 4). Arriving in Galilee once more, he seems to have gone back to fishing. But when John the Baptist was imprisoned and Jesus began a more extensive ministry, Andrew gave up all to follow Him (Mark 1:17). Thereafter Andrew was present on many notable occasions, including the healing of his sister-in-law (Mark 1:29–31), and for the Olivet Discourse (Matthew 24–25). At least at the time when Jesus healed Simon's mother-in-law, Andrew was living with Simon (Mark 1:29) and presumably was not married. Eusebius of Caesarea (fourth century) preserved a tradition that Andrew preached to the Scythians in the area of what is now the southern steppes of Russia and the Ukraine. The third century apocryphal *Acts of St. Andrew* tells of his persecution and crucifixion in Achaia (Greece).

Bartholomew

Bartholomew is mentioned in the New Testament only in the four lists of the apostles. But since he is generally identified with Nathanael, he appears elsewhere by that name. He is thought to have been the brother of Philip. At least Philip stands next to him in the apostolic lists, and it was Philip who invited him to come to Jesus (John 1:45). Initially, he had a prejudice against Jesus because He came from Nazareth. Probably this attitude was not brought on by any scorn for Nazareth but by the belief that the Messiah would come from a more significant place. At any rate he responded to the invitation to "come and see for yourself," and changed his opinion. No doubt present on many occasions during the ministry of Christ, he is not mentioned by name. He is named, however, as one of the seven disciples to whom Jesus appeared after the resurrection (John 21:2). In that connection we learn that his occupation possibly was fishing and his original home was Cana. According to tradition he was flayed alive in Armenia.

James, the Son of Alphaeus

James, the son of Mary and Alphaeus, is generally identified with James the Less, the brother of Joses (Matthew 27:56; Mark 15:40). *"The Less"* is the translation of a Greek word that refers to age. The Revised Standard Version rendering of "the younger" gives the correct idea. Evidently he was younger than James, the son of Zebedee. Some feel that James' father is the same Alphaeus as the father of Matthew, but this is probably not the case. From John 19:25, it would seem that Alphaeus was also called Cleopas. Outside of the appearance of his name in the four lists of the twelve, he is not mentioned specifically elsewhere in the New Testament. Obviously, he was present on numerous occasions, however, such as the Last Supper, when all of the twelve were together, and during at least four of the post-resurrection appearances of Christ, to say nothing of His earlier ministry.

James and John, the Sons of Zebedee

From a comparison of Mark 15:40 and John 19:25, many infer that the mother of James and John, Salome, was the sister of the virgin Mary. Therefore James and John were cousins of Jesus. This may account in part for their closeness to the Lord as members of the inner circle along with Peter, and their presumption that they had a right to some special place in the Kingdom (Matthew 20:20–23). James and John were fishermen who lived at Bethsaida on the Sea of Galilee. Since James is always mentioned before his brother in the lists of the apostles, he was probably the older of the two. Apparently the family possessed some wealth because they had hired servants (Mark 1:20). It seems, too, that the family of Zebedee were partners with Peter and Andrew in the fishing business and that together they owned several boats (Matthew 4:18–21; Mark 1:19–20; Luke 5:11).

From all we can learn in the New Testament, the brothers were alike in temperament. They were called *Boanerges,* which means "sons of thunder." Generally it is thought that this applied to their hot temper. The commonly given illustration of that temper is their reaction to the Samaritan rejection of Jesus: "Lord, do you want us to command fire to come down from heaven and consume them?" (Luke 9:54). But it could be that they were jealous for the Lord on this occasion and were moved with righteous indignation. Perhaps the transfiguration scene flashed before their eyes as they thought about their Lord's rejection. At any rate, Boanerges might as easily allude to boisterousness or loud boastfulness, or even some other more favorable trait.

Probably James and John were both prepared for the Lord's call by John the Baptist and were introduced to Him by the Baptist. Later, before His early Judean ministry, Jesus called them to follow Him (Matthew 4:18–22; Mark 1:16–20; Luke 5:1–11), providing them with a miraculous catch of fish as further evidence of His identity. As favored apostles, the brothers, along with Peter, were the only members of the twelve present at the raising of Jairus' daughter (Mark 5:37; Luke 8:51), at the Transfiguration (Matthew 17:1–8; Mark 9:2–8; Luke 9:28–36), and at the agony in the garden (Matthew 26:36–46; Mark 14:32–42). They were two of the four present for the Olivet discourse (Mark 13:3–4). Also, they were among the seven at the Sea of Galilee when Jesus made a third postresurrection appearance to the disciples (John 21:1–14). Of course, they were constantly present with the Lord during other phases of His ministry. As already noted, James met his death at the hands of Herod Agrippa I. John, singled out as the disciple whom Jesus loved and to whom He revealed the identity of His betrayer, later ministered in the Roman province of Asia, suffered exile on the Isle of Patmos offshore during the reign of the Emperor Domitian, and seems to have died a natural death at an advanced age in the city of Ephesus. The traditional site of his grave is located under the altar in the ruins of the Church of St. John at Ephesus.

Judas Iscariot

Judas, a son of Simon (John 6:71), came from the Judean village of Kerioth, south of Hebron (according to the indication of his name). Probably he first met Jesus during His early Judean ministry, but he did not officially become one of Jesus' disciples until the middle period of the Galilean ministry.

Why he joined the Apostolic band is a matter of debate. Perhaps at the beginning he shared the hope of many other Israelites in a coming Messiah. But like them his thoughts centered around a political deliverer, and his self-aggrandizing nature may have led him to join the band with the hope of a position of importance in the new Kingdom. But gradually he grew at odds with Jesus and finally betrayed Him.

Possibly the fact that he was a Judean and the rest were Galileans brought friction. Then, too, his business ability earned him the position of treasurer of the group, and he seemingly grew ever more greedy. He apparently embezzled funds entrusted to him (John 12:6), resented it when Mary "wasted" a large sum in anointing Jesus, professed an interest in the poor (John 12:5), and finally betrayed Jesus for thirty pieces of silver[1] (Matthew 26:14–16; Mark 14:10–11; Luke 22:3–6).

Moreover, Judas gradually came to realize that the Kingdom would not be political but spiritual; so his dreams for power were blasted. For these and other reasons the gap widened between him and Jesus to the point of betrayal. But having obtained his price, Judas became very depressed. The money did not satisfy, and he was conscience-stricken for having betrayed innocent blood. He tried to return the thirty pieces of silver to place the blame more squarely on the shoulders of the religious leaders, but they would not accept the money. Finally, in a fit of frustration and remorse, he rushed out and committed suicide. With the coins he had flung on the temple floor the chief priests purchased the potter's field, afterward called "the field of blood" (Matthew 27:7–8).

Judas (of James)

Whether Judas was the "son" or "brother" of James is open to question (Luke 6:16; Acts 1:13). It seems clear, however, that he is to be equated with Thaddaeus and Lebbaeus (Matthew 10:3; Mark 3:18). What these alternate names signify cannot be discerned with certainty. Outside of the lists of the disciples, this Judas is mentioned only once specifically, when he asked Jesus a question on the way to the Garden of Gethsemane (John 14:22). Of course, he was present on numerous occasions when all the disciples were together, such as for the Sermon on the Mount, at the Last Supper, and at least two post-resurrection appearances.

Matthew

During His early Galilean ministry, Jesus met Levi, who was engaged in his business of tax collecting near the Sea of Galilee. Levi heard Him gladly and promptly responded to the call of discipleship. Whether or not he had any spiritual preparation in having heard John the Baptist, or Jesus' message from another, we cannot determine. After his conversion, Levi put on a banquet in his own home in Jesus' honor (Luke 5:27). Thereafter he seems to have been known as Matthew (meaning "gift of God"). In three of the apostolic lists, Matthew appears next to Thomas, also called Didymus, which means "twin," and on this basis some have felt that the two were brothers. His home was probably Capernaum, and his father's name Alphaeus (Mark 2:14), likely not the same as the father of James the Less. Outside of these facts, we have no specific statement about him in the New Testament, though he, like several of the others, was present on numerous occasions during the ministry of Christ. (See references under Judas of James, etc.).

Philip

A native of Bethsaida of Galilee (John 1:44), Philip was among the group that had journeyed across the Jordan to hear John the Baptist. While there, Philip met Jesus and became His disciple. Like Andrew, he immediately won another to the Lord—Nathanael. Philip then accompanied Jesus back to Galilee and must have been present for the miracle of Cana. He probably also followed Jesus into Judea for the early Judean ministry.

While present at numerous events during our Lord's ministry, he is mentioned by name only in connection with the feeding of the five thousand (John 6:5–7), the appeal of the Greeks at the Passover in Jerusalem (John 12:20–33), and during the address of Jesus after the Last Supper, when he said, "Lord, show us the Father, and it is sufficient for us" (John 14:8). That his name is Greek implies that he had some Greek connections, and it may be why the Greeks came to him at the Passover in Jerusalem, thinking they would get a better hearing from him than from the other disciples. Another item of interest is Philip's allusion to the Old Testament prophecies, indicating his knowledge of the Scripture and some Messianic longing on his part (John 1:45).

Simon the Cananite or Zealot

Simon is called *Cananaean* in Matthew 10:4 and Mark 3:18, the *Zealot* in Luke 6:15 and Acts 1:13 (all KJV). Actually, both terms refer to the same thing. Cananaean has nothing to do with *Cana* or *Cananaite*, but is the Greek form of the Aramaic word for *Zealot*. The Zealots were a fierce party of nationalists working for the recovery of Jewish freedom. If he was a member of such a group, Simon would readily have welcomed a Messiah who might accomplish his cherished aim. Apart from his listing among the twelve, Simon is not mentioned elsewhere in the New Testament. We can be certain of his presence with the Lord only at those times when the entire group, the eleven (minus Judas), or the ten (minus Judas and Thomas) were together. He does not appear on the scene until the middle period of Jesus' Galilean ministry.

Simon Peter

A native of Bethsaida on the Sea of Galilee, Simon was a fisherman by trade (John 1:44). In this occupation he and his brother, Andrew, seem to have been business partners with Zebedee and his sons, James and John (Matthew 4:21; Luke 5:10). Later he moved to Capernaum, where apparently his mother-in-law and Andrew lived with him and his family. His father was Jona, Jonas, or John (Matthew 16:17; John 1:42). His mother is not named.

It is evident that Peter early had strong religious inclinations, for he and Andrew had gone to Bethabara, beyond Jordan, to hear the preaching of John. While there, Jesus came along and met Andrew, who brought his brother to Jesus. At that time Jesus gave Simon his new name, *Peter*, meaning "rock," perhaps symbolic of his strong character (John 1:40–42). With the others, Peter accompanied Jesus on His return to Galilee and therefore witnessed the miracle at Cana. Soon Peter accompanied the rest to the Passover at Jerusalem and during the early Judean ministry.

Upon returning to Galilee, the disciples must have returned to their customary occupations for some time. Then, when John was imprisoned, Jesus began His ministry in earnest, calling disciples to full-time service. Among them was Peter (Matthew 4:19; Mark 1:17; Luke 5:3). Soon after this call, Peter's mother-in-law became ill and Jesus healed her (Matthew 8:14 ff.). Later, during the second period of the Galilean ministry, Jesus commissioned the Twelve, Peter heading the list (Matthew 10:4; Mark 3:14, 16; Luke 6:13–14).

Thereafter, the name of Peter is predominant in the Gospels. He is mentioned often as a member of the inner circle (Peter, James, and John) as they accompanied the Lord on specific occasions, including the raising of Jairus' daughter, the Transfiguration, and Jesus' agony in the Garden. He uttered the great confession that Jesus was the Christ and soon thereafter tried to stand in the way of the Lord's suffering and death (Matthew 16:13–23). He objected to having the Lord wash his feet at the time of the Last Supper (John 13:1–10). He sliced off Malchus' ear when the mob sought to take the Lord in the Garden (John 18:10–11). But he also denied the Lord three times during the Passion and repented bitterly for having done so (Matthew 26:56–58; Mark 14:66–72; Luke 22:54–62; John 18:15–27).

On resurrection morning, Peter was the first to investigate the women's story of the empty tomb (John 20:1–10). Christ made a special appearance to him after the resurrection, giving him the opportunity to reaffirm his loyalty (John 21:1–23). After the ascension he took a position of leadership in the Church, as may be seen from Acts 1–15. Peter was bold, courageous, impulsive, and faithful to the Lord, except for his defection prior to the crucifixion. These characteristics led him to make some admirable as well as foolish moves. But after Pentecost, when these qualities were sublimated and strengthened by the filling of the Holy Spirit, there was no stopping him.

Thomas

As noted above, Thomas is also called Didymus (John 11:16; 20:24; 21:2), which means "twin."

Some have thought he was the twin of Matthew; others have related this to his twin-mindedness—the struggle within him between unbelief and faith. He did not appear as a member of the apostolic company until the middle period of the Galilean ministry, when his selection to the twelve occurred (Matthew 10:3; Mark 3:18; Luke 6:15; Acts 1:13). The first time Thomas was vocal occurred just before the healing of Lazarus. When Jesus proposed that they return to Judea to heal Lazarus, the other disciples tried to stop Him, fearing that the Jews might seek to kill them (John 11:8). But Thomas, in a burst of faith and loyalty, declared, "Let us also go, that we may die with him" (John 11:16).

Later, during the upper room discourse, Thomas revealed his spiritual limitations in responding to Christ's assuring words about His absence and second coming: "Lord, we know not where you are going, and how can we know the way?" (John 14:5). After the crucifixion, he dropped out of sight for a while, not being present with the ten on resurrection Sunday. He disbelieved when told of the Lord's appearance (John 20:25), but he was present with the apostolic company the following week when the Lord appeared again. Then he made a clear profession of faith: "My Lord and my God" (John 20:28). Later he was among the group to whom Jesus appeared in Galilee (John 21:1–11). Thomas is like those who today demand empirical support for their faith. But once they have fought through their intellectual difficulties, they come into a clear cut, triumphant stand for the truth.

His Relatives

His Mother

Any reliable account of the virgin Mary must come from an objective interpretation of Scripture, not from imaginary apocryphal works or Church dogma. The biblical indications reveal that she was a deeply meditative and devout believer with no "inside track" to the favor of her Son, but certainly enjoying His highest respect and loving care.

As to her kinship, Mary was a descendant of David through Nathan (Luke 3), whereas Joseph was descended from David through Solomon (Matthew 1). One sister is mentioned (John 19:25), probably Salome, the wife of Zebedee and mother of James and John (Matthew 27:56; Mark 15:40). According to Luke 1:36, Mary was also related to Elisabeth, mother of John the Baptist. The biblical biography of Mary begins with the period of her engagement to Joseph, while they were both living in Nazareth of Galilee. One day she was startled by the angel Gabriel, who told her that she was to be the virgin mother of Jesus, the Son of God. Her absolute devotion to God in the face of almost certain shame and suspicion is expressed in her reply, "Behold the handmaid of the Lord; be it unto me according to your word" (Luke 1:38, KJV).

But she was human; she fled to Elisabeth in Judea for comfort and encouragement. (Gabriel had told her that Elisabeth too was to have a child—in old age.) There she received great encouragement and uttered her beautiful magnificat (Luke 1:46–55). Remaining with Elisabeth about three months (Luke 1:56), she returned home to face Joseph, who, after a period of internal struggle, received assurance from God of the divine nature of his betrothed's conception and was reconciled to her and they married (Matthew 1:18–25). Before long, Augustus Caesar ordered a census and taxing, and no doubt with great hardship Mary made the difficult trip to Bethlehem, where Jesus was born. What Mary thought as the shepherds and wise men came to adore her infant Son is left to the imagination: "Mary kept all these things and pondered them in her heart" (Luke 2:19).[2] After the flight to Egypt and return to Nazareth, Mary assumed greater responsibilities with the increase in her family. Besides Jesus, she had four sons and an unspecified number of daughters (Matthew 13:55–56).

Glimpses of Mary appear several times during Christ's ministry. At His first miracle at Cana, she called attention to the exhausted wine supply—apparently with the faith that He could do something about it (John 2:3) and after the miracle, accompanied Him, His disciples, and the rest of the family to Capernaum (v. 12). On another occasion Jesus' mother and brothers became very solicitous for His welfare. His health was in danger because of constant demands on Him by the multitudes, and now He was faced by an angry group of religious leaders who even accused Him of casting out demons by the power of Satan. Perhaps He should get away for a rest. But Jesus continued with His Messianic responsibilities (Matthew 12:46–50; Mark 3:21–25).

At the cross, Mary stood with John, no doubt pondering all the inexplicable events which had occurred in the short lifetime of her Son. Jesus observed the pair and tenderly committed His mother into the care of the beloved disciple, whom we may conclude fulfilled his duties well (John 19:25–27). After the ascension, Mary was with her family in the upper room, awaiting the baptism of the Holy Spirit (Acts 1:14). Apparently she and His brothers had advanced by various steps of faith to full belief in and service to the divine Messiah. No doubt it is a tribute to Mary's influence that the rest of the family kept within the apostolic circle.

Joseph

Like Mary, Joseph was of the house of David (Matthew 1:1–17), though a very humble representative of it indeed. At the time of Jesus' birth his home was in Nazareth (Luke 2:4), where he was a carpenter (Matthew 13:55). When the New Testament first reveals his private life, he is engaged to a hometown girl by the name of Mary (Matthew 1:18). As the wedding day approached, Mary suddenly left town and stayed away three months. When she returned she was pregnant (Matthew 1:18). Joseph, full of consternation, just about made up his mind to call off the wedding, when the Lord revealed to him that Mary was to be the mother of the Savior. Then, fearless, he married her (Matthew 1:18–25).

Soon afterward, the decree of Caesar Augustus came ringing through the land. Joseph and Mary made their way to Bethlehem, their ancestral home, for taxing and census taking. There Jesus was born and adored by shepherds (Luke 2) and later by wise men (Matthew 2). In the face of Herod's threat against Jesus' life, Joseph fled to Egypt with his wife and child. Returning after the death of Herod the Great, Joseph settled in Nazareth again (Matthew 2:13–23). During successive years other children were born into the home.[3] Joseph is usually presumed to have died sometime between Jesus' visit to the temple at the age of twelve and the inauguration of His ministry. But John 6:42 may indicate that Joseph was still alive near the beginning of Jesus' ministry. Certainly he was no longer living at the time of the crucifixion, when Jesus entrusted His mother alone to the care of the apostle John.

As to character, Joseph was a devout man, strict in the observance of Jewish law. Immediately responsive to the command of God, he married Mary in the face of almost certain gossip or slander and moved quickly into Egypt to save the Holy Child. In the latter instance the difficulties of the situation are often passed by. Here was a young father with an infant, carrying his belongings and walking across a rather arid territory to settle in a strange land. Truly his faith was great. He demonstrated his careful observance of Jewish law in the circumcision of Jesus, the presentation of the Babe in the temple at the end of forty days, when the purification of Mary was accomplished, and in the annual trek to the Passover in Jerusalem (Luke 2:21–24, 41).

His Brothers and Sisters

That Mary and Joseph had other children after the birth of Jesus is clear from at least five incidents in the New Testament.[4]

- After Jesus' first miracle at Cana, His mother and *brothers* accompanied the apostolic group to Capernaum (John 2:12).
- During the middle period of Jesus' Galilean ministry, He became involved in quite a debate with the scribes and Pharisees. During the discussion, His mother and *brothers* sent Him a message, evidently in an effort to break up the disputation (Matthew 12:46 ff.; Mark 3:31 ff.; Luke 8:19 ff.).
- Later, when Jesus taught in Nazareth, His neighbors could not understand His remarkable claims because they had watched Him grow up and knew His mother, *brothers,* and *sisters* (Matthew 13:54 ff.; Mark 6:2 ff.). In this instance, His brothers were named (James, Joses, Simon, and Judas), but His sisters never were.
- On another occasion, before the Feast of Tabernacles, His unbelieving *brothers* ridiculed Him and taunted Him to go up to Jerusalem to the Feast and display His works (John 7:1–10).
- It would appear, however, that after the resurrection His *brothers* became believers because they were present with Mary and the disciples in the upper room, waiting for the Pentecostal blessing (Acts 1:14).

Other references to the Lord's brothers include 1 Corinthians 9:5, Galatians 1:19, and Jude 1.

Beyond what has already been said about our Lord's brothers, not a great deal can be added. Of Joses (Joseph) and Simon we can say nothing more. Jude was rather insignificant in the early Church, but it is commonly conceded that he was the author of the epistle that bears his name. The situation is different with James, however. The Lord appeared to him after the resurrection (1 Corinthians 15:7). According to Galatians 1:19, he interviewed Paul in Jerusalem after the latter's conversion. Other references indicate his gradual rise to prominence in the Jerusalem church until in 49 or 50, and at the great Council of Jerusalem (Acts 15) he was chairman. He is generally acknowledged to be the author of the epistle that bears his name.

His Followers

John the Baptist

Whether to list John the Baptist among the relatives or followers of Jesus is something of a problem, for he was both. He was related to Jesus through his mother, Elisabeth, who was a cousin of the virgin Mary (Luke 1:36). But John's divine commission was in announcing the Messiah and thus in serving Him. So he should be classified here.

John was born about six months before Jesus, of priestly parents, Zacharias and Elisabeth (Luke 1:5). According to Luke, they were a truly godly pair (1:6). From all that is said about them, they were eminently qualified for rearing a child "filled with the Holy Spirit, even from his mother's womb" (Luke 1:14–16). Apparently John spent much of his life in desert places, probably in meditation and communion with God (Luke 1:80). No doubt he gave much thought to the prophecy made before his birth that he would go before the Lord in the spirit and power of Elijah and turn many to the Lord (Luke 1:16–17).

The forerunner's ministry began in the fifteenth year of Tiberius Caesar (Luke 3:1), probably A.D. 29, and could hardly have lasted three years. He preached in the Jordan Valley (Bethabara or Bethany, John 1:28), in Judea (Aenon near Salim, John 3:23), and probably for a while in Perea or Galilee, since he was taken prisoner by Herod Antipas (governor of those two areas). As he ministered, he made a rustic appearance, clad in a coarse garment woven from camel's hair (Mark 1:6). John's message was a call to repentance in view of the soon coming of the Messiah, who would rule in righteousness and judgment during the Messianic age. He spared no one in his vigorous condemnation of evil, and was particularly jolting to the religiously smug Pharisees. Even rulers came in for their share of warning (Luke 3:1–19).

Conspicuous in connection with John's ministry was his baptism, which signified a break with the old life and forgiveness of sin. His hearers were prepared for such a baptism by their familiarity with Jewish ceremonial washings and the ceremony used to initiate proselytes into the Israelite community. In performing his ministry, John utilized the help of disciples and trained them to carry on in his steps. Among other things, he taught them forms of prayer and fasting (Matthew 9:14; Mark 2:18; Luke 5:33). The effectiveness of John's ministry is demonstrated by the fact that almost twenty years later Paul met his followers in distant Ephesus (Acts 19:1–7). The Jewish historian Josephus took note of the popularity of John in referring to John's preaching and baptism and in attributing Herod's murder of the Baptist to the king's fear that a revolt might gather force around the person of John.[5]

Though fearless in dealing with evil, John was retiring and humble before his Lord: "He it is, who coming after me is preferred before me, whose shoe's latchet I am not worthy to unloose" (John 1:27, KJV); "He must increase, but I must decrease" (John 3:30). Moreover, he felt unworthy to baptize Jesus (Matthew 3:14). Recognizing Jesus as the Lamb of God, he willingly turned his disciples over to the Lord (John 1:35–36). Jesus' estimate of John could not have been more complimentary: "Among them that are born of women there has not arisen a greater than John the Baptist" (Matthew 11:11, KJV).

Four Other Followers

In addition to John the Baptist, there are four other men that should come in for discussion here. At the time of Jesus' presentation in the temple shortly after His birth, a devout man named Simeon recognized Him as the Messiah and Savior of Israel (Luke 2:25–35). Nothing more is recorded of him.

Joseph was a rich man and an honorable counselor (Mark 15:43) who lived at Arimathaea, probably to the northwest of Jerusalem (Matthew 27:57). He was a member of the Sanhedrin, but apparently absented himself from the trial that condemned Jesus (Luke 23:50–51). A secret disciple earlier in the Master's ministry (John 19:38), Joseph discarded all reticence when he went in "boldly" to Pilate and asked for the body of Jesus (Mark 15:43), and took Jesus' body from the cross himself (Luke 23:53), wrapped it in linen, and laid it in his own tomb (Matthew 27:60).

Because of his mention in one of the best known chapters of the Bible (John 3), Nicodemus is a familiar figure. He was a ruler of the Jews and a member of the Sanhedrin. In John 3, he came to Jesus by night (whether out of fear, timidity, or a desire for privacy is unknown) to inquire about spiritual things. On that occasion, Christ explained the new birth. How successful He was is uncertain because Nicodemus' response is not recorded. Eventually, however, the interview bore fruit. When the Sanhedrin sought to condemn Jesus during the Feast of Tabernacles, because of His sermon on the "living water" (John 7:37–38), Nicodemus defended him on a point of Jewish law (John 7:50–51). After the crucifixion of Jesus, Nicodemus helped Joseph of Arimathaea prepare the body of Jesus for burial, furnishing the spices with which to embalm Him (John 19:39–42). We may assume that Nicodemus came to full faith in Christ, but the New Testament never clearly states that he did.

After His resurrection, Jesus appeared to two disciples on the road to Emmaus. One of these was Cleopas (Luke 24:18). Of him nothing further is known. Probably he was a faithful disciple or Jesus would not thus have honored him.

Women Disciples

In addition to these men, several women are also mentioned by name as followers of Jesus. One, Anna, a prophetess in Jerusalem, is distinguished for having recognized the infant Jesus as the Messiah at the time of His presentation in the temple (Luke 2:36–38).

Several women ministered to Jesus during His preaching tours. For the most part, they had experienced Jesus' healing ministry (Luke 8:2–3). A few of the most faithful are named, but there must have been many more.[6] One of the group was Susanna, a woman of some wealth, who is mentioned only in connection with Christ's Galilean ministry (Luke 8:3). Among others accompanying Him was Joanna, the wife of Chuza, one of Herod Antipas' stewards. Apparently, Joanna accompanied Him on many of His preaching tours because she was present in Jerusalem at the time of His crucifixion and went to His tomb on resurrection Sunday (Luke 24:10).

Another of the group was Salome. She was present at the crucifixion and was among those who came to the tomb on resurrection morning (Mark 16:1–2). From a comparison of Mark 15:40–41, Matthew 27:56, and John 19:25, we may gather that she was the sister of the virgin Mary and the wife of Zebedee and therefore the mother of James and John. She was the one, then, who requested that her sons be given a privileged place in the kingdom (Matthew 20:20–24). A mother of one of the other apostles also accompanied the apostolic group: Mary, the mother of James and Joses. All we know of her is that she lingered late at the cross (Mark 15:40), observed the burial (Mark 15:47), was among the group who came to anoint Jesus on resurrection morning (Mark 16:1–8), and met the risen Lord soon thereafter (Matthew 28:1–10).

Probably of prominence in this group of women was Mary Magdalene, out of whom Jesus cast seven devils. She was probably healed early in Jesus' Galilean ministry and joined Him in His ministry shortly afterward. No doubt she remained with Him regularly during following months, becoming prominent again during the Passion Week. She was at the cross (Matthew 27:61; Mark 15:40) and at the tomb early on resurrection Sunday (Matthew 28:1; Mark 16:1; Luke 24:10). Lingering behind when the other women went to report Jesus' missing body to the disciples, Mary was the first to see the resurrected Lord (Mark 16:9–11; John 20:11–18).

Two other women converts merit our consideration: Mary and Martha of Bethany. Jesus' contact with this household came rather late in His ministry—during the Judean ministry. Martha received him into her home and bustled around with the household tasks, while Mary sat down with their guest and engaged Him in relaxing conversation, listening eagerly to His teachings. Soon Martha had worked herself into a frenzy and erupted: "Lord, do You not care that my sister has left me to serve alone?" Jesus tenderly rebuked Martha, commenting that Mary had chosen a better way (Luke 10:38–42). But let us not sell Martha short. Jesus did not condemn service rendered for Him. Service must not be performed to the exclusion of fellowship with Him, however. And in service for the Master we must not allow ourselves to fly into a frenzy but must demonstrate the serenity of spirit that flows from constant dependence on Him.

Two or three months later, Lazarus, brother of Mary and Martha, fell ill, and the sisters sent Jesus a message to come and heal him. When Jesus finally arrived near the town, Martha ran out to meet Him and scolded Him for not having come sooner, to which He answered with comments about the resurrection. But when Mary met Him, He was so shaken that He wept. Then Jesus went to the grave and raised Lazarus from the dead. The comment on this episode is interesting: "Then many of the Jews which came to *Mary*, and had seen the things which Jesus did, believed on Him" (John 11:45, KJV).

A few weeks later, when Jesus entered Bethany to take up His abode during the Passion Week, a supper was given for Him. Martha served. But Mary gave vent to her intense devotion and, breaking from her usual retiring manner, flung herself at His feet and anointed His head and feet with a costly perfume and began to wipe His feet with her hair. Apparently she had gained a spiritual understanding of the great events that were about to take place, because Jesus commented, "Against the day of my burying hath she kept this" (John 12:7, KJV).[7] Perhaps there is real significance in John's statement; his gospel usually gives a more spiritual interpretation. Note that he says, "hath she *kept this*." If we are not reading too much into the text, Mary had been anticipating this event for some time and kept the perfume on hand, knowing she would have an opportunity to use it.[8]

Others

There are many other individuals mentioned in the Gospels as having come in contact with our Lord during His earthly ministry. Those involved in His political life, such as Pilate and Herod Antipas, have been discussed in chapter 3. Objects of His miracles of healing are mentioned in chapter 7. But five other individuals need a brief comment.

For His first hearing before His Jewish accusers during the Passion Week, Jesus was taken before Annas, father-in-law of Caiaphas, titular high priest (John 18:12–13). Annas held an informal hearing and then sent Jesus to Caiaphas for a formal trial. Annas had been appointed high priest by Quirinius in A.D. 6 or 7 and removed by Valerius Gratus in A.D. 15. But Annas remained the controlling figure in the high priesthood for many years to come, his five sons and son-in-law all holding the position. Probably he was the real power behind the office, though Caiaphas held the title at the time. As such, he would have been the prime mover behind all of the efforts to destroy Jesus of Nazareth. Annas continued to stir up trouble for the Christian movement after the ascension (Acts 4:6). Edwards characterizes the family as wealthy and greedy and indicates that the chief source of their wealth was the sale of animals, birds, oil, and wine for temple sacrifices. For this they had four "booths of the sons of Annas" on the Mount of Olives and one inside the temple. Holding a monopoly on such provisions, they could extort high prices.[9] This helps to explain the attitude of Jesus during His two cleansings of the temple, as well as the increasing determination of the priesthood to dispose of Him.

Caiaphas, son-in-law of Annas, held the high priesthood A.D. 18–36, being deposed by the procurator Vitellius. While he served during the ministry of John the Baptist (Luke 3:2), he was particularly important for his part in the crucifixion of our Lord. After the raising of Lazarus, when Jesus' followers began to increase rapidly, Caiaphas saw clearly the danger of the new movement to high priestly leadership and possibly even to Roman rule in Palestine. In order to eliminate this cause for Roman vengeance upon them and to solidify the position of the Sadducees, Caiaphas said, "It is expedient for us, that one man should die for the people" (John 11:50). Later, during the Passion Week, following a preliminary hearing before Annas, Christ was brought to the palace of Caiaphas (John 18:24). The High Priest saw to it that the Sanhedrin declared Jesus guilty of blasphemy and worthy of death (Matthew 26:57–66). Later, Caiaphas was active in the persecution of the apostles (Acts 4:5–22).

Perhaps a word should be added about three Simons mentioned in the Gospels. One is described as "a leper" of Bethany. Since lepers were outcasts from society, he obviously had been healed, probably by Jesus. It was in his house that Mary anointed Jesus (Matthew 26:6–13; Mark 14:3–9; John 12:1–8). Possibly this Simon was Martha's husband, as some suggest. A second Simon, often identified with the one above, is singled out by Jesus for his ingratitude. While the Master was dining in Simon's home, an unidentified woman came in and anointed His feet. Jesus then spoke the parable of the two debtors to Simon (Luke 7:36–50). On the matter of identifying these two Simons, it should be noted that the woman in the second instance is described as a woman of the street and an implication of lewdness is present in the original. Mary of Bethany would hardly have been so described. A third Simon was from Cyrene (Cyrenaica, part of modern Libya) in North Africa. He apparently was a Jew of the Dispersion in Jerusalem for the Passover and therefore was not Black, as some have suggested. He was forced to carry Jesus' Cross to Calvary. This Simon was the father of Alexander and Rufus (Matthew 27:32; Mark 15:21), who apparently later became prominent Christians.

NOTES

1. Efforts have been made to compute this sum in modern currency, and the resultant amount has always been paltry and therefore unrealistic. As a matter of fact, we are not sure which silver coin is meant here; but it is one which represents at least the daily wage of a worker. Thirty coins would then equal the wages to be earned during six five-day weeks. If another silver coin were chosen, the total could easily run to four times that amount.

2. Luke gives a very personal account of Mary's attitude toward her role in the divine mystery. Many have suggested that he obtained these intimations directly from Mary.

3. See second paragraph following.

4. Many have sought to make these "brothers" of our Lord "cousins" (Roman Catholic view) or Joseph's children by a previous marriage. But the indications that these "brothers" were children of Mary and Joseph seem

too numerous to be set aside. There is no real reason why Mary shouldn't have had other children later; such a fact would detract in no way from the uniqueness of Christ. The dogma of "perpetual virginity" built up by the Roman church cannot really be *proved* from Scripture. Is not Jesus called Mary's "first-born son" in Luke 2:7? Does not Matthew 1:25 imply that other children were born into the home after the incarnation of Jesus?

5. Josephus, *Antiquities* 18:5.2.

6. The presence of such women of wealth, or at least moderately well-to-do, indicates where Judas got some of the contents of the "bag," and helps to explain the apparent freedom of the disciples from economic restraints. The complete absence of charges against Jesus, His disciples, or these women of any inappropriate male-female relations indicates that they all must have been very discreet indeed, for Jesus' enemies used many pretexts to discredit Him; but this one is not mentioned.

7. It is impossible to equate this event with the anointing of Luke 7:36–50, as some have done. That anointing took place much earlier, probably during the Galilean ministry, in the house of Simon the Pharisee, who is reproved for his ingratitude. Moreover, the woman of Luke 7 is uninvited and is a questionable character of the street, with all that implies. All the circumstances of the two events are different. The frequency of anointing in Palestine for one purpose or another does not preclude the possibility of several such events during Jesus' ministry.

8. Admittedly, however, there is some difficulty in understanding the Greek text at this point.

9. D. Miall Edwards, "Annas," *International Standard Bible Encyclopedia,* 2d ed., 1:137.

TEN

Prophecies Fulfilled in the Life of Christ

AS WE look at the life of our Lord, we find many references to Old Testament prophecies fulfilled by events in His life. Since most of the key predictions concerning Christ's life appear in Isaiah, Jeremiah, and Ezekiel, this chapter is largely devoted to those prophets. Here then are the highlights.

Lineage of the Messiah

Background of Christ's lineage is found in a number of Old Testament prophecies, going back to the book of Genesis. God promised Abraham, "In you all families of the earth shall be blessed" (Genesis 12:3; 22:18; cf. Matthew 1:1; Luke 2:29–32; Galatians 3:16). He guaranteed David, "And your house and your kingdom shall be established forever before you. Your throne shall be established forever" (2 Samuel 7:16). In line with the Davidic Covenant, Isaiah prophesied, "There shall come forth a Rod out of the stem of Jesse, and a Branch shall grow out of his roots" (11:1). Hengstenberg's translation is a little closer to the Hebrew: "And there cometh forth a twig from the stump of Jesse, and a branch from his roots shall bear fruit."[1] The "twig" refers to the new life or new hope to arise in the line of Jesse. The "stump" signifies the humbled condition of the Davidic dynasty when

Christ came. Joseph was a carpenter, and Mary was his wife.

This prophecy of a Great One to come was fulfilled in the birth of Christ in Bethlehem (Micah 5:2; cf. Matthew 2:1). He declared Himself to be the Messiah and some recognized Him as such. As the New Testament closes, the Holy One speaks from Heaven: "I am the Root and the Offspring of David, the Bright and Morning Star" (Revelation 22:16).

As the New Testament opens, the lineage of the Messiah appears in detail. The genealogy is divided into three groups of fourteen generations each: Abraham to David, David to the captivity of Israel, and the captivity to Christ. This is probably a description of the ancestry of Joseph. The genealogy is traced through Solomon and Jeconiah, and is the *legal* line of Joseph, the *legal* father of Christ. The Holy Spirit guards, lest it be thought that Christ was born of Joseph, for the "of whom" following "Mary" in Matthew 1:16 is in the feminine in the original.

Scholars have experienced great difficulty when comparing Matthew's genealogy with Luke's. From Abraham to David the two lists agree, but after that the divergence is great. Also, the Luke account gives names in the reverse. Some have tried to account for the difference in change of purpose; others have endeavored to make Joseph the heir of Heli and Jacob, without too much success.

Godet makes a strong appeal for considering Luke's account as the genealogy of Mary.[2] In this way almost all difficulties are removed at once. It is interesting to note that the Talmud refers to Mary as the daughter of Heli.[3] Scofield follows this same line of thought:

> In Matthew, where unquestionably we have the genealogy of Joseph, we are told (1:16) that Joseph was the son of Jacob. In what sense, then, could he be called in Luke "the son of Heli"? He could not be by natural generation the son of both Jacob and of Heli. But in Luke it is not said that Heli *begat* Joseph, so the natural explanation is that Joseph was the son-in-law of Heli, who was, like himself, a descendant of David. That he should in that case be called "son of Heli" ("son" is not in the Greek, but rightly supplied by the translators) would be in accord with Jewish usage (cf. 1 Samuel 24:16). The conclusion is therefore inevitable that in Luke we have Mary's genealogy; and Joseph was "son of Heli" because espoused to Heli's daughter. The genealogy in Luke is Mary's, whose father, Heli, was descended from David.[4]

Further study of this problem requires some such genealogical arrangement in order to fulfill prophecies set forth in the book of Jeremiah. The prophet writes of King Coniah (Jeconiah, Jehoiachin), "Thus says the LORD, 'Write this man down as childless, a man who shall not prosper in his days; for none of his descendants shall prosper, sitting on the throne of David, and ruling anymore in Judah'" (Jeremiah 22:30). Jeremiah writes further of Jehoiakim, father of Coniah: "Therefore thus says the LORD concerning Jehoiakim king of Judah: He shall have no one to sit upon the

throne of David: and his dead body shall be cast out
to the heat of the day, and the frost of the night"
(36:30).

According to these prophecies, Christ could never
have reigned on the throne of David by virtue of His
descent through the line of Joseph because that line
was doomed. It is interesting to note that Luke traced
Mary's lineage to David through the line of Nathan,
against whom no curse was made. This accounts for
the difference of names in the two lists. Thus the
prophecy concerning Christ's Davidic lineage has been
fulfilled. He did come from the family of Jesse but
through a grandson whose posterity had not fallen
under God's condemnation.

The Virgin Birth

Another problem involved in the fulfillment of
prophecy relative to the birth of Christ is that of the
virgin birth. The King James Version states, "Behold,
a virgin shall conceive, and bear a son" (Isaiah 7:14).
Many scholars have long contended that the Hebrew
word here translated "virgin" *('almah)* means only "a
young married woman" or "a woman of marriageable
age." Brown, Driver, and Briggs do not help the conservative much, for they describe *'almah* as a "young
woman (ripe sexually; maid or newly married)."[5] The
Septuagint (Greek translation of the Old Testament)
does improve the situation. There the Greek is *par-
thenos,* which is the same word used in the original of
Matthew 1:23. Arndt and Gingrich give the meaning
of the word as "virgin"; and they note it may also be

used of men who have had no sexual intercourse with women.[6]

The answer to the problem is not found in the view that the term comes from a word meaning "to conceal," as some have suggested, though it is true that virgins led a concealed life; all recent expositors teach that the word comes from a similar verb meaning "to be strong." Others have sought in the past to solve the issue by a differentiation between *bethulah* (a young woman) and *'almah* (a virgin). But a study of Genesis 24:16 and 43 shows that those words can be used interchangeably.

In addition to the help provided by the Septuagint and Matthew 1:23, as noted above, the solution to the problem is to be found in the use of the Hebrew word *'almah* (translated "virgin" in Isaiah 7:14, A.V.) as it appears in the rest of the Old Testament. Bout-flower observes:

> The word occurs seven times in the Old Testament, and always of unmarried persons. (See Gen. xxiv. 43, Ex. ii 8, Ps. lxvii. 25, Prov. xxx. 19, Cant. 1.3, vi. 8, and the present passage.) We may reverently believe that in Isa. vii. 14 the prophet, led by the Spirit, uttered an oracle, which in its primary sense involved no miracle, whilst at the same time it was couched in such language as to suit the miraculous conception and birth of our Lord and Saviour Jesus Christ, in which events it found its second and grander fulfilment.[7]

There has been some question concerning the Proverbs passage mentioned above, however. Various

scholars have linked verses 19 and 20 and so made
the young woman an adulteress. Hengstenberg has
developed this problem sufficiently to show that the
maiden is not the renegade many have made her.[8]
Discoveries at Ras Shamra (ancient Ugarit) on the Syr-
ian coast also show that 'almah signifies "virgin."[9]

Some further insight will help clarify the situation.
First of all, if the Hebrew term in Isaiah 7:14 means
"virgin," so should its Greek equivalent in the Septuagint. If that is true, then the fulfillment of the prophecy, definitely mentioned as such in Matthew 1:23,
also speaks of a virgin and not just a marriageable girl
or a young married woman. Second, the woman
could not have been the prophetess (Isaiah's wife) as
some have claimed. Hardly could the Hebrew noun
apply to an older married woman; it could never be
stretched to mean more than a young married woman.
Also, it seems that the prophet would have referred to
his wife as either "my wife" or "the prophetess"
instead of in such vague terms. Third, the question
must be answered as to the time of fulfillment of this
prophecy. Three views have been suggested: (1) it
was to be immediate and in an ordinary way; (2) the
prophecy relates to two births, one at the present and
one later; (3) it refers to the Messiah (Jesus Christ).
The first idea is not in keeping with the context, which
demands something spectacular. The second is a possibility and should not be completely discarded. The
third would have been a real sign and encouragement
to the people. They were threatened with destruction;
the promise of a Savior at a future date would insure
that some of them would be left to receive Him and

that there would be a people left to redeem. With regard to the futurity of the coming of this Great One, Delitzsch points out that in Isaiah "behold" *(hineh)* always introduces something belonging to the future.[10]

In conclusion, it appears that the passage does refer to a virgin and not to the wife of Isaiah. From the nature of the verse and its context, it seems that the prophecy has a far off and spectacular fulfillment. This fulfillment is best accomplished in the Messiah—the Christ, at whose advent the prophecy is declared to be fulfilled, according to Matthew 1:23. The verse also speaks of the deity of Christ.

The Deity of the Messiah

The verse just considered provides one of the first references in Isaiah to the deity of the Messiah: "Behold, the virgin shall conceive and bear a son, and shall call His name Immanuel" (7:14b). Immanuel means "God with us." Of this One, Cook says: "The child must be such that the doctrine of God's presence with Israel (so long represented by the Shekinah) shall be realized in His person. The dignity of the child must not fall short of that assigned to Him in the prophet's own expansion of the name 'Immanuel' in ix. 6."[11] The direct fulfillment of this passage is noted in Matthew 1:22–23, where the evangelist says, "So all this was done that it might be fulfilled which was spoken by the Lord through the prophet, saying: 'Behold, the virgin shall be with child, and bear a Son, and they shall call his name Immanuel,' " which is translated,

"God with us." While Immanuel could hardly designate anything other than a divine child, the following passage is even more specific: "For unto us a child is born, unto us a son is given: and the government shall be upon his shoulder: and his name shall be called Wonderful, Counsellor [Wonder-Counsellor], The mighty God, The everlasting Father [Father of Eternity], The Prince of Peace" (Isaiah 9:6, KJV).

Such terms as *God* and *Everlasting Father* certainly speak of deity. They look forward to New Testament revelation concerning Christ. There the writers ascribe deity to Him, i.e., "The beginning of the gospel of Jesus Christ, the Son of God" (Mark 1:1). God speaks of Him, saying, "You are My beloved Son, in whom I am well pleased" (Mark 1:11). Christ claimed to be divine: "For I proceeded forth and came from God" (John 8:42). Other pertinent Scriptures include John 5:36–39; 6:29, 57; 7:28; 10:36; 11:42; 17:18, 21–25. Also, all through His earthly ministry, Christ acted as if He were God. His heavenly lineage also appears in John 1:1–3: "In the beginning was the Word, and the Word was with God, and the Word was God. He was in the beginning with God. All things were made through him, and without him was nothing made that was made." If it is true that "in the mouth of two witnesses it shall be established," then Christ, the Messiah, the Immanuel, certainly was divine.[12]

The Humanity of Christ

But Christ was also human. In the prophecies previously discussed, He was described as being *born*. The

New Testament fully reveals the nature of His human, earthly life and His death, burial, and resurrection—all connoting a human body.

Events of Christ's Early Life

Slaying of Bethlehem's Children

After Herod heard of the birth of Christ from the inquiring Magi, he ordered them to return to him with news of the child. But God overruled Herod's selfish request and sent the wise men home by a different way. Tricked, Herod decided to take matters into his own hands, that he might be rid of this supposed contender for his throne. He decreed that all infants of Bethlehem and its environs, two years old and under, be killed to satisfy his fiendish desires. Meanwhile Joseph had been warned to take his family to Egypt, so Jesus was spared. "Then was fulfilled that which was spoken by Jeremiah the prophet, saying, In Rama was there a voice heard, lamentation, and weeping, and great mourning, Rachel weeping for her children, and would not be comforted, because they are not" (Matthew 2:17–18, KJV; cf. Jeremiah 31:15).

Residence

The following verses could hardly be interpreted, at first glance, to refer to the location of residence of the coming Messiah:

Nevertheless the dimness shall not be such as was in her vexation, when at the first he lightly afflicted the land of Zebulun and the land of

Naphtali, and afterward did more grievously afflict her by the way of the sea, beyond Jordan, in Galilee of the nations. The people that walked in darkness have seen a great light: they that dwell in the land of the shadow of death, upon them hath the light shined (Isaiah 9:1–2).

The Holy Spirit does, however, interpret them in that way. Matthew records that, after the temptation, Jesus departed into Galilee. Then the evangelist remarks:

And leaving Nazareth, he came and dwelt in Capernaum, which is upon the sea coast, in the borders of Zebulun and Nephthali: That it might be fulfilled which was spoken by Esaias the prophet, saying, The land of Zebulun, and the land of Nephthali, by the way of the sea, beyond Jordan, Galilee of the Gentiles; The people which sat in darkness saw great light; and to them which sat in the region and shadow of death light is sprung up (Matthew 4:13–16, KJV).

The ministry of Christ in Galilee is related in numerous passages—Matthew 4:12–18:35; Mark 1:14–9:50; Luke 4:14–9:50; John 4:43–8:59. Obviously Christ spent much of His life in Galilee. Though Galilee was the headquarters of Christ during His ministry, it was also His home during His boyhood, the period of special consideration in this section. Joseph, as he returned from Egypt with his family, was warned of God and turned aside into Galilee. "And he came and dwelt in a city called Nazareth: that it might be fulfilled which was spoken by the prophets, He shall be called a Nazarene" (Matthew 2:23, KJV).

Preparation for Ministry

Ministry Announced

In addition to details concerning the early life of Christ, the major prophets also speak of preparation for His ministry on earth. First, the work of His forerunner is foretold:

> The voice of him that cries, in the wilderness Prepare the way of the Lord [Hebrew punctuation], make straight in the desert a highway for our God. Every valley shall be exalted, and every mountain and hill shall be made low: and the crooked shall be made straight, and the rough places plain (Isaiah 40:3–4, KJV).

In the ancient East, sovereigns sent heralds ahead to announce their coming; so God used the figure here: "prepare the way."

Who was the herald? The New Testament answers the question:

> In those days came John the Baptist, preaching in the wilderness of Judea, And saying, Repent, for the kingdom is at hand. For this is he that was spoken of by the prophet Esaias, saying, The voice of one crying in the wilderness, Prepare the way of the Lord, make his paths straight (Matthew 3:1–3, KJV).

Luke 3:4–5 also alludes to Isaiah 40:3 and adds the quotation of Isaiah 40:4—"Every valley shall be filled, and every mountain and hill shall be brought low; and the crooked shall be made straight, and the rough ways shall be made smooth." For further evidence of the fulfillment of this prophecy, see Matthew 11:10, cf. Malachi 3:1; Mark 1:2; Luke 7:27–28; and John 1:23.

Power of the Holy Spirit

Not only was the way to be prepared for Christ but He was to have a unique personal enduement for His ministry. Three passages especially refer to this:

> And the spirit of the LORD shall rest upon him, the spirit of wisdom and understanding, the spirit of counsel and might, the spirit of knowledge and of the fear of the LORD (Isaiah 11:2, KJV).[13]
>
> Behold my servant, whom I uphold; my elect, in whom my soul delights; I have put my spirit upon him: he shall bring forth judgment to the Gentiles (Isaiah 42:1, KJV).
>
> The Spirit of the Lord God is upon me; because the LORD hath anointed me to preach good tidings unto the meek (Isaiah 61:1, KJV).

The descent of the Spirit upon Christ is recorded in Matthew 3:16 (KJV):

> And Jesus, when he was baptized, went up straightway out of the water: and, lo, the heavens were opened unto him, and he saw the Spirit of God descending like a dove, and lighting upon

him (cf. Mark 1:10; Luke 3:22; John 1:32; Acts 10:38).

And in Luke 4:18 Jesus Himself testified, "The Spirit of the Lord is upon me." The results of the coming of the Spirit upon Christ, according to Isaiah 11:2, are evident in His earthly life.[14] He demonstrated supreme wisdom and understanding in dealing with such difficult situations as the woman taken in adultery, the question of rendering allegiance to Caesar, and the conversation with the woman at the well. The Spirit of might was upon Him; it was that Spirit by which He arose from the dead (1 Peter 3:18; Romans 8:11).

Scope of Ministry

After Jesus' preparation for His lifework, He entered upon a ministry very different in scope and nature from what the Jews expected of their Messiah. Their ideas centered mainly on a political deliverer; His involved spiritual deliverance. Their concern was for the Jewish nation; His included the rest of the world as well.

Isaiah characterized the general nature of Christ's ministry as follows:

> The Spirit of the Lord God is upon me; because the LORD hath anointed me to preach good tidings unto the meek; he has sent me to bind up the broken hearted, to proclaim liberty to the captives, and the opening of the prison to them that are bound; To proclaim the acceptable year of the LORD (61:1–2a; cf. Luke 4:18, KJV).

This passage describes preeminently a ministry of grace. His promises are peculiarly to the brokenhearted and to the captives taken by the god of this world. He opens blind eyes, imparting the true light. He proclaims the acceptable year of the Lord.

The ministry of Christ as described in the New Testament is so familiar that a demonstration of the way in which the verse quoted above fits His earthly ministry is hardly needed. Aside from Jesus' comment in Luke 4:18–21, perhaps the verse which most nearly answers to the Isaiah statement is Luke, KJV 7:22:

> Then Jesus answering said unto them, Go your way, and tell John what things you have seen and heard; how that the blind see, the lame walk, the lepers are cleansed, the deaf hear, the dead are raised, to the poor the gospel is preached (cf. Matthew 4:23; 9:35; Mark 1:38–39; Luke 8:1).

While Christ's ministry was bestowed largely on the Jews, He was also sent to the Gentiles:

> Behold my servant, whom I uphold; my elect, in whom my soul delights; I have put my spirit upon him: he shall bring forth judgment to the Gentiles . . . I the LORD have called you in righteousness, and will hold your hand, and will keep you, and give you for a covenant of the people, for a light of the Gentiles; To open the blind eyes, to bring out the prisoners from the prison, and them that sit in darkness out of the prison house (Isa. 42:1, 6–7, KJV).

That Christ had a worldwide compassion is evident in His ministry. He cast the demon from the Syrophoenician woman's daughter; He healed the centurion's son; He spoke parables indicating that the Gospel also would be preached among the Gentiles. Just before Christ ascended to Heaven He gave the command: "Go into all the world and preach the gospel to every creature" (Mark 16:15; cf. Matthew 28:19–20). Recognition of the Isaiah 42 prophecy and claim to its fulfillment are recorded in Matthew 12:17–18, 21, KJV):

> That it might be fulfilled which was spoken by Isaiah the prophet, saying, Behold my servant, whom I have chosen; my beloved in whom my soul is well pleased: I will put my spirit upon him, and he shall show judgment to the Gentiles. And in his name shall the Gentiles trust.

Other passages that refer to Christ's ministry to Gentiles include Matthew 15:21–28; Luke 2:10; John 10:16; Acts 1:8.

Character of Ministry

Meek and Lowly

As prophesied, the character of the Messiah's earthly ministry was to be meek and lowly, of a somewhat retiring nature, in direct contrast to His second advent. Urquhart well sums up Isaiah's picture of the Messiah in this respect:

They [the prophecies] speak of the patience of Jesus. There was to be no rude haste to snatch an early victory. He was to be no leader in tumultuous assault even upon wrong. "He shall not cry, nor lift up, nor cause his voice to be heard in the street" (Isa. 42:2). They tell of the lowliness of Jesus. The greatness of Christ was not to remove Him from us and shut Him up in a world of His own. There was to be might without its pride, wisdom without its haughty disdain, holiness without its blighting scorn of weakness and sin. "A bruised reed shall he not break, and the smoking flax shall he not quench" (Isa. 42:3). "He shall feed his flock like a shepherd, he shall gather the lambs in his arm, and carry them in his bosom, and shall gently lead those that give suck" (Isa. 40:11). Can we see the Redeemer more clearly in the Gospels themselves than He is revealed here? And if not, is not this fact alone enough to prove that He is God's gift to us? That life no man could have looked for, far less painted. It was an absolutely new experience for humanity. Its appearance caused a new departure in thought and morals. It revolutionized human ideas of greatness and excellence.[15]

Certainly the Gospels bear out this Old Testament picture of Christ. He very rarely asserted His kingly authority; there is little hint of the great potentate of Psalm 2.

Opposition and Rejection

In spite of the humility and tender love manifest in Christ's ministry, He met great opposition and hate on the part of His nation. Speaking of the Messiah, Isaiah uses the expression "to him whom man despises, to him whom the nation abhors" (49:7, KJV). *Nation* signifies the mass of the people; they hated him. The nation as a whole did reject Him, the leaders plotted against Him; the mobs yelled, "Crucify him!" The Lord Jesus felt this opposition keenly, as is evidenced in His denunciation of the cities of Galilee (Matthew 11:20–24), but more especially in His lament over Jerusalem: "O Jerusalem, Jerusalem, the one who kills the prophets and stones those who are sent to her! How often I wanted to gather your children together, as a hen gathers her chicks under her wings, but you were not willing!" (Matthew 23:37).

The Death of the Messiah

While the birth, life, and ministry of the Messiah are described by the prophets, other important prophecies concern His death. Christ was born to die, that His people might be redeemed and live. A suffering and dying Messiah was not the one for whom the Jews looked, however; their yearning was for a political strong man who would deliver them from the heel of foreign oppression. But God's ways were different. He knew that their spiritual needs were greater.

Since a large part of this section deals with Isaiah 53, it is necessary at the outset to discover the identity of the one or ones to whom the prophecy refers. The older Jewish interpretation of this passage admitted the messianic element, but the modern Jewish and liberal views apply it to the Jewish nation or the pious nucleus of the Jewish nation. In refutation of the modern position, Baron states:

> Here, too, as in chapter 42:1–9, where the ideal personal Servant of Jehovah is contrasted with the nation whose failure and unfaithfulness is depicted in verses 18–25 of the same chapter, His mission extends, not only to Israel, whom He is to raise up and restore, and to whom He is to be, not only the mediator, but the very embodiment of "the covenant" which shall be everlastingly established between them and their God, and is to be the light also of the Gentiles, and God's salvation unto the very ends of the earth.
>
> And as in chapters 42 and 49, so also in Isa. 53 itself, "Where the figure of the Servant of Jehovah unfolds its entire fullness of meaning," He is clearly and definitely distinguished from the nation.[16]

Other reasons which Baron gives as to why this can be no other than Christ are: (1) the subject of the prophecy is an innocent sufferer not worthy of death; (2) a voluntary sufferer; (3) an unresisting sufferer; (4) one whose sufferings end in death. None of these characteristics is to be found in the Jewish nation.[17] Eight New Testament quotations show that this chapter refers to the Messiah: Matthew 8:17; Mark 15:28; Luke 22:37; John 1:29; 12:38; Acts 8:28–35; Romans 10:16; 1 Peter 2:21–25. Further discussion on this point may be found in any detailed conservative commentary on Isaiah.

Purpose of Messiah's Death

The theme of Isaiah 53 is substitution: "He was wounded for our transgressions, he was bruised for our iniquities." Hodgkin remarks:

> Seven times we are told He has borne our sins:
> (1) Wounded for our transgressions; (2) Bruised for our iniquities; (3) The Lord hath laid on Him the iniquity of us all; (4) For the transgression of My people was the stroke upon Him; (5) Thou shalt make His soul an offering for sin; (6) He shall hear their inquities; (7) He bare the sin of many.[18]

While these phrases have to do with the Jews particularly, God broadens the application in His address to the Messiah in Isaiah 49:6: "I will also give You as a light to the Gentiles, That You should be My salvation to the ends of the earth."

Need there be any further discussion of the purpose for which Messiah died? Is it not clear? His followers may not have comprehended the value of such a seeming catastrophe; His enemies may have thought they were accomplishing their ends and getting rid of Him forever, and the crowds may not have understood Him, but God in His eternal counsels was laying "on him the iniquity of us all."

Some New Testament references demonstrate clearly how Christ in His death fulfilled this preview of Him.

1. "He was wounded for our transgressions" (Isaiah 53:5); "Christ also suffered once for sins, the just for the unjust" (1 Peter 3:18).

2. "And the LORD has laid on Him the iniquity of us all" (Isaiah 53:6); "He made Him who knew no sin to be sin for us" (2 Corinthians 5:21).

3. "For the transgressions of My people was he smitten" (Isaiah 53:8); "that Jesus would die for that nation" (John 11:51–52).

4. "When You make His soul an offering for sin" (Isaiah 53:10); "He who did not spare His own Son, but delivered Him up for us all" (Romans 8:32).

5. "For He shall bear their iniquities" (Isaiah 53:11); "who Himself bore our sins in His own body on the tree" (1 Peter 2:24).

6. "He bore the sin of many" (Isaiah 53:12); "Christ was once offered to bear the sins of many" (Hebrews 9:28).

Treatment of the Accused

When the Messiah died He underwent a great deal of suffering. This may be divided into two classes: suffering at the hands of men and suffering at the hand of God. The former was largely physical, while the latter was mostly spiritual. Chafer has well said:

> Human hands might inflict physical suffering and death as any victim would die, but only the hand of God could make Christ a sin offering, or could lay on Him the iniquity of others (2 Corinthians 5:21; Isaiah 53:6) . . . Had Pontius Pilate been moved with superhuman compassion for lost souls and had he crucified the Saviour with that in view, he could have done no more than to

crucify Him. God alone might provide a sinbearer and God alone could impute sin to the One He provided.[19]

Suffering at the Hands of Men

Isaiah 50:6 provides the first three elements in Christ's suffering: (1) "I gave my back to those who struck Me," (2) "and My cheeks to those who plucked out the beard;" (3) "I did not hide My face from shame and spitting." Many verses show the fulfillment of the first point, but two will suffice here: "Then they spat in his face and beat him; and others struck Him with the palms of their hands" (Matthew 26:67). "And when he had scourged Jesus, he delivered him to be crucified" (Matthew 27:26). Concerning the second point Fausset says, "To 'pluck the hair [beard]' is the highest insult that can be offered an Oriental"[20] (cf. 2 Samuel 10:4; Lamentations 3:30). Though the second prophecy does not have a literal fulfillment mentioned in Scripture, it may be assumed that the event occurred. Jesus said: "Behold, we are going up to Jerusalem, and all things that are written by the prophets concerning the Son of Man will be accomplished" (Luke 18:31). Of the third prophecy Fausset remarks, "To spit in another's presence is an insult in the East, much more on one; most of all, in the face."[21] Job 30:10 and Matthew 27:30 may be noted in point. Matthew 26:67, quoted above, records the fulfillment of this prediction. A number of other New Testament passages mention the fact.

Three other events in the sufferings of the Messiah are found in Isaiah 53: The first speaks of His rejection

by man: "He is despised and rejected by men" (v. 3).
In fulfillment the New Testament answers: "He came
to his own and his own did not receive him" (John
1:11). The second recounts more physical suffering:
"But He was wounded for our transgressions, He was
bruised for our iniquities . . ." (Isaiah 53:5). Hardly
any reference to Christ's physical sufferings is necessary: it is usually the physical torture which evangelists
and preachers emphasize, to the exclusion of the spiritual. Matthew records:

> And they stripped him, and put on him a scar-
> let robe. And when they had platted a crown of
> thorns, they put it upon his head, and a reed in
> his right hand: and they bowed the knee before
> him, and mocked him, saying, Hail, King of the
> Jews! And they spit upon him, and they took
> the reed, and smote him on the head (27:28–30,
> KJV).

The third prophecy of suffering inflicted by men occurs in verse 8: "He was taken from prison and from
judgment." He was taken from prison and judgment
by death. Judgment here refers to the judicial proceed-
ings, in which He was put on trial, accused, and
convicted as worthy of death. In other words, His
unjust judgment, hostile oppression, and judicial
prosecution were the circumstances out of which He
was carried away by death. The trial and imprisonment
of Christ are well-known New Testament events.
Other prophecies concerning Jesus' suffering at the
hands of men include His betrayal by a friend (Psalm

41:9; cf. John 13:18–19), the betrayal price of thirty
pieces of silver (Zechariah 11:12; cf. Matthew 26:15),
the return of the betrayal money when the betrayer
grew remorseful over his misdeed (Zechariah 11:13;
cf. Matthew 27:7–10), and being forsaken by His
disciples (Zechariah 13:7; cf. Matthew 26:56).

Suffering at the Hand of God

Great though the suffering imposed by man must
have been, the suffering imposed on Christ by God
was far greater. Becoming sin for the race was the
extreme of suffering. Two verses speak of this especially: ". . . and the LORD has laid on Him the iniquity
of us all" (Isaiah 53:6). The New Testament answers,
"He made him who knew no sin to be sin for us"
(2 Corinthians 5:21). Delitzsch says of the Hebrew for
iniquity that it:

> is not merely iniquity, but the guilt it entails, and
> the punishment it produces; the whole multitude
> of sins, mass of guilt, and weight of punishment,
> came, by the arrangement of the God of salvation,
> whose grace is enshrined in holiness, upon the
> servant of Jahve.[22]

No one will ever comprehend what it meant for Christ
to bear the world's load of sin in His own body on the
tree.

Another prophecy about God's infliction of suffering is in Isaiah 53:10: "Yet it pleased the LORD to
bruise him." The significance of this passage is that,
while men carried on the actual afflicting of the Mes-

siah, God was behind the scenes controlling it all. Delitzsch remarks:

> It was men who inflicted on the servant of God such crushing suffering, such deep pain; but the highest *causa efficiens* in all was God, who made the sins of men subservient to His own will and decree. The suffering of His servant was destined to be for the latter the way to glory; this his way through suffering to glory was destined to establish a community of redeemed ones, originating from him; it was to be the beginning of the execution of the divine plan of salvation, a plan henceforth to be carried out by the servant in his future life of unceasing action.[23]

New Testament echoes of Isaiah 53:10 are found in Romans 8:32 and John 3:16.

Attitude and Description of the Accused

Attitude

Evident in the sufferings and death of the Messiah was His willingness to perform the task to which He was sent. He gave Himself to punishment (Isaiah 50:6). A later statement says, "He poured out his soul unto death" (Isaiah 53:12). Reflecting this attitude on the part of Christ, the author of Hebrews writes, "Then said he, Behold, I have come to do Your will, O God" (10:9). A third indication of the attitude of the accused appears in Isaiah 53:12: "He . . . made intercession for the transgressors." What greater demonstration could the Messiah give of His utter selflessness and concern for the mission He came to perform?

Luke records the fulfillment of this verse: Then said Jesus, "Father, forgive them, for they do not know what they do" (23:34).

Description

First of all, the Messiah may be characterized by His reaction to the situations He met: "a Man of sorrows and acquainted with grief" (Isaiah 53:3). "A Man of sorrows" signifies heart-sorrow in all forms, one whose distinguishing characteristic was sorrow. Being "acquainted with grief" means an associate, one familiar with grief by constant contact with it. The Hebrew for *grief* is really a term for sickness, yet Christ was not sick in the sense that He had a sick body. Delitzsch says it:

> is not that he had a feeble body, falling out of one sickness into another; but that the wrath evoked by sin, and the ardour of his self–sacrifice (Psalm 69:10), consumed him, in soul and body, like a fever; so that, although he had not died a violent death, he would have succumbed to the violence of those destructive forces, which sin has domesticated in humanity, and of his own self-consuming struggles against them.[24]

Another indication that grief was always close to Jesus is seen in Luke 19:41: "Now as He drew near, He saw the city and wept over it." Christ was not a morbid person, but He keenly felt the sin and degradation of the people, more so because of the perfection which He Himself was. Then, too, He never lost sight of the great mission which He had come to perform.

Second, the Messiah's submission was also prophesied. "He was oppressed and He was afflicted, yet He opened not His mouth; He was led as a lamb to the slaughter, and as a sheep before its shearers is silent, so He opened not his mouth" (Isaiah 53:7).

Matthew and Peter provide New Testament fulfillments of this prophecy:

> And while he was being accused by the chief priests and elders, He answered nothing. Then said Pilate to Him, "Do You not hear how many things they testify against You?" But He answered him not one word, so that the governor marveled greatly (Matthew 27:12–14).
>
> Who when he was reviled, reviled not again; when he suffered, he threatened not (1 Peter 2:23, KJV).

Third, the moral character of the Messiah was also prophesied, ". . . He had done no violence, nor was any deceit in His mouth" (Isaiah 53:9). The New Testament records the absolutely spotless life of Christ in many passages. In one, a Gentile attests: "When Pilate saw that he could prevail nothing, but rather a tumult was made, he took water, and washed his hands before the multitude, saying, I am innocent of the blood of this just person; see ye to it" (Matthew 27:24, KJV).

Death of Christ

In addition to the facts noted above, Isaiah makes several prophecies about events surrounding the Messiah's death. The appearance of the dying one is first of all. "His visage was marred more than any man, and His form more than the sons of man" (Isaiah 52:14). The true significance of the Hebrew here is that His visage was so marred that one could scarcely recognize Him. In fact, it was so marred that it could be said He no longer looked like a man. Likewise, His body was so disfigured that it did not look like the form of man. While the New Testament does not describe the face of Christ as He hung on the Cross, one can imagine His physical condition after the inflictions described in Matthew 26:67–68; 27:27–30.

Another prophecy concerns the companions of Christ at His death. Isaiah foresees: "And he made his grave with the wicked" (53:9, KJV); "and he was numbered with the transgressors" (53:12, KJV). This was fulfilled at Christ's death: "With Him they also crucified two robbers; the one on His right and the other on His left" (Mark 15:27).

Also, it was declared that the Messiah would make His grave with the rich in His death (Isaiah 53:9). Some modern scholars have sought to explain the Hebrew for *rich* as being synonymous with the original for *wicked,* which appears in the previous clause; but a large number of them have rejected this identification as untenable. Certainly New Testament references demonstrate the incorrectness of this identification. The fulfillment of this prophecy is particularly interesting, for, in the words of Delitzsch,

If we reflect that the Jewish rulers would have given to Jesus the same dishonourable burial as to the two thieves, but that the Roman authorities handed over the body to Joseph the Arimathaean, a "rich man" (Matthew 27:57), who placed it in the sepulchre in his own garden, we see an agreement at once between the gospel history and the prophetic words, which could only be the work of the God of both the prophecy and its fulfillment, inasmuch as no suspicion could possibly arise of there having been any human design of bringing the former into conformity with the latter.[25]

Christ's burial attests to the reality of His death, and consequently, to the reality of His resurrection; for where there was no true death there could be no true resurrection. But before we move on to the resurrection, let us note several other prophecies in Zechariah and Psalms concerning Jesus' death. Prediction is made concerning the piercing of His hands and feet (Psalm 22:16; cf. Luke 23:33; John 20:25), the piercing of His side (Zechariah 12:10; cf. John 19:34–37), the parting of His garments and casting lots for His cloak (Psalm 22:18; cf. John 19:23–24), the fact that His bones were not broken (Psalm 34:20; cf. John 19:33, 36), and His cry of forsakenness, "My God, my God, why have You forsaken me?" (Psalm 22:1; cf. Matthew 27:46).

The Resurrection of Christ

The resurrection of the Messiah is also intimated in Isaiah 53:

Yet it pleased the LORD to bruise Him; He has put Him to grief. When You make His soul an offering for sin, He shall see His seed, He shall prolong His days, and the pleasure of the LORD shall prosper in His hand (v. 10).

The phrases "His seed" and "prolong His days" are the type of language which requires resurrection of the Messiah. Of the first Baron says:

The Messiah's "seed," of which the spirit of prophecy speaks here, is the glorious *spiritual* progency which He has begotten with "the travail of His soul," and the new family which He came to found, and which sprang, so to say, at His resurrection out of His empty tomb, is the new "seed of Israel," or the Household of Faith. This spiritual "seed"—the "bringing of many sons into glory"—was the chief joy which was set before Him, for the sake of which He endured the cross, despising the shame. [26]

Psalm 16:10 also predicts the resurrection of the Messiah: "For You will not leave my soul in Sheol, neither will You allow Your Holy One to see corruption." Fulfillment is referred to in Acts 2:25–31.

Truly marvelous has been the fulfillment of prophecy, even to the minutest details, relating to the first advent of Christ. Chafer notes that upwards of three hundred detailed predictions concerning Christ were fulfilled by His first advent. [27] Certainly this presents a tremendous argument for the inspiration and veracity of Scripture.

NOTES

1. E. W. Hengstenberg, *Christology of the Old Testament* (Edinburgh: T. & T. Clark, 1878), II, 101.

2. Louis M. Sweet, "The Genealogy of Jesus Christ," *International Standard Bible Encyclopedia,* 2nd Edition, II, 1198.

3. *Ibid.*

4. C. I. Scofield, editor, The Scofield Reference Bible (New York: Oxford University Press, 1909), pp. 1075–76.

5. F. Brown, S. R. Driver, and C. A. Briggs, *A Hebrew and English Lexicon of the Old Testament* (Boston: Houghton Mifflin Company, 1891), p. 761.

6. William F. Arndt and F. Wilber Gingrich, *A Greek-English Lexicon of the New Testament* (Chicago: University of Chicago Press, 1957), p. 632.

7. Charles Boutflower, *The Book of Isaiah, Chapters I–XXXIX* (London: Society for Promoting Christian Knowledge, 1930), p. 47.

8. Hengstenberg, *op. cit.,* pp. 46–47.

9. Robert Dick Wilson, *A Scientific Investigation of the Old Testament,* revised by Edward Young (Chicago: Moody Press, 1958), Appendix 2*b.*

10. Franz Delitzsch, *Biblical Commentary on the Prophecies of Isaiah* (New York: Funk & Wagnalls, *n.d.*), I, 174.

11. F. C. Cook, editor, *The Holy Bible with an Explanatory and Critical Commentary* (New York: Scribner, Armstrong & Co., 1875), p. 80.

12. A good treatment of the deity of the Messiah may be found in Hengstenberg, *op. cit.,* IV. 282–331.

13. That this verse refers to Christ is evident because it speaks of the Branch of verse one, whom previous study has identified as the Messiah.

14. The fact that the Spirit came upon Christ in some

special sense at the entrance upon His public ministry probably does not mean that He was without the ministry of the Spirit before. If John the Baptist was filled with the Spirit from birth, could we expect less in the life of Christ?

15. John Urquhart, *Wonders of Prophecy* (London: Pickering & Inglis, 1939), pp. 152–53.

16. David Baron, *The Servant of Jehovah* (New York: George H. Doran Company, 1921), p. 37.

17. *Ibid.* p. 38.

18. A. M. Hodgkin, *Christ in All the Scriptures* (London: Alfred Holness, 1914), p. 150.

19. Lewis Sperry Chafer, *Systematic Theology* (Dallas: Dallas Seminary Press, 1948), III, 51.

20. Robert Jamieson, A. R. Fausset, and David Brown, *A Commentary on the Old and New Testaments* (Philadelphia: J. B. Lippincott & Co., 1866). III, 722.

21. *Loc. cit.*

22. Delitzsch, *op. cit.,* p. 287.

23. *Ibid.* p. 295.

24. *Ibid.* p. 281.

25. *Ibid.* p. 115.

26. *Ibid.* p. 122.

27. Chafer, *op. cit.,* p. 117.

ELEVEN

The Present Ministry of Christ

FOR many, the story of Jesus Christ virtually ends with His resurrection and ascension. Though they may have a vague idea of the return of Christ and His judgment of the world at some future time, they often fail to recognize what Christ is doing now. While it is impossible for us to peer into the remotest recesses of heaven to observe Christ's present work, we can learn much about it from the nine names or descriptives which Scripture applies to Him in connection with this work. Of these, one (priest) refers primarily to His work in heaven; the other eight have to do largely with His work on earth: king, prophet, shepherd, vine, head of the Church, the stone, last Adam, and bridegroom.

Since Christ is Deity, He is everywhere present, because omnipresence is an attribute of Deity. That He is spiritually present, especially among believers today, is further obvious from such statements as "Christ in you, the hope of glory" (Colossians 1:27); "Lo, I am with you always, even unto the end of the age" (Matthew 28:20); and "If a man love me, he will keep my words: and my Father will love him, and we will come to him, and make Our home with him" (John 14:23). Because Christ is spiritually present everywhere, He can continue great works on earth, though bodily present in heaven.

Priest

Foundational to the rest of Christ's present ministry is His priesthood. According to Hebrew religious institutions, a priest was one duly constituted to minister in sacred things—to offer sacrifices and, on the basis of those sacrifices, to serve as a mediator between man and God. Christ was constituted a priest by God Himself (Hebrews 5:4–10), made a perfect sacrifice (Himself) that would suffice for all sin for all time (Hebrews 7:27; 9:26), and now continuously intercedes (Hebrews 7:25; Romans 8:3–4) and advocates (1 John 2:1) on behalf of believers.

Priestly Advocate

That we need an advocate or defense attorney is obvious from such a passage as Revelation 12:10, where Satan is called the accuser of the brethren. It would appear from this verse that Satan now has access to the throne of God, where he levels accusations against sinning saints in an effort to destroy their salvation. But Christ as our attorney pleads our case, demonstrating that He has already paid the penalty which Satan now demands. The one who has received Christ has benefited by the sacrifice of Christ for all sins (before or after salvation, 1 John 2:2), and the decision of the Supreme Judge of the universe can only be, "Case dismissed!" That the foregoing description of the heavenly tribunal is not a mere figment of the imagination is demonstrated by Romans 8:33–34, where an attack upon and a defense of the believer is implied: "Who shall bring a charge against God's elect? It is

God who justifies. Who is he who condemns? It is Christ who died, and furthermore is also risen, who is even at the right hand of God, who also makes intercession for us."[1]

Priestly Friend

Christ also prays for us as a solicitous Friend. Two verses in Hebrews show how He succors us or lends a helping hand: "For we have not an high priest which cannot be touched with the feeling of our infirmities; but was in all points tempted like as we are, yet without sin" (4:15, KJV); "For in that he himself has suffered being tempted, he is able to succour them that are tempted" (2:18, KJV). Evidently, Christ prays for the keeping power of God to be exercised on behalf of His disciples and for those who in the future should believe on Him (John 17:6–26).

Also, His statement to Peter (that though Satan had desired to sift Peter as wheat, He had prayed for Peter that his faith fail not) in Luke 23:31–32 is another indication of Christ's prayer for us. It should be a great comfort to us that the prayers of Christ as very God would hardly be denied by God the Father. Furthermore, Christ in His omniscience would always pray in the perfect will of the Father. The keeping and protecting care of God is noted in the beautiful benediction of Jude: "Now unto him that is able to keep you from falling [stumbling], and to present you faultless before the presence of his glory with exceeding joy, To the only wise God our Saviour, be glory and majesty, dominion and power, both now and ever. Amen" (Jude 24–25, KJV).

Prophet

While the prophetic work of Christ was prominent during His years of public ministry, it continues during the present age—through the agency of the Holy Spirit. During our Lord's conversation with His disciples before His betrayal, He told them that He still had much to teach them but they were not yet prepared for those deeper truths. Therefore, after the ascension, the Holy Spirit would come to continue this instructional ministry—imparting to them the message of Christ (John 16:12–15). In this connection, it should be remembered that prophecy includes both forthtelling (proclaiming the truth) and foretelling (predicting the future), and that the emphasis in the New Testament is on the former.

King

Christ offered Himself as king to Israel during His public ministry, but He was rejected. This does not mean, however, that He will not one day rule on the throne of David in Jerusalem. Meanwhile, even though Christ is not on the throne of David, He does sit at the right hand of the Father and exercise a great deal of authority. According to Ephesians 1:20–22, He has been exalted above all principality, power, might, and dominion, and God has put all things under His feet. Philippians 2:9–11 affirms this. Of course it should be recognized that some of this dominion is potential rather than actual at the present time; but Christ now has tremendous power over the universe. In fact, Colossians 1:17 states that through Him the universe holds together (literal translation).

Head of the Church

The New Testament also speaks of Jesus Christ as Lord or Head of the Church, which is His Body (Ephesians 1:22–23; 5:23–24; Colossians 1:18). So, while He is viewed as head of the organism, He is also part of it. As a head directs a human body, Christ rules over the Church. Individual members of the Church are likened to the foot, hand, eye, and ear—all having an important part to play in the effective functioning of the organism (1 Corinthians 12:4–27). Moreover, Christ, like a human head, is the means of nourishing the body (Colossians 2:19). As ruler over the Church, Christ also presents her with gifted leaders: apostles, prophets, evangelists, pastors, and teachers (Ephesians 4:11–12), for the perfecting of the saints. In this connection, we know He also has a part in bestowing the spiritual gifts mentioned in 1 Corinthians 12.

Last Adam

As the Last Adam (1 Corinthians 15:45) or the Second Adam (1 Corinthians 15:47), Christ is contrasted with the first Adam. The primary emphasis, however, concerns the relation of both Adams to their posterity. The first Adam transmitted physical life with all of its tendencies to sin and death to his posterity (1 Corinthians 15:22; Romans 5:12), while Christ as a "quickening spirit" constantly imparts spiritual life to all who place their faith in Him (1 Corinthians

15:22, 45; Romans 5:15–21). While one in the first Adam is dead in sin and possesses a body subject to death and corruption, the one in Christ possesses a new divine nature that will some day be placed in an incorruptible body (1 Corinthians 15).

Shepherd

As the Good Shepherd, Christ laid down His life for His sheep (John 10:11, 15), and on that basis He has been busy seeking and saving lost sheep ever since (v. 16). Whenever lost ones by saving faith become members of the divine flock, they can expect the continual watchcare of the Shepherd. This interest in believers on the part of Christ closely relates to His high priestly intercession on their behalf. The Shepherd's watchcare particularly involves the leading of our Lord (John 10:3–4, 27). Believers, like sheep, are dependent on the Shepherd for guidance in right paths, for protection from evil, and for provision for daily needs.

The Vine

On the way to the Garden of Gethsemane, Jesus gave a beautiful message on fellowship with Himself by analogy with the vine and the branches (John 15). In it He described Himself as the true vine—the source of life for its branches. The true branches are so related to Christ that they continually experience divine life flowing through them, which produces spiritual fruit. This fruit may be considered in a general sense as success in witnessing and edifying the Church or in a specific sense as the sevenfold fruit mentioned in

Galatians 5:22–23 (love, joy, peace, etc.). The passage itself (John 15) indicates that abiding in Christ brings fruitfulness (v. 5), great joy (v. 11), and effectiveness in prayer (v. 16). The disciples are warned, however, that a fruitful plant is occasionally pruned that it might become more fruitful; therefore they may expect some corrective experiences that will ultimately result in a more productive spiritual life.

On the other hand, unfruitful branches are severely judged (v. 6). Exactly what this judgment is has been a matter of controversy and does not concern us here. The emphasis in the chapter focuses on abiding in Christ, with resultant fruitbearing, and on the fact that Christ is the source of life and enablement for believers. It is vital to Christians who aspire to victorious living that they come to grips with Christ's pronouncement, "Without me you can do nothing" (John 15:5*b*).

The Rock

The New Testament frequently describes Christ as a rock or stone. He is called the foundation (1 Corinthians 3:11–15), the chief cornerstone (Ephesians 2:20; 1 Peter 2:6), a living stone (1 Peter 2:4–8), a stumblingstone (1 Corinthians 1:23; Romans 9:32–33; 1 Peter 2:8), and a stone of judgment (Matthew 21:44). The first three apply more particularly to Christ's present ministry than do the others. As the foundation, He is the one upon whom we rest for salvation and upon whom the spiritual building of the Church depends. As the cornerstone, Christ gives significance and symmetry to the structure. As the living stone, He imparts life to the individual stones of the building. The figure of the living stone and the stones of the building bears a message similar to that of the head and the body and the vine and the branches. The spiritual house (the Church) is in view in all three. Members, branches, and stones have life as they are related to Christ, the source of life. In each case the same divine life animates the whole and together the parts form a living unity. Moreover, the individual members, branches, and stones all have a necessary and significant part to play in the functioning of the whole organism.

The Bridegroom

On a number of occasions Christ referred to Himself as the Bridegroom and believers as the bride (Matthew 9:15; 25:1, 5–6, 10; Mark 2:19–20; John 3:29). Paul supplements these references by likening the relation of Christ and the Church to the relation of husband and wife (Ephesians 5:21–32). This figure looks to the future much more than the others mentioned in this chapter. And it has in view the love of Christ for the Church and a new future unity of the Church not yet realized—when all members will be gathered in one place and when the bride will be taken to her new home.

As the Bridegroom, Christ is now engaging in two activities. First, He is preparing a place for the bride (John 14:2). When the Bridegroom returns to take the bride to her new home, He will surprise and please her with a beautiful and perfect dwelling place. A question might be raised as to why it would take Christ so long to prepare a place for us and why He should delay His coming on that account. Perhaps the answer is found in the second activity of Christ as the Bridegroom: He is preparing the bride for her place, sanctifying and cleansing the Church (Ephesians 5:26), "That He might present her to himself a glorious church, not having spot or wrinkle or any such thing, but that she should be holy and without blemish" (Ephesians 5:27). Here an extended time element is involved. In the first place, He withholds judgment while individuals receive Him by faith and become members of the bride. Second, since He works with obstinate human wills, a greater lapse of time will be required to achieve His purposes.

Conclusion

Of course it is impossible for finite minds to come to a complete understanding of the infinite glories of the work of the divine Trinity. But God never leaves us completely in the dark concerning Himself or His works. These nine New Testament descriptions of the work of Christ in relation to believers in the present age at least give us a glimpse of what He is now doing.

NOTE

1. Job 1 and 2 also indicate that Satan has access to God and that he does accuse or condemn believers before the Father.

TWELVE

The Future Activity of Christ

IMMEDIATELY after Jesus delivered the shocking news to His disciples that He was about to leave them, He promised that He would return: "And if I go and prepare a place for you, I will come again, and receive you to Myself; that where I am, there you may be also" (John 14:3). Commenting on the ascension, Luke asserted, "This same Jesus, who was taken up from you into heaven, will so come in like manner as you saw Him go into heaven" (Acts 1:11). Paul declared, "For the Lord Himself will descend from heaven with a shout, with the voice of an archangel, and with the trumpet of God" (1 Thessalonians 4:16). John exulted, "Behold, He is coming with clouds, and every eye will see Him, even they who pierced Him. And all the tribes of the earth will mourn because of Him" (Revelation 1:7).

While Scripture is clear in proclaiming the return of Christ, it is equally clear that when He comes a resurrection and judgment will occur. Jesus Himself said, "For the hour is coming in which all who are in the graves shall hear His voice and come forth—those who have done good, to the resurrection of life, and those who have done evil, to the resurrection of condemnation" (John 5:28–29). John also prophesied, "The sea gave up the dead who were in it, and Death and Hades delivered up the dead who were in them. And they were judged, each one according to his works" (Revelation 20:13).

Concerning the facts of the second coming, a resurrection, and a judgment, Christians are generally agreed. But in explaining the meaning of these, they diverge greatly. Many do not follow a literal interpretation of the Bible's prophecies about future events and therefore deny a literal Tribulation and Millennium. Of these, some are known as amillennialists and others postmillennialists. The latter regard the Tribulation symbolically, usually holding that prophecies in Revelation concerning the Tribulation have already been fulfilled. They view the Millennium as a utopian era of indefinite length that comes as the result of a triumph of the Gospel throughout the world; it will be followed by the return of Christ, a general resurrection, and judgment.

The former generally agree with the postmillennialists concerning the Tribulation, but they disagree on the Millennium, denying any literal golden age on earth. Sometimes they hold that whatever Millennium exists is experienced by believers in heaven now, protected as they are from the power of Satan and sin. Christ could return at any time for a general resurrection and a general judgment. Premillennialists, however, hold to a literal interpretation of prophecies concerning the Tribulation and Millennium. Moreover, they do not lump all the judgments and resurrections into one but see an order of events in prophecy. In all of those events, Christ assumes a position of preeminence.

To the writer, the premillennial position seems to be the one that can be most effectively defended from Scripture. In the first place, consistency in biblical interpretation demands it. On what basis can one view the prophecies of Christ's first coming literally but spiritualize away even the general teachings concerning His second coming? Second, as far as the Tribulation is concerned (and a literal Tribulation is part of the premillennial system), Christ Himself spoke in unequivocal language about a coming Tribulation, after which He would return to the earth (Matthew 24—25). Paul paralleled our Lord's message with his description of the day of the Lord, to be followed by the Lord's coming (2 Thessalonians 2:1–12) and His kingdom.

If we admit a literal Millennium, a literal Tribulation, both pre- and posttribulation comings of Christ, and in general a literal interpretation of Scripture, we are ready to outline the future ministry of Christ. (For discussion of these end-times events, see the Appendix.)

1. Next on the prophetic calendar, then, is the rapture of the Church, which includes both living and dead believers. All will be caught up to meet the Lord in the air and will receive new incorruptible bodies. In heaven believers will stand before the judgment seat of Christ, where rewards for Christian service will be given (1 Thessalonians 4:13–18; 1 Corinthians 15:51–57; John 14:2–3; 1 Corinthians 3:12–15; 9:16–27; 2 Corinthians 5:9–11).

2. Then the Tribulation will occur. During this period, described in Revelation 4–19 and Matthew 24, Christ will be instrumental in bringing much, if not all, of the terrible judgments on the earth. He opens the seals (Revelation 6:1, 3, 5, 7, 9, 12)

and may be responsible for giving the order to the angels to pour out the seven vials of wrath (16:1).

3. At the end of the Tribulation Christ will return to earth. His first act apparently will be to destroy the forces of evil in the war of Armageddon (Revelation 19:11–19; cf. 16:16; Matthew 24:27–31; 25:31). This is accompanied by His destruction of the man of sin (2 Thessalonians 2:1–12) and the judgment of the beast and false prophet (Revelation 19:20). The binding of Satan may also occur at this point (Revelation 20:2–3).

4. Then everyone on earth is gathered before the Lord for judgment. Those judged righteous (sheep) enter the Kingdom (the Millennium). Those judged unrighteous (goats) are cast into everlasting punishment, prepared for the devil and his angels. The basis of judgment is treatment of the "brethren," probably Jews. But we should not conclude that befriending a Jew during the Tribulation period merits salvation. No doubt it will be such a risky business that only believers will do it; therefore it becomes an evidence of salvation (Matthew 25:31–46).

5. The judgment over, the Millennium is ushered in. During this period Christ will rule the earth from Jerusalem, perhaps as a kind of international capital. As noted above, this period will be characterized by peace, prosperity, justice, a rejuvenation of nature, a removal of animosity in the animal kingdom, and knowledge of the truth of God.

6. At the end of the Millennium Satan is released and gathers himself a host of opponents to the truth, described as Gog and Magog.

7. After the battle of Gog and Magog and the final doom of Satan (Revelation 20:7–10), the great white throne judgment will take place (Revelation 20:1–15). Probably Christ will be the judge,[1] and He will deal with people according to their works. Seemingly the dead raised here are only the wicked dead. If believers are raised at the rapture (1 Thessalonians 4:13–18) and Tribulation martyrs are raised at the end of the Tribulation (Revelation 20:4), we may conclude that these are wicked dead. Of course it is possible that some believers of the Millennium will be involved in this judgment, but there does not seem to be any reason for the death of an individual during the Millennium unless he openly rebels against the rule of Christ. At any rate, there is nothing said of the destiny of believers after the great white throne judgment—only of unbelievers.

8. Following this judgment, the old heavens and earth flee away and the new heavens and new earth are created.

9. Then the new Jerusalem, beautiful beyond description, comes down out of heaven. In it the Father and the Son are the center of worship (Revelation 21:22), the Lamb is the source of light (Revelation 21:23), and from the throne of the Father and the Son flows the river of life (Revelation 22:1). Christ as Alpha and Omega (the beginning and the ending, Revelation 22:13), rules forever in the New Jerusalem.

Although it is good for Christians to discover the details of the prophetic scheme and therefore to know the future ministry of Christ, the most important event for them is the rapture of the saints. To Christians, the Lord's coming should be a purifying hope and a stimulus to service. Perhaps it would be well for us to close this discussion of the future as John closed his: "He who testifies to these things says, 'Surely I am coming quickly.' Amen. Even so, come, Lord Jesus" (Revelation 22:20).

NOTE

1. "The throne" should be read for "God" in Revelation 20:12.

THIRTEEN

Walking as Christ Walked

JOHN urged, "He who says he abides in Him ought himself also to walk just as He walked" (1 John 2:6). Note that John addressed the one who "says he abides in Him." That is, his message is for the Christian, and especially for the Christian who maintains a daily fellowship with Christ. Many believers feel that this is an impossible exhortation. Christ was in a class by Himself. He was divine. How can we ever approach the standard of perfection set by Him?

Remember, Jesus was also human and that He lived in the power of the Holy Spirit: "The Spirit of the Lord is upon me, because he has anointed me to preach the gospel to the poor; he has sent me to heal the brokenhearted, to preach deliverance to the captives, and recovering of sight to the blind, to set at liberty them that are bruised" (Luke 4:18, KJV). The believer is indwelt by the same Holy Spirit and therefore has, up to a point at least, the same potential for holy living as Christ Himself. The fact that one will never attain the perfect standard set by Christ's example should not deter his striving in that direction. Inability to achieve a high standard does not stop a student from seeking to emulate a great scholar, or a political novice from following in the steps of a great diplomat. Nor should it prevent a Christian from pursuing the example of his Lord.

Christ's World and Life View

Before we note Christ's relations with others as a pattern for the believer's walk, we should seek to discover the attitudes which motivated Him in those relationships. They were part of His world and life view.

Regarding God

1. To begin with, Christ anchored His faith in an unquestioning acceptance of the existence of God as full appreciation of His nature. Consequently He spoke of God's holiness, love, mercy, justice, and the importance of His purposes and will.
2. He viewed humanity as a creation of God fashioned in His image; therefore He recognized the dignity of the human personality. Human welfare was more important than the mere keeping of a law or tradition. The rehabilitation of humanity was the supreme goal of His ministry.
3. Christ possessed a thorough perception of sin and its effects and the disorder of the world. Human beings were helpless without divine enablement and experienced an incompleteness without Him.
4. Christ repeatedly emphasized the importance of the incarnation and the death, burial, and resurrection of the Son of Man.

Regarding People

In His dealings with men and women, Christ was never impressed with their station in life. He was never deferential because He saw all equally lost before God.

Their wealth, social position, religiosity, and culture counted nothing toward their legal standing before God. But neither was Jesus interested in running them down; rather, He wanted to raise them to higher levels. To Him, the tax collectors and sinners were not to be shunned and further repressed but to be born anew in the Kingdom of God. The woman taken in adultery was not merely to be judged for her sinfulness but redeemed. In short, He was not so interested in what people were as what they could become in the hands of God.

Regarding Life

Also, in Jesus' general outlook on life, He never sacrificed the ultimate on the altar of the immediate. He always lived with eternity's values in view. During the temptation, He chose not to accept Satan's offer of the kingdoms of this world and thereby to obtain honor and glory without the cross. He saw the greater importance of a few who fully recognized and accepted His Messiahship than vast crowds merely impressed with His miracle working powers. Therefore He frequently told people not to spread the news of their healing. He could have had greater popularity for a brief time, but the solidity of the foundation of the Christian movement was more important.

Christ's Relations with Others

With a general view of Christ's outlook on life before us, let us try to discover how that outlook influenced His relation to the Father, to Satan and evil, to relatives, friends, and coworkers, to officialdom, and to unbelievers.

Christ's Relation with the Father

Though divine, Jesus Christ took upon Himself humanity and submitted to the limitations of the flesh. Moreover, as divine, the Second Person of the Trinity followed the will of the First. So, in a dual sense Jesus Christ was under the directive of the Father. When Scripture says, "For God so loved the world, that He gave His only begotten Son" (John 3:16), it records the divine initiative in providing for man's salvation. Christ was always obedient to the desires of the Father, and aware of the mission on which the Father had sent Him. This is revealed early in His life when at the age of twelve He inquired of Mary and Joseph, "Did you not know that I was bound to be in my Father's house?" (Luke 2:49, NEB). And obedience characterized His entire life so that when He came to the end He could pray, "O my Father, if it is possible, let this cup pass from Me; nevertheless not as I will, but as You will" (Matthew 26:39). Hebrews 10:7, 9 further show the desire of Christ to do the will of the Father: "Behold, I have come to do Your will, O God."

Closely related to Christ's obedience to the Father was His dependence upon Him. This dependence is best demonstrated in His prayer life. For instance, before choosing the twelve He prayed all night (Luke 6:12); after feeding the five thousand He departed into a mountain to pray (Mark 6:46); before raising Lazarus from the dead He prayed (John 11:41); in

His great high priestly prayer He sought the Father's keeping power on behalf of believers (John 17:1–26). Christ's dependence on the Father also appears during the temptation. He refused to act independently and exercise His own power in providing food for His hunger, in calling upon the angels to care for Him if he jumped off the temple, or in bypassing the cross in favor of a counterfeit road to glory (Matthew 4:1–11).

Jesus always sought to carry out the purposes of the Father. In the temple at the age of twelve He was already concerned about this (Luke 2:49). After His interview with the Samaritan woman, Jesus told His disciples, "My food is to do the will of Him that sent Me, and to finish His work" (John 4:34). During His discourse on the bread of life Jesus said, "For I have come down from heaven, not to do My own will, but the will of Him who sent me" (John 6:38). This will of God included salvation and the resurrection of humanity: "And this is the will of Him who sent me, that every one who sees the Son and believes in Him may have everlasting life; and I will raise him up at the last day" (John 6:40). In giving the model prayer, Christ prayed to God, "Your will be done on earth as it is in heaven" (Matthew 6:10). This might as easily be translated, "Your program be carried out on earth." If this was Jesus' example to the disciples, certainly it was an echo of His own conviction (see also Matthew 18:14; 26:39, 42; John 5:30; 9:31).

Christ's Relation to Satan and Evil

Jesus' dealing with Satan and evil is best illustrated in the temptation narrative (Matthew 4:1–11; Mark

1:12–13; Luke 4:1–13). It is significant to note that Jesus entered His temptation experience filled with the Holy Spirit (Luke 4:1; cf. Ephesians 5:18 for the believer). In this way He was eminently prepared, from the human standpoint, to cope with the onslaughts of Satan. Available to Him were all the wisdom and discernment necessary for the emergencies of life. Moreover, Christ knew the Scripture well; so the Holy Spirit had something to work with in meeting the evil one.

In this connection, note that Christ knew Scripture so well that when Satan started to quote Scripture, Jesus recognized it was being distorted. Christ's temptation was extensive; the threefold testing came at the end of the forty day period of temptation. Whether or not most of Christ's temptations came during these days, Hebrews 4:15 declares that He was tempted in all areas of life that we are—yet without yielding. Christ met His temptations successfully, in the power of the Holy Spirit, and through the knowledge and use of Scripture. The believer can do this also.

Christ's Relation to Earthly Powers

Two incidents reveal Christ's relationship to the officialdom of His day. On one occasion the Pharisees came to trap Him with a question about whether or not it was lawful to pay tribute to Caesar. To this He made His famous reply, "Render therefore to Caesar the things that are Caesar's, and to God the things that are God's" (Matthew 22:21). In other words, He recognized two spheres or realms of human responsibility: the temporal or political and the spiritual.

The believer has an obligation in each. Before this event the collectors of the annual half-shekel head tax for the temple asked Peter whether his Master paid the tax, to which Peter replied in the affirmative, indicating that Jesus was in the habit of doing so. Jesus prepared to do so again, lest He give offense (Matthew 17:24–27). The meeting of one's religious and political obligations constitutes an important part of his testimony before unbelievers.

Christ's Relation to Relatives, Friends, Coworkers

We come next to Jesus' relations with His relatives, friends, and coworkers. A book could be written on Jesus' relationship with His disciples, but a few basic principles must be noted.

1. In all things Jesus always put God first. To those who would become His disciples He said, "He who loves father or mother more than Me is not worthy of Me. And he that loves son or daughter more than Me is not worthy of Me" (Matthew 10:37). When His mother and brothers laid a special claim on Him and sought to break up one of His discussions, He revealed a new principle of relationships: "Whoever does the will of My Father in heaven is my brother and sister and mother" (Matthew 12:50). That is to say, relatives according to the flesh should not have first claim on us; following God comes first. In dealing with Martha, who was distraught because Mary had forsaken her household tasks in favor of fellowship

with the Master, Jesus said, "Mary has chosen that good part" (Luke 10:42), namely, communion with the Son.

2. While Jesus seemed at times to deprecate human ties and responsibilities, He always cared for those who were closest to Him. At the Cross He tenderly entrusted His mother to John. There is no hint that He ever had real trouble with His brothers. Later they believed in Him. He appeared to James after the resurrection (1 Corinthians 15:7). When Peter's household was plunged in sorrow, he healed Peter's mother-in-law. To His disciples who had borne the burden and heat of the day He gave assurance of special reward at the end of the way (Matthew 19:27–29). And He reminded them of the full provision of the Father on their behalf. Surely if God cared for the lily of the field and the birds of the air, His provision for them would be most adequate (Matthew 6:25–34).

3. Jesus sought to lead those closest to Him to a deep appreciation of the nature and work of God and to faith in Him. By means of such miracles as the feeding of the five thousand and the feeding of the four thousand, He demonstrated that God is able to provide in impossible situations for those who have faith. Certainly His other miracles were performed to the same end. As noted above, He exhorted His followers to lay aside their anxiety in view of the Father's care of the lilies and birds (Matthew 6:25–34). In fact, faith as a grain of mustard seed could remove mountains (Matthew 17:20).

4. Jesus set before His disciples an example of humility. To James and John, who wanted to rule on His right and left hands in the kingdom, He pointed out that the one who wished to be great must be the servant of others, even as He was (Mark 10:43–45). On another occasion He set a child in their midst and gave them an object lesson on humility (Matthew 18:1–5). During the Last Supper He washed the feet of the disciples (John 13:2–16). Paul comments that Jesus' whole outlook was characterized by walking in humility (Philippians 2:1–4).

5. Christ was a wise administrator. First the disciples served a period as observers while He performed miracles and taught. Then they served as apprentices, carrying on under His supervision such tasks as He assigned to them. Then He sent them out as His coworkers, in pairs, to preach and heal. Moreover, after they returned from their ministry, He gave them a rest period and time to discuss problems they had met (Mark 6:30–31).

Christ's Relation with Unbelievers

In an effort to discover how Jesus lived and walked, we must also consider His relation to unbelievers. To those who sought Him He was compassionate. He healed the blind, lepers, deformed, and diseased. He honored the requests of both Gentile and Jew. He received little children. He had compassion on hungry multitudes and fed them. He willingly mingled with sinners, even though it involved criticism. He served the needy until He was exhausted.

In all of His dealings with unbelievers, He began where the people were (in their thinking and social standing) and injected His principles into the situations. With the woman at the well (John 4), He started a conversation about the water of life and true satisfaction. He confronted Nicodemus, who came for information on how to live better, with the fact that one could not even see the kingdom of God unless he had been born anew (John 3). With a lawyer who came to inquire about eternal life, Jesus began a conversation about the teachings of the law (Luke 10:25–29). How much better was His approach than the one we often follow: laying down general principles and leaving them detached from the life situation.

For those who had hardened hearts, Jesus had little time. He answered them on occasion and exposed their religious sham (especially that of the Pharisees). But He made it clear that His interest was in those who were lost and knew it, for those who really wanted the truth. This was the point of the three parables of Luke 15: the lost sheep, the lost coin, and the lost son. Jesus had little interest in the ninety nine sheep, nine coins, or an elder brother who represented religiously smug Pharisees. But He would spend no end of time on a lost sheep—one who was obviously lost by everyone's standards.

Christ's Sense of Urgency

Above all, Jesus was compelled with a sense of urgency, a sense of mission. Even at the age of twelve, this urgency was present. In the temple He said to Mary and Joseph, "Did you not know that I was bound to be in my Father's house?" (Luke 2:49, NEB). Returning to Galilee from Judea, "He needed to go through Samaria" (John 4:4). Later in the same chapter He told the disciples, "My food is to do the will of him that sent me, and to finish his work. Do you not say, 'There are yet four months, and then comes the harvest'? Behold, I say to you, Lift up your eyes, and look on the fields; for they are white already for harvest" (John 4:34–35, KJV).

As He gave Himself fully to His ministry, one day during the Galilean period of service, "When his friends heard of it, they went out to lay hold on him: for they said, He is beside himself" (Mark 3:21, KJV). As Jesus came to the end of His earthly ministry, He prayed to the Father: "I have glorified You on earth: I have finished the work which You have given me to do. And now, O Father, glorify me together with Yourself with the glory which I had with You before the world was. I have manifested Your name to the men whom You have given me out of the world" (John 17:4–6, KJV).

How Christ Walked: Implications for Believers

This is how Jesus walked among men. It would almost seem unnecessary to spell out what we should do to follow His example. Intimations have been numerous. In addition, the New Testament presents a number of exhortations and commands for the believer that closely relate to the pattern of Christ's life. In general, we are commanded to "abstain from every form of evil" (1 Thessalonians 5:22), to "walk worthy of the calling with which you were called" (Ephesians 4:1), to "walk not as other Gentiles walk, in the vanity of their mind" (Ephesians 4:17, KJV), to "walk in love" (Ephesians 5:2), to "walk as children of light" (Ephesians 5:8), to "walk circumspectly, not as fools but as wise" (Ephesians 5:15), and to "walk in the light, as He is in the light" (1 John 1:7).

In Relation to Governmental Authority

We are to obey those in authority over us (Romans 13:1–7), to pray for our rulers (1 Timothy 2:1–3), and to submit to the ordinances of men for the Lord's sake (1 Peter 2:13–14). In relation to Satan, we are exhorted to "resist the devil" (James 4:7), and we are promised that "there has no temptation taken you but such as is common to man: but God is faithful, who will not suffer you to be tempted above that you are able; but will with the temptation also make a way of escape, that you may be able to bear it" (1 Corinthians 10:13, KJV).

In Relation to the Father

We are exhorted to total devotion: "I beseech you therefore, brethren, by the mercies of God, that you present your bodies a living sacrifice, holy, acceptable unto God, which is your reasonable service. And be not conformed to this world: but be transformed by the renewing of your mind, that you may prove what is that good, and acceptable, and perfect, will of God" (Romans 12:1–2, KJV). And we are commanded to "pray without ceasing" (1 Thessalonians 5:17).

In Respect to Our Mission

We have the direct command, "Go therefore and make disciples of all nations, baptizing them in the name of the Father and of the Son and of the Holy Spirit, teaching them to observe all things that I have commanded you; and, lo, I am with you always, even to the end of the age" (Matthew 28:19–20). As we carry out this commission, we are to redeem the time (Ephesians 5:16), and are to be constrained or impelled by the love of Christ (2 Corinthians 5:14).

It is all very well to list such lofty exhortations and to talk about walking as Christ walked, but Christians are helpless to fulfill such commands in their own strength. They can only hope to have success as they are filled with (or controlled by) the same Holy Spirit that energized Christ in His walk (Luke 4:1). Paul urges, "Be filled with the Spirit" (Ephesians 5:18) and "walk by the Spirit" (literal translation, Galatians 5:16). The filling or control of the Holy Spirit can be the experience of all believers who yield themselves wholly to God as living sacrifices (Romans 12:1–2). When so yielded and filled, believers will experience in full measure the teaching ministry of the Holy Spirit (John 16:12–15) and to a remarkable degree the leading of the Holy Spirit (Romans 8:14). With such enduement it is possible in some measure to walk as Christ walked.

Appendix

Further Discussion of End-Time Events

While John speaks symbolically in the Revelation concerning a time of great trial on the earth, he has some *specific* things to say about the results of God's works of judgment. For instance, the third part of the trees and grass are burned up; a third part of the sea becomes blood; a third part of the sea creatures and ships are destroyed; a third part of the waters are poisoned; and great monsters come upon the earth and kill a third of the inhabitants (Revelation 8:7–9, 11; 9:18). Certainly nothing of this magnitude has taken place since John's day; we await a future fulfillment of these horrible predictions. In an era of nuclear fission, such destruction is not unthinkable.

A Literal Understanding of the Millennium

While admittedly the Millennium is mentioned only in Revelation 20, and Revelation is a book filled with symbols, other passages of Scripture demand a literal kingdom of God on earth. The covenants and prophecies of the Old Testament must be taken into account. The Abrahamic Covenant requires an earthly kingdom. The covenant and its confirmations appear in Genesis 12:2–3; 13:14–17; 15:1–18; 17:1–19; 26:3–5, 24; 28:13–15. God promised Abraham a multitude of descendants who would inherit the land of Canaan everlastingly. The boundaries of the promised land would be the River of Egypt on the south and the Euphrates on the north.

Temporary sojourns outside of the land would not annul the general provisions of the covenant. With Isaac and Jacob God renewed this covenant. Also, the Davidic Covenant requires an earthly kingdom. In it God unconditionally promised David and his seed a king forever, a throne forever, a kingdom forever, and a land forever (2 Samuel 7). It is clear from the New Testament genealogies (Matthew 1; Luke 3) and statements from Paul and Luke (Galatians 3:13–16; Luke 1:32–33; cf. Isaiah 9:7) that the unconditional and everlasting covenants made to Abraham and David are to be fulfilled in Christ. Certainly only an infinite person could fulfill an infinite promise.

Numerous Old Testament prophecies speak of future glory for Israel, a time when she will be gathered from among the nations of the world to the promised land. Then she will enjoy a highly favored position among the nations of the earth because the Messiah will rule from Zion. The kingdom age will be characterized by universal peace, social justice, economic prosperity, rejuvenation of nature, an abundance of plant life, a removal of animosity from the animal kingdom, lengthened life for human beings, and a widespread knowledge of the truth. The glorious picture presented in Scripture seems to be almost too wonderful for us to apply to an earthly scene, short of the new earth.

Yet, observe that Isaiah 2:2–5 mentions that these indeed are the conditions that will exist during the "last days," indicating the new earth has not yet come into being. Isaiah 65:20 alludes to the lengthening of physical life. And many references speak of animals, the building of houses and planting of crops—in addition to numerous other features of a very physical nature and certainly not what we would expect the eternal state to be like. Moreover, if Satan is bound during the Millennium (Revelation 20:1–7), we would anticipate remarkably good conditions on the earth. (Especially helpful references include Psalm 2:6–8; Isaiah 2:2–5; 11:1–13; 35:1–10; 65:20–25; Jeremiah 23:5–8; Ezekiel 37:21–28; Zechariah 9:10; 14:4–21.) It should be noted that the predictions concerning Christ's rule on the throne of David also have an eternal aspect. The Millennium is merely the first stage of fulfillment. He continues to rule in the new earth.

Christ's Activity in the End-Times

If we accept literally the prophecies concerning the second coming, the Tribulation, and the Millennium, it becomes possible to discover an order of events at the end times and therefore to outline the future ministry of Christ. But before we can speak further about the order of these events, we must first tackle the pretribulation rapture question.

The Time of the Rapture

Pretribulationists[1] have many arguments to say that the Church will not go through the Tribulation. Some of the strongest are included here. First, the purpose of the Tribulation is the purification of Israel and preparation for her restoration. It is a time of "Jacob's trouble." It concerns "Daniel's people," the temple, flight on the Sabbath, the "sacrifice and oblation" of the temple ritual, the land of Judea, false messiahs, and the preaching of the Gospel of the Kingdom. The picture is entirely Jewish; the Church is never mentioned specifically in any of the passages on the Tribulation (Deuteronomy 4:29–30; 30:1–6; Jeremiah 30:4–11; Daniel 9:24–27; 12:1, 3; Matthew 24:15–31; 1 Thessalonians 1:9–10; 5:4–9; Revelation 4–19). It is obvious, of course, that the Tribulation also constitutes a judgment on a Christ-rejecting world.

For example, Christ in His great Olivet Discourse (Matthew 24–25) gave the basic order of these future events: a tribulation (Matthew 24:6–26), His second coming (25:27–31), and then after some illustrative parables (25:32—24:30), a judgment (25:31–46), with the righteous (sheep) going on into the Kingdom and the unrighteous (goats) going into everlasting punishment. In this order of events there is a posttribulation coming of Christ.

Second, the restrainer of sin mentioned in 2 Thessalonians 2:7 is best identified as the Holy Spirit. It is argued that the restraining ministry of the Holy Spirit cannot be removed from the earth until the rapture of the Church, which He indwells. In this connection, it is interesting to note that 2 Thessalonians 2:3 may be translated "except the departure come first." If so construed, it might support the pretribulation rapture view. Third, the exhortations to constant expectancy of Christ and the purifying effect of His coming are nullified if a period of seven years must pass before He can come (Titus 2:13; 1 John 3:2–3; Mark 13:35; 1 Thessalonians 5:6; Revelation 3:3).

But more pertinent than the first three arguments is the fact that in the references to Christ's second coming two stages are implied. There are such great differences described in the verses surrounding this theme that we must conclude they do not all refer to one event. First, at the rapture saints meet Christ in the air (1 Thessalonians 4:17), while at the posttribulation coming Christ returns to the earth (touching the Mount of Olives and dividing it) with His saints (1 Thessalonians 3:13; Zechariah 14:4–5; Acts 1:11). Second, the pretribulation coming seems to be secret (1 Thessalonians 4:13–17), whereas the posttribulation coming is public and accompanied by signs in the heavens (Matthew 24:27–31; 25:31).

Third, at the pretribulation rapture, living saints leave the earth (1 Thessalonians 4:17), while at the posttribulation coming living saints remain on the earth (Matthew 25:31–46). Fourth, at the rapture believers receive a glorified body (1 Corinthians 15:51–57), while at the posttribulation revelation believers go on into the Millennium to engage in normal pursuits, including rearing of children (Matthew 25:34; cf. references under discussion of Millennium above). Fifth, at the rapture there is no indication of judgment on sinful mankind, but this does take place at the posttribulation coming (Matthew 25:41–46). Other differences could be listed.[2] A faithful interpretation of the Bible seems to necessitate both a pretribulation and posttribulation coming of Christ. Thus we have a basis for a pretribulation rapture, a literal Tribulation, a posttribulation coming of Christ, and a literal Millennium.

NOTES

1. The writer realizes he has omitted many issues about the Millennium and the Tribulation. This is not a volume on theology; the purpose of this appendix and chapter 12 is merely to give a brief survey of Christ's future activity on earth.

2. For further discussion see W. E. Blackstone, *Jesus is Coming* (Westwood, N.J.: Revell, 1898), pp. 75–82.

Books for Further Study

Hundreds of books could be listed here on various phases of the life of Christ. No doubt the reader would lose himself in such a list. Therefore the following books have been selected with a view to their *general* theological acceptability, factual accuracy, and availability in church or Christian college libraries. They have been arranged under headings of special interest.

General Works on the Life of Christ

Edersheim, Alfred. *Life and Times of Jesus the Messiah.* Reprint. Grand Rapids: Eerdmans, 1945.

Foster, R. C. *Studies in the Life of Christ.* 3 vols. Grand Rapids: Baker, 1962–68.

Green, Joel B. and others, eds. *Dictionary of Jesus and the Gospels.* Downers Grove, Ill.: Inter-Varsity, 1992.

Guthrie, Donald. *Jesus the Messiah.* Grand Rapids: Zondervan, 1972.

_____. *A Shorter Life of Christ.* Grand Rapids: Zondervan, 1970.

Harrison, Everett F. *A Short Life of Christ.* Grand Rapids: Eerdmans, 1968.

Hoehner, Harold. *Chronological Aspects of the Life of Christ.* Grand Rapids: Zondervan, 1977.

Hunter, A. M. *The Work and Words of Jesus.* London: S.C.M., 1950.

Lockyer, Herbert. *Everything Jesus Taught*. New York: Harper & Row, 1976.

Morgan, G. Campbell. *Crises of the Christ*. New York: Revell, 1936.

Pentecost, J. Dwight. *The Words and Works of Jesus Christ*. Grand Rapids: Zondervan, 1981.

Robertson, A. T. *Epochs in the Life of Jesus*. New York: Scribners, 1920.

Smith, David. *The Days of His Flesh*. New York: Doran, n.d.

Smith, James E. *The Promised Messiah*. Nashville: Thomas Nelson, 1993.

Stalker, James. *The Life of Jesus Christ*. Rev. ed. Westwood, N.J.: Revell, 1891.

Vollmer, P. *The Modern Student's Life of Christ*. Westwood, N.J.: Revell, 1912.

Walvoord, John F. *Jesus Christ Our Lord*. Chicago: Moody, 1969.

Whyte, Alexander. *The Walk, Conversation and Character of Jesus Christ our Lord*. Westwood, N.J.: Revell, 1905.

Background Studies

Brownrigg, Ronald. *Who's Who in the New Testament*. London: Weidenfeld and Nicolson, 1971.

Fairweather, William. *Background of the Gospels*. 4th ed. Edinburgh: T. & T. Clark, 1926.

Filson, Floyd V. *The New Testament Against Its Environment*. London: S.C.M., 1950.

Finkelstein, Louis. *The Pharisees*. 2 vols. 2d ed. Philadelphia: Jewish Pubn. Soc., 1938.

Geer, Russel M. *Classical Civilization: Rome*. 2d ed. Englewood Cliffs, N. J.: Prentice-Hall, 1950.

LaSor, William S. *The Dead Sea Scrolls and the Christian Faith*. Rev. ed. Chicago: Moody, 1962.

_____. *The Dead Sea Scrolls and the New Testament*. Grand Rapids: Eerdmans, 1972.

Moore, G. F. *Judaism*. 2 vols. Cambridge, Mass.: Harvard, 1946.

Pelikan, Jaroslav. *Jesus Through the Centuries*. New Haven: Yale, 1985.

Perowne, Stewart. *The Later Herods*. New York: Abingdon, 1958.

_____. *The Life and Times of Herod the Great*. London: Hodder & Stoughton, 1956.

Pfeiffer, Charles F. *The Dead Sea Scrolls and the Bible*. Grand Rapids: Baker, 1969.

Scroggie, W. Graham. *A Guide to the Gospels*. London: Pickering & Inglis, 1948.

Sherwin-White, A. N. *Roman Society and Roman Law in the New Testament*. Oxford: Clarendon, 1963.

Sinnigen, William G., and Arthur E. R. Boak. *A History of Rome to 565 A.D.* 6th ed. New York: Macmillan, 1977.

Tenney, Merrill C. *New Testament Survey*. Rev. ed. Grand Rapids: Eerdmans, 1961.

_____. *New Testament Times*. Grand Rapids: Eerdmans, 1965.

Whyte, Alexander. *Bible Characters*. Grand Rapids: Zondervan, n.d.

Witherington, Ben. *Women in the Ministry of Jesus*. Cambridge: Cambridge U. Press, 1984.

Miracles

Brown, Colin. *Miracles and the Critical Minds*. Grand Rapids: Eerdmans, 1984.

Bruce, Alexander B. *The Miraculous Element in the Gospels*. London: Hodder & Stoughton, 1886.

Laidlaw, John. *The Miracles of Our Lord*. Grand Rapids: Baker, 1956.

Lewis, C. S. *Miracles*. New York: Macmillan, 1947.

Machen, J. Gresham. *The Virgin Birth of Christ*. Grand Rapids: Baker, 1967.

Smith, Wilbur M. *The Supernaturalness of Christ*. Boston: Wilde, 1944.

Trench, Richard C. *Notes on the Miracles of Our Lord*. Grand Rapids: Baker, 1949.

Parables

Hunter, Archibald M. *Interpreting the Parables*. Philadelphia: Westminster, 1960.

Jeremias, Joachim. *The Parables of Jesus.* 2nd rev. ed. New York: Scribner's, 1954.

Morgan, G. Campbell. *The Parables and Metaphors of Our Lord.* Westwood, N.J.: Revell, 1943.

————. *The Parables of the Kingdom.* Westwood, N.J.: Revell, 1907.

Pentecost, Dwight. *The Parables of Jesus.* Grand Rapids: Zondervan, 1982.

Trench, Richard C. *Notes on the Parables of Our Lord.* 10th ed. London: Macmillan, 1866.

Death of Christ

Denney, James. *The Death of Christ.* 1903. Reprint. Downers Grove, Ill.: Inter-Varsity, 1967.

Krummacher, F. W. *The Suffering Saviour.* Chicago: Moody, 1947.

Morris, Leon. *The Cross in the New Testament.* Grand Rapids: Eerdmans, 1965.

Nicholson, William R. *The Six Miracles of Calvary.* Chicago: Moody, 1927.

Schilder, K. *Christ Crucified.* Grand Rapids: Eerdmans, 1940.

Stalker, James. *The Trial and Death of Jesus Christ.* London: Hodder & Stoughton, 1894.

Resurrection of Christ

Miethe, Terry L., ed. *Did Jesus Rise from the Dead?* New York: Harper & Row, 1987.

Milligan, William. *The Resurrection of Our Lord*. 3d ed. London: Macmillan, 1890.

Morison, Frank. *Who Moved the Stone?* Grand Rapids: Zondervan.

Moule, C. F. D. *The Significance of the Message of the Resurrection for Faith in Jesus Christ*. Naperville, Ill.: Allenson, 1968.

Moule, H. C. G. *Jesus and the Resurrection*. London: Seeley, 1893.

Orr, James. *The Resurrection of Jesus*. London: Hodder & Stoughton, n.d.

Osborne, Grant R. *The Resurrection Narratives*. Grand Rapids: Baker, 1984.

Tenney, Merrill C. *The Reality of the Resurrection*. Chicago: Moody, 1972.

Walsh, John Evangelist. *The Man Who Buried Jesus*. New York: Macmillan, 1989. A novel with useful approaches to the Resurrection.

Westcott, B. F. *The Gospel of the Resurrection*. 4th ed. London: Macmillan, 1879.

_____. *The Revelation of the Risen Lord*. 6th ed. London: Macmillan, 1898.

Return of Christ

Blackstone, W. E. *Jesus Is Coming*. Westwood, N.J.: Revell, 1898.

Hoyt, Herman. *The End Times*. Chicago: Moody, 1969.

Ludwigson, R. *A Survey of Bible Prophecy*. Grand Rapids: Zondervan, 1973.

McClain, Alva J. *The Greatness of the Kingdom*. Grand Rapids: Zondervan, 1959.

Pache, Rene. *The Return of Jesus Christ*. Trans. William S. LaSor. Chicago: Moody, 1955.

Ryrie, Charles C. *The Basis of the Premillennial Faith*. New York: Louizeaux, 1953.

Walvoord, John F. *The Millennial Kingdom*. Grand Rapids: Dunham, 1959.

Index

About the Author

HOWARD F. VOS is the Professor of History and Archaeology at The King's College, Briarcliff Manor, New York. He holds the Th.D. from Dallas Theological Seminary and the Ph.D. from Northwestern University and has authored 23 books.

Nelson's Quick-Reference™ Series

Nelson's Quick-Reference™ Bible Concordance

Gives you easy access to over 40,000 key Bible references that are most often sought. Save time and avoid the tedium that goes with wading through long lists of references less sought after. Keyed to the New King James Version, but useful with any.

400 pages / 0-8407-6907-5 / available now

Nelson's Quick-Reference™ Bible Dictionary

More like a "mini-encyclopedia" than a standard dictionary, this compact reference offers an A-Z way to discover fascinating details about the Bible—its characters, history, setting, and doctrines.

784 pages / 0-8407-6906-7 / available now

Nelson's Quick-Reference™ Bible Handbook

Helps you read each of the Bible's 66 books, plus those of the Apocrypha. Offers book introductions, brief summaries, historical and faith-and-life highlights, at-a-glance charts, and detailed teaching outlines. Suggests individual reading plans and schedules for group study.

416 pages / 0-8407-6904-0 / available now

Nelson's Quick-Reference™
Bible Questions and Answers

Learning is fun, lively, and exciting with the over 6,000 questions and answers covering the whole Bible. Variety keeps interest high—short answer, true/false, multiple choice, fill in the blank, and sentence completion.

384 pages / 0-8407-6905-9 / available now

Nelson's Quick-Reference™
Introduction to the Bible

Introduces the Bible as a whole and describes all its parts from an historical and evangelical theological perspective. Explore the fascinating variety in Scripture—story and song, poetry and prophecy, and more. Discover its divinely revealed answers to the most important questions of life.

approx 400 pages / 0-8407-3206-6 / available now

Nelson's Quick-Reference™
Bible People and Places

From Aaron to Zurishaddain, and from Dan to Beersheba, quickly identify each person and place in the Bible—and many key events. One list, arranged from A to Z, gives brief descriptions and Scripture references, and tells what the names mean, how to say them, and which refer to the same person or place. Variant spellings make this guide useful with any translation.

approx 400 pages / 0-8407-6912-1 / available now

Nelson's Quick-Reference™
Bible Maps and Charts

Make any Bible a study Bible with this unique collection of maps, book charts, and other visuals that present clear information about Bible people, events, and teachings in ways that heighten your interest, retention, and understanding in Bible study. Seeing it helps you believe it!

approx 300 pages / 0-8407-6908-3 / April, 1994